Praise for the book

A timely and relevant book for today's India. It clearly brings out that GDP alone will not make us a powerful nation, unless we also focus on issues of accountability and misgovernance that keep large numbers of our people deprived of their most fundamental needs .... A must read for those who want to see a better India.

—Anu Aga, Director, Thermax Limited

This is an excellent, well-researched book which combines the dimensions of economics, politics and law to highlight the governance deficit in our country. It sets out an actionable agenda to take accountability to the next level in India. Fascinating read!

—Davinder S. Brar, Promoter Chairman, GVK Biosciences Private Limited

Jay's meticulous research and attempt to connect the dots, including going back in time, is commendable. *Accountability* helps put in perspective this decline in governance prevalent across India and provides a practical call to action for us to do a lot more, to make our contribution to building the nation.

—Amit Chandra, Managing Director, Bain Capital Advisors (India) Pvt. Ltd

Accountability is a very timely contribution to the current debate over accountability in India. Desai brings critical thinking, creative conceptualization and compelling empirical evidence to bear on this important topic. He traces the historical origins and current multidimensional reality of this issue, shows how it hampers India's progress, and suggests a comprehensive but practical approach to corrective action.

—Patricia M. Danzon, Ph.D., Celia Moh Professor, The Wharton School, University of Pennsylvania

Nothing is as important to India's future well-being as governance. Jay P. Desai rightly focuses on accountability, which is at the heart of our governance deficit. Jay brings in considerable skills as a business consultant to diagnose the problem and offer solutions.

—Gurcharan Das, author, *India Unbound* and *The Difficulty of Being Good*

Desai provides an insightful, analytical and practical assessment of the current situation in India and what can be done to take this cherished country to the next level. With his focus on accountability in public administration and among citizens, he lays out how the country might embrace long-term economic and societal change. You will find provocative ideas on virtually every page.

—Thomas J. DeLong, Philip J. Stomberg Professor of Management Practice, Harvard Business School

Accountability is a very timely publication on the deficit in accountability, probity and transparency in India. An excellent read to better understand the current debate about governance in the country.

—Adi Godrej, Chairman, Godrej Group

Desai's book is an important contribution to the literature on the governance deficit that plagues the world's second-fastest growing economy. It makes us aware of what is wrong, how it must be addressed and, above all, that we must never forget our tragedies.

—Samar P. Halarnkar, Editor-at-Large, *Hindustan Times*

Accountability is a well-studied account examining India's progress against the world's other great democracies. Desai skilfully employs statistical evidence and insight to illuminate Indian performance gaps and establish key links among governance, accountability and performance …. This important book deserves our attention and a central role in any debate about the future course of India.

—Michael L. Hand, Professor of Applied Statistics and Information Systems, Willamette University

There are few who would be able to apply the full power of their analytical skills to such a complex issue. This book manages to list all the excuses in the category 'we are like that only', and debunk them one at a time. *Accountability* will provide you with all the tools you need to develop your own roadmap of engagement. Highly recommended.

—Abhay Havaldar, Managing Director, General Atlantic Private Limited

Desai outlines the critical role that good governance must play for India to achieve its full economic and democratic potential. In this passionate study, he argues for the benefits of increased accountability. Drawing from numerous historical examples, Jay shows how accountability lapses contributed to social challenges. Most importantly, he offers an action-oriented framework designed to improve accountability in India—and bolster the nation's long-term prospects.

—Dipak C. Jain, Dean, INSEAD

At a time when the whole issue of governance is at centre-stage, Jay P. Desai's book … is timely. The book covers a vast canvas, taking us through the historical to the current global context. It identifies the causes of low accountability, provides possible solutions and makes for very interesting reading.

—K. V. Kamath, Non-Executive Chairman, ICICI Bank Limited

I resonate strongly with the objective of providing the public with an accessible discussion of accountability and governance in India, in a way that goes beyond hand-wringing. I love the historical anchor and the practical suggestions … Desai has done us all a service.

—Tarun Khanna, Jorge Paulo Lemann Professor, Harvard Business School

Dissatisfaction with the working of governments seems to have peaked worldwide. In *Accountability*, Desai attacks this issue with a plan to bring cooperation between public administration and citizens. The book also provides detailed statistical correlation analysis between socio-cultural factors and good governance. This is a well-researched book…. The lessons are applicable worldwide.

—Gerald J. Lynch, Interim Dean and Professor of Economics, Krannert School of Management, Purdue University

Desai has done a remarkable job analysing the state of accountability in the Indian legislative, executive and judicial systems …. What makes this book stand out is the amount of honest research effort that has gone into it.

—Luis Miranda, Chairman, IDFC Private Equity

An insightful and in-depth study on accountability which lends clarity to an area which otherwise suffers from low visibility…. I have no doubt that this book will become one of the leading commentaries on the subject in our country, and rightly so. A must-read for all those who have a desire to invest in the future of this country.

—Zia Mody, Managing Partner, AZB & Partners

A perfectly timed and important book! … Jay Desai's incisive but caring examination of the astonishing lack of accountability in India is essential reading for anyone trying to fathom and fix the problem.

—Jehangir S. Pocha, Former Editor, *Businessworld*; and Co-Promoter, INX News

This is an important book, written at a crucial time. Desai has brought together many fields—history, politics, economics and law. The book is well-written with strong conceptual foundations and empirical rigor and has many actionable implications for how the Indian system needs to change, to make progress in the years to come.

—Jaideep Prabhu, Jawaharlal Nehru Professor of Indian Business and Enterprise, Judge Business School, University of Cambridge

From examples of lapses in individual responsibility to looming gaps in systemic responsibility, Jay's work provides a well-reasoned, inter-disciplinary and practical approach to addressing the most critical challenge to India's development—the challenge of governance.

—Roopa Purushothaman, Head of Research, Everstone Capital Management, Co-author, *Dreaming with BRICs: The Path to 2050*

A brilliant and detailed sociological exposition on accountability and governance; a comprehensive primer which should be a compulsory read for all those associated with governance, whether from the executive, judiciary, legislature, or civil society. Jay's book is most timely and illuminating.

—V. Raghunathan, author, *Games Indians Play*

As India grapples with its challenges of delivering inclusive development to its people, the subject of governance has come to occupy centre-stage. But 'governance' is a fuzzy, catch-all word, one that can be best appreciated through various instruments of accountability. In this excellent book, Desai gives us a framework to assess accountability in our public institutions and provides specific pointers for practical action. It is a must-read for those interested in India's transformation.

—Ramesh Ramanathan, Co-founder, Janaagraha Centre for Citizenship and Democracy

Accountability is the cornerstone of good governance and Desai's incisive but succinct presentation of this premise helps the reader navigate the challenge of remedying contravening behaviour. There are very few treatises on the subject where you see personal passion balanced neatly with erudite essay, and it is captured in this book.

—Ranjit Shahani, Vice Chairman & Managing Director, Novartis India Limited

A highly engrossing and monumental treatise on the role of citizens, media, businesses and civil societies in making public officials accountable. *Accountability* is full of concrete suggestions about how India, as a nation, can transform from a culture of '*Chalta Hai*' (being indifferent) to one of action and achievement.

—Jagdish N. Sheth, Charles H. Kellstadt Professor of Marketing, Goizueta Business School, Emory University

Desai's book is a must read for India's administrative reformers, business leaders and ordinary citizens. The book shows step by step how to carry out a winning accountability campaign and its value …. Highly recommended.

—Fred Thompson, Grace and Elmer Goudy Professor of Public Management and Policy, Atkinson Graduate School of Management, Willamette University

Desai's book … is a meticulous, systematic and holistic study of the neglect of governance due to poor accountability mechanisms …. Using modern analytical tools, he provides solutions, at the core of which is the need for greater participation and awareness of the ordinary citizens in enforcing accountability. Timely, topical and exceptionally relevant, this book is a must read for all those concerned about the current drift and future aspirations of India.

—Pavan K. Varma, writer-diplomat, author, *Becoming Indian* and *Being Indian*

A wonderfully timely and rigorous look at governance and accountability, the issues which most determine our country's future. Jay does an excellent job provoking thought and offering practical solutions so the reader is left with energy and hope rather than just angst.

—Ravi Venkatesan, Former Chairman, Microsoft India

Accountability

··

Angst, Awareness, Action

Jay P. Desai
Founder & CEO
Universal Consulting India Pvt. Ltd

Delhi • Chennai • Chandigarh

Assistant Editor – Acquisitions: Saumya Chawla
Editor – Development: Proteeti Banerjee
Associate Editor – Production: Vipin Kumar

The views and opinions expressed in this book are those of the author, and the facts are as reported by him. They do not necessarily represent the official position or the views of the publisher.

ISBN 978-81-317-6705-4

First Impression
Second Impression, 2012
Third Impression, 2013

Published by Dorling Kindersley (India) Pvt. Ltd, licensees of Pearson Education in South Asia.

Head Office: 7th Floor, Knowledge Boulevard, A-8(A), Sector 62, Noida 201 309, UP, India.

Registered Office: 11 Community Centre, Panchsheel Park, New Delhi 110 017, India.

Cover design by Krsna Mehta.
Cover design copyright © 2012 by Jay P. Desai.

Composition: Mukesh Technologies Pvt. Ltd.
Printer: Gopsons Papers Ltd., Noida

For my parents,
Meena and Praful,
who exemplify the importance of public
service, having dedicated their lives to
healing the unwell.

Contents

List of Figures

Foreword

. . . .

'India will be prosperous, but not happy, if we do not fix our governance,' laments the well-known writer, Gurcharan Das. Good governance is the link between economic prosperity and a fulfilling life. India's citizens and public officials have finally begun to sense its importance, as we see from the events of the last few months. This realization, however, needs to be firmly grounded on a clearly designed pathway that can ultimately lead to improved governance.

Jay P. Desai presents the book *Accountability: Angst, Awareness, Action* at indeed a crucial juncture in India's post-independence history. The current nation-wide concern over corruption and poor governance is fundamentally driven by the poor accountability of those who walk the corridors of power. This book sets out a roadmap to improve governance in India, through a three-dimensional construct of accountability. Jay brings a fresh perspective to this national debate—not through the eye of an academic or the heart of an activist, but rather, through the mind of an engaged citizen. Here, he examines the three key institutions of governance—the Legislature, the Executive and the Judiciary, and suggests 'Six Initiatives' to address the deeply rooted issues of poor governance and low accountability.

The challenge of fostering a sense of accountability applies equally to all sectors of society—private companies, public companies, NGOs and the government. The famous economist and Nobel laureate Milton Friedman, in his classification of 'Four Ways to Spend Money', explains that this challenge is a particularly difficult one for any government, since they 'spend someone else's money on somebody else'. The likelihood of effectively spending taxpayers' money is naturally lower, rendering accountability in government spending a rather difficult task.

A robust system of accountability should impose similar standards and penalties for non-performance on the government, as are imposed on private providers of goods and services. Unfortunately, the Consumer Protection Act excludes many of the goods and services provided by the state. In reality, citizens must be able to hold all service providers accountable, regardless of whether they are private or public. Some interesting examples of this have emerged recently. The Madhya Pradesh Public Services Guarantee Act 2010 is a pioneering effort in assuring minimum standards of service; it imposes clear penalties on public officials for dereliction of their duties. Bihar has followed suit and several other states may adopt this practice. The Union government has also proposed an Electronic Service Delivery Bill, which will guarantee the quality of all online services. The Bill is likely to extend even to services provided non-electronically, within a decade. Progress is being made.

Accountability and monopoly cannot coexist. All monopolies, whether private or public, are more inclined to serving their own interests, rather than those of consumers. For any government to be truly accountable, it should concentrate its attention only on doing what individuals, organizations and communities cannot effectively do themselves. This is not merely ideology; it is more a pragmatic realization that even a well-intentioned government cannot, by itself, build a prosperous and happy society. India's experience with the liberalization of several industries has clearly displayed the benefits of competition. The same principle applies equally to social services like education, healthcare, subsidized food, fuel and fertilizers. Choice and competition keep providers accountable. Simple instruments such as vouchers and conditional cash transfers serve as effective tools to create competition among suppliers of social services, provide choice to consumers and help to increase accountability. In the sphere of education, instead of funding only government schools, the authorities should give school vouchers to parents, who can use them to access education at either government or private schools. In the area of food, Madhya Pradesh has recently implemented a food voucher system in place of the Public Distribution System, to provide access to subsidized food. These are small changes that will have a big impact.

One of the 'Six Initiatives' proposed in this book to improve accountability is the Information Initiative, and this should be the spearhead in the battle for accountability. Without complete information, there can never be complete accountability. The Right to Information (RTI) Act is the crowning achievement of this movement to ensure accountability in government. There are two different obligations imposed on the government by the RTI Act. The first is the government's obligation to provide information when requested, and the second is the government's obligation to publish information, even when it has not been explicitly sought. The government should also publish online all information that is provided in response to any RTI application, to prevent duplication of effort.

In conclusion, Jay P. Desai's book is an engaged citizen's wake-up call to the rest of us. It should move us from angst, to awareness and finally into action. I deeply hope that all citizens heed this call, so that India achieves not only prosperity, but also the happiness it so richly deserves.

Dr Parth J. Shah
President, Centre for Civil Society
New Delhi, September 2011

The Centre for Civil Society is an independent, non-profit research and education think tank based in New Delhi, India.

Acknowledgements
....

Writing a book of this breadth and scope invariably meant that I had to rely on extensive research and engage in continuous dialogue with a large number of knowledgeable people. I am truly grateful to all those who supported me in this effort and educated me on the subject of accountability and governance in India. As a result, there is a rather long list of people I need to thank profusely.

My Universal Consulting colleagues at the UC Centre for Strategic Synthesis, our internal think-tank, provided unflagging support to me for three years since December 2008, when we commenced this research project. The team, admirably led by the ever-smiling Shweta Gadia and the quietly confident Neha Tulsiani, worked tirelessly through the process, from conception to conclusion, over this long period. I was also extremely well-supported by Rhea Cordeiro in the last few months of our research and by Shreekant Khaitan in the initial phase. Jyoti Bijlani Shah and Asgari Pagarkar from UC's office staff were a great help in the concluding phase of our work. This book could not have been written without the entire team's devotion, diligence and determination. Thank you.

I have to thank, in particular, Dr Parth J. Shah, President of the Centre for Civil Society, who readily agreed to write a Foreword for this book.

My friend, Bobby Parikh, asked me 'a question of accountability' that literally ignited this effort and helped bring focus to the research. Thank you.

We interviewed a large number of Civil Society Organizations (CSOs) in the early stages of our research, and they were kind enough to give us their perspective on the subject. I would also like to express gratitude to Professor Michael L. Hand at Willamette University (Oregon, USA), for taking the time to examine our statistical analysis. My friends Anshu Chatterjee and Anand Krishna were generous with their time and gave me their views on the draft manuscript. Senior industry leaders Mr Ranjit Shahani, Mr Cyrus Guzder and Mr Ashok Barat were helpful in early discussions on the topic.

Global institutions and think tanks like the World Bank, Transparency International, World Economic Forum, United Nations Development Programme, Economist Intelligence Unit, UNESCO Institute for Statistics, Institute for Democracy and Electoral Assistance, Center for Systemic Peace, John Wiley & Sons, Inc., Global Integrity and Geert Hofstede granted us permission to use their data to conduct our analysis. I thank all of them.

I am truly grateful to the people at Pearson Education, especially Vivek Govil, K. P. R. Nair, Preeta Priyamvada, Saumya Chawla, Proteeti Banerjee and Vipin Kumar, who were very supportive and guided us through this long process.

My childhood friends Kapil and Jayashree Bhalla provided the inspiration for the cover design, in conjunction with artist Krsna Mehta and his assistant, Mayur Palekar. Thank you.

A big thank you to all those who took the time to read the draft manuscript and provide their views and comments on this book.

I would like to thank my four Partners at Universal Consulting, Ryan Albuquerque, Shankar Rajesh, Jagat Parikh and Samir Sathe, for giving me full support and freedom to undertake this research study. Their boundless energy, enthusiasm, motivation, good humour and maturity has helped to build a successful strategy consulting firm over the past 17 years.

My parents have always led by example and emphasized the importance of working for society and country, without expecting anything in return. Thank you.

Lastly, I would like to express gratitude to my effervescent wife Madhavi and my darling son Arjun for being part of my life, and being supportive of my writing moments.

If I have forgotten to thank somebody, it has been purely unintentional.

Important note: This research was not supported or funded by any external organization, and was entirely an initiative of Universal Consulting India Pvt. Ltd and our internal think-tank, the UC Centre for Strategic Synthesis.

Introduction
....
A Question of Accountability

A prudent question is one-half of wisdom.
Francis Bacon, 1561–1626

The horrific night of 26 November 2008 is one that most Indians would want to cast out of their memories. Terror descended on India's financial capital, Mumbai, with deathly armed attacks by terrorists on two premier downtown hotels, the main train station and a house of religious affiliation. Like many of my fellow citizens around the country, I sat transfixed by the television, shock, fear and outrage my three companions. A worried call to the Partners at our consulting firm thankfully confirmed that our team members were safe and accounted for. Word trickled in through telephone, email and text messages that close friends and family were also safe. With these immediate concerns at rest, a question ricocheted through my mind: what could have led to this gross failure of intelligence processes and the visible absence of preparedness? With my immediate world seemingly secure, I reluctantly turned in for the night, breaking in and out of a fragile sleep. The next morning I would awaken to the sad news that a student from my school and another from my college had fallen victim to the terrorists' bullets.

Over the next few days, the citizens of India rallied against the public administration, which they saw as our Achilles heel, deftly exploited by the terrorists. The sorrow, anger and frustration of the people was palpable. Protest marches, media debates and online forums demanded greater accountability from public officials. The pulsating force of this movement, both on-the-ground and in the ether-world, triggered more questions—why was nobody taking ownership, why was nobody being held responsible and, most importantly, who should be blamed—the public officials, or the normally apathetic citizens who had elected them in the first place? A gnawing realization dawned within; nothing I had done in 45 years of life as an Indian citizen qualified to absolve me of some of the blame, even if it was a failure of public administration.

A few days later, on a flight to Mumbai, I was seated next to Bobby Parikh, a friend and professional colleague since two decades. Just 10 days earlier, he had survived a harrowing escape from the 26/11 attacks after a horrendous night at the Taj Mahal Hotel. As he finished recounting the heart-stopping events, I asked him a question: 'Now that you have been granted another life, has it changed your view of the world?' Bobby thought for a few moments and in his characteristically measured manner, replied, 'I would like to know what I can do to improve accountability in our country, but where do I start?' With this question was launched a voyage of exploration into the world of accountability, a journey that has taken me three years. The continuous unravelling of corruption scandals over this period has only lent credence to the view that accountability in India is under threat, as never before.

My objective in writing this book was to increase the public understanding of the concept of accountability among the citizens of India. The assumption was that there were many like me, who knew little about accountability, were deeply concerned by its absence, but did not know what role they could play in improving it. I intend to explain to you why accountability is a critical element of governance, without which India will never be able to achieve its full economic, social and political potential. I also present a range of actions that individuals and businesses can pursue to improve accountability. Your role as a citizen of India is critical to this process, more than you might imagine. I would consider all my effort worthwhile if I can transport you from a feeling of helplessness about the current state of accountability, to one of hope for the future.

Many among us harbour a desire to see India as a respected global power, wielding significant influence on the world stage. For many more Indians, though, this mirage will reveal itself only after they see substantial improvements in the basics of life—healthcare, education, roads, power, water and housing. India is among the few countries that has blatantly neglected the fundamental needs of ordinary living for so large a population of its people, for so long a time. Right from our founding days, India was designed to be a liberal democracy, with free and fair elections through universal suffrage and a political framework with personal liberty and sanctity of the rights of an individual as its centre-piece. In practice, India has evolved to operate in many ways like a semi-liberal democracy, with inefficient public institutions, rampant unaccountability among many public officials, and delayed judicial recourse for violation of personal rights. The mis governance that we see around us is a strong signal that our liberal democracy is disobeying the principles of its grand design.

At the heart of our dismal economic, social and political performance lies the irregular and arrhythmic drum-roll of poor governance; non-standard, ad-hoc, whimsical. What drives poor governance is the absence of accountability in public office. Accountability is the heartbeat of good governance. Accountability fixes responsibility for outcomes on specific individuals, positions, departments, ministries or organizations. The culture of accountability appears not to have percolated into the Indian psyche, be it for citizens or for public officials. India is a country where collusion between law-breakers, law-keepers and law-makers often feeds the cancer of misgovernance. Not surprisingly, the 'rule of law' is often the exception and the 'rule of power', often the unwritten rule. The inability to swiftly penalize public officials and citizens who violate policies designed to ensure accountability, is the key to our malfunctioning governance system.

The maladies spawned by the unaccountable are many. Hundreds of millions of our citizens accept their undignified destiny with a sense of stoicism, almost resigned to a fate that ostensibly has a larger purpose than their miserable lives. It is from this turbid cesspool of despair and destiny that corrupt public officials draw their strength, to live their lives of self-aggrandizement. The realization that they exist to serve the people is alien to them. The reverse is more endemic to their thinking. Our citizens, in fact, feel accountable to public officials, perhaps a legacy of our feudal and colonial past. Noted economist Raghuram Rajan writes in his book *Fault Lines*, '... This will require a change in mindset of those in power, a change from thinking that public services, especially for the poor, are acts of charity by the government service provider rather than the due of the citizen. When government servants serve the people instead of ruling over them, India will have arrived ....'

It is a fallacy, of course, to assume that all public officials shun accountability. India has its fair share of outstanding public officials; unfortunately, they are often strait jacketed by a system that does not permit them to be accountable.

The absence of accountability strikes at the heart of many of the greatest tragedies that we have stood witness to over the past six decades. Some are chronic maladies, so widespread that we have been numbed into a state of silent acceptance. Others are acute ailments that have struck without warning, searing our collective psyche. In every instance, the epidemic of unaccountability has conquered the spirit of the Indian. There are several examples of these maladies, and I will touch upon some of them briefly.

The Bhopal gas tragedy of 1984 was a lethal disaster in which thousands of people lost their lives and many more were badly injured, due to the leakage of highly toxic methyl isocyanate gas from a manufacturing plant. The callousness of public officials that followed in its aftermath was even more tragic for those affected by the disaster. The world's worst industrial catastrophe should have resulted in quick justice. Unfortunately, this process took 25 years. Thousands of victims still suffer ill-health from that tragic accident.

In July 2005, excessive rains and unprecedented floods crippled the city of Mumbai for days, highlighting the absence of accountability and coordination among city authorities. The natural flood-protection barrier of mangrove swamps ravaged by rampant construction, an antiquated suburban drainage system weighed down by uncontrolled urban development, a river choked with untreated sewage and industrial effluents, all resulting from poor urban management, contributed to the floods. Ineffective disaster management by public authorities showered its curse on an already struggling populace.

The 2010 Commonwealth Games in New Delhi revealed the ugly and corrupt face of India for the world to see. The run-up to the event was studded with allegations of large-scale corruption, poor quality of infrastructure, and glaring inefficiencies in planning as well as in the execution of key projects. Reports revealed that in spite of there being around 21 governmental organizations engaged in preparing for the event, the absence of leadership and accountability among them resulted in the Prime Minister of India having to assume command to rescue the situation, barely two months before the Games (*International Herald Tribune* 2010). An opportunity to create a spectacular impact was lost to embarrassing front-page global press, highlighting the spectre of poor governance. Absence of accountability was at the heart of this disastrous spectacle.

The dust had barely settled on the new stadiums of the Commonwealth Games when another storm was brewing a few miles away. Irregularities in the allocation of the 2G telecom spectrum licenses in 2008 were being reported. The regulatory protocol of auctioning appeared to have been flouted, reportedly causing the government large amounts of notional monetary losses. Preliminary investigations revealed the absence of any competitive bidding and the allotment of 2G spectrum licenses at 2001 prices, instead of market prices (*The Economic Times* 2010). Again, the absence of accountability and sheer misgovernance acted in concert to create the cacophony of corruption.

There are also a multitude of chronic national issues that arise due to the culture of unaccountability prevalent in our public administration. Poor accountability plagues our creaking public healthcare infrastructure and services, especially in rural areas. High absenteeism among doctors and support staff, chronic shortage of medicines, primitive facilities, unhygienic conditions and sub-standard care are the norm. Healthcare in India is inequitable and ineffective, out of reach for much of the populace. Our public education infrastructure displays very little that is different. The pathetic schooling conditions are responsible for 25 per cent of rural children and more than 50 per cent of urban children opting to study in private schools, rather than in the free government-run schools. Reportedly, 25 per cent of government primary school teachers are absent on any given day and of those present, 25 per cent are found not to be engaged in teaching (*The Times of India* 2010). This absence of accountability impacts our future generations, who certainly deserve a better chance at a good life. The callous hand of accountability is not content with just ravaging our public healthcare and education infrastructure.

Millions of tonnes of food grains rot in warehouses every monsoon due to inefficiencies in the Public Distribution System (PDS), notwithstanding the fact that India houses 27 per cent of the world's under-nourished population and has more poverty than Sub-Saharan Africa (*The Times of India* 2010). While the examples are varied, endless and always disturbing, the underlying story remains the same: poor accountability and poor outcomes.

A number of scholars have studied specific areas of governance and accountability in India in great depth. I have attempted to present here what I hope is a more accessible framework to help increase the public understanding of accountability, by using a broad brush-stroke to paint a 'systems-overview' of this landscape. With this approach, I believe the reader will be in a better position to grasp the power of accountability. Understanding and unravelling the intricacies of accountability turned out to be a rather complex task. A multitude of intertwined cultural, social, political and economic factors are inextricably linked together, to create the flavour of accountability we experience today. To tease out the nuances of accountability, we asked a series of layered questions—how is accountability defined; how did accountability evolve in India over recorded history; can accountability be measured in some way; what is the relationship between accountability and the socio-economic potential of a country; which socio-economic factors are closely linked to accountability; and what role do existing policies, mechanisms and institutions play in ensuring accountability? We then went on to examine the broad initiatives that should be taken to improve accountability and, most importantly, what ordinary citizens and businesses can do to improve accountability in India. Over the next few pages, I will walk you through the evolution of our thinking on these questions, with a snap-shot of what you will read in the chapters that follow.

Chapter 1, 'The Origin of Angst', examines the evolution of accountability in India through the eyes of 3,500 years of recorded history, way back from the Vedic Age through to modern-day, post-colonial India. You will see how the silhouette of our ancestors still casts its long shadow over twenty-first century India, and how it shapes our expectations of accountability from public officials and from each other.

Chapter 2, 'The Accountability Deficit', will give you an overview of the concept of accountability and discuss the four foundations of accountability: *Appropriate Representation, Participative Conduct, Legitimate Conduct* and *Liability Enforcement*. Only if these four foundations are truly stable can you expect an environment where accountability will be strong. We then compare the level of accountability in India with other countries. To quantify accountability in India, we refer to cross-country governance indicators like the Corruption Perceptions Index, the Bribe Payers Index and the Worldwide Governance Indicators. These indices clearly showcase India's poor performance on governance and accountability. Another indicator, the Global Integrity Index, a study on the effectiveness of key accountability mechanisms, highlights the weaknesses in the implementation of accountability mechanisms in India. The poor quality of governance and accountability in India is also reflected in India's sub-standard economic and social performance, with the Doing Business Index, the Global Competitiveness Index and the Human Development Index providing empirical evidence of this. Accountability is a potent force with cascading power. It impacts the quality of governance, it impacts economic performance, and it impacts a country's performance on social indicators. Harnessed appropriately, accountability can be a powerful catalyst for the improvement of a country's all-round performance. But poor accountability threatens to shroud our future if it remains unchecked.

Chapter 3, 'Unveiling the Shroud', examines the societal fabric of India to explain the role that socio-economic factors could be playing in influencing the state of accountability, our cultural predisposition to the idea of being accountable, and our ability to extract accountability from those in power. India's socio-economic environment is characterized by low literacy, low income, high social inequality, and tremendous social diversity. Do these factors influence the quality of governance? Is low literacy a key constraint to achieving better governance? Does the high degree of social inequality predispose us towards poor governance? Does high social diversity act as a barrier to achieving better governance? To obtain greater clarity, we conducted a correlation analysis between those socio-economic factors that we thought may have some relationship with accountability, and the corresponding governance scores for a large number of countries. Factors such as adult literacy, social diversity, voter turn-out and population size, which we intuitively thought would hinder governance, show only a weak-to-moderate correlation with governance scores. On the other hand, factors like income per capita, the level of individualism in a society and social hierarchy have a moderate-strong correlation with governance. Sadly, India's relative position on those socio-economic factors that have a strong correlation with governance is weak. Our current standing on these socio-economic factors is therefore unlikely to be the springboard from which we launch into an era of good governance.

We then shift gears to review the institutions and mechanisms of accountability, which are designed to hold our democracy together. In Chapter 4, 'Three-Dimensional Accountability', we present the 3D construct that we built to optically examine and dissect the quality of accountability in the institutions that are responsible for good governance. With this 3D model as a frame of reference, the reader will be in a better position to understand how a particular action taken by the government fits into the overall schematic of accountability. We first talk about the three *mechanisms* of accountability: internal mechanisms (imposed by a government department on itself), horizontal mechanisms (imposed by one government department on another) and external mechanisms (imposed by citizens, civil society organizations, and the media, on the government). We then move on to introducing the three *institutions* of government: the Legislature, the Executive and the Judiciary, which are held accountable by these mechanisms. A three-dimensional scaffold of accountability is then constructed, with the four *foundations* of accountability (mentioned earlier), the three *mechanisms* of accountability, and the three *institutions* of government. The construction of this 3 D scaffold is the lens through which we examine the quality of accountability over the next three chapters.

Chapter 5, 'Legislative Accountability', Chapter 6, 'Executive Accountability', and Chapter 7, 'Judicial Accountability', examine the effectiveness of accountability mechanisms in each of the three institutions of government, the Legislature, the Executive and the Judiciary. These mechanisms are evaluated to assess whether they support or weaken the four foundations of accountability—*Appropriate Representation, Participative Conduct, Legitimate Conduct* and *Liability Enforcement*—for each of the three institutions. We conclude that these foundations are unstable due to several weaknesses in implementing the accountability mechanisms. The study of these weaknesses leads us to six potential areas of improvement to enhance accountability. That is the focus of the next chapter.

Chapter 8, 'The Six Initiatives', begins by summarizing and categorizing all the weaknesses in the accountability mechanisms of the Legislature, the Executive and the Judiciary, in the form of *six inadequacies*. These inadequacies point us to a broad roadmap for the improvement of accountability, in the form of six areas that we need to focus on. These *six initiatives* are classified as follows: *Information, Impartiality, Implementation, Infrastructure, Independence* and *Involvement*. The key action points needed to improve our performance in each of these areas are then set out. We then subjectively rate the government's current progress in each of these six areas to understand what needs to be done to bridge the performance gap between the current state and the desired state.

Finally, in Chapter 9, 'The Five-Fold Path', we turn our attention to the critical role that Civil Society Organizations (CSOs), citizens and the media play in strengthening accountability. We take a closer look at how CSOs create awareness, conduct assessments and advocate to support their cause. Building institutional capacity in these CSOs is critical, and is the easiest way for a citizen to play a role in the process of improving accountability. We recommend five avenues that citizens and businesses can pursue to support these CSOs: volunteering time, providing media access, providing intellectual capacity, providing technology and infrastructure, and providing monetary support.

The 'Epilogue' brings our travels to an end. First, we compare the paucity of accountability reforms over the past six decades with the intensity of economic reforms over the same period. Clearly, a burst of accountability and governance reforms is long overdue. We then discuss the concept of the 'Accountability Change Curve', where we comment on how the passage to a higher level of accountability will likely play out over the next decades.

As we conclude our reconnaissance across the landscape of accountability, I cannot help but feel a sense of fearful anticipation at the magnitude and gravity of the uphill journey that we must embark upon. It appears to me that India has been endowed with every political, economic and social obstacle that a country in search of its global position would not want to encounter on its pathway to modernity. Creating these obstacles are the endemic maladies of weak accountability and poor governance. Failure to circumvent these obstacles could result in disastrous consequences for the nation, if we collapse into the unending downward spiral of crony capitalism, oligarchic somnolence, stumbling growth, and the ever-waiting, middle-income trap that swallows promising economies with gusto. Yet, amidst the constant cascade of corruption scandals, there are clear signs of hope. Spurred by the efforts of the media, civil society organizations, citizens, and even the government, a process of change appears to have begun. The cesspool of despair and destiny promises not to remain stagnant forever.

Mahatma Gandhi famously said, '... You must be the change you want to see in the world...'. With these words, the father of our nation committed each of us to a path of action. More than any other entity, the ordinary citizens of India, you and I are responsible and accountable for the political, economic and social condition in which we live. It is my hope that those who read this book will transit from a state of *angst* about accountability, to a state of *awareness*, and ultimately, to a resting state of *action*.

PART I

Angst

1   The Origin of Angst

Set up eyes and ears in your kingdom that pick up weak
signals before your enemies.

Machiavelli, 1469–1527

Every country's culture represents a refracted image of its past, a reflection of its present, and is a repository of its future. The convoluted trajectory of India's history has an ambidextrous impact on our lives, sometimes positive, and occasionally negative. Social institutions like the caste system, which originated thousands of years ago, are still pervasive and impinge on the political and social environment of modern-day India. Similarly, the deficit in accountability visible today is not just a product of the present, but also a victim of our past.

The current concept of accountability originated more than 3,500 years ago. Ancient Indian texts like the *Ramayana* and the *Mahabharata* alluded to the idea of accountability and the need to check even the actions of the Kings, with the help of political and administrative regulations. An adage from the *Ramayana* says, '*Yatha raja tatha praja*' (as the ruler is, so shall be the subjects), emphasizing that rulers should lead by example, since their intellect, ability and righteousness impact the welfare of the citizens. The *Mahabharata* even approved a protest against a King who failed to perform his duty to protect his subjects. Another ancient Indian treatise, the *Arthashastra*, elaborated a system of vigilance and penalties designed to ensure that appointed officials perform their duties effectively.

Apart from these external controls, ancient Indian texts also highlighted the significance of self-monitoring one's actions for fear of the likely consequences. The concept of *karma* in Hinduism implies that each person is responsible for his or her actions. Depending on the moral quality of an action, individuals are rewarded or punished, either in this life or in a future life. This fear of 'bad *karma*' forces people to be more responsible for their actions, and therefore makes them more accountable (Reichenbach 1988).

Over many centuries, the concept of accountability evolved from a few informal guidelines to more formal mechanisms, established more recently. As India progressed to becoming a democratic nation, the citizens' ability to demand their rights and liberties also increased. Today, public officials are beginning to feel the responsibility that accountability bestows upon them. But for the moment, unroll the carpet of time and witness accountability evolving over the ages.

India's densely storied past can be broadly classified into five historical eras (Figure 1.1): the Vedic age, the Mauryan and Gupta ages, Medieval and post-Medieval India, Colonial India and, lastly, Independent India. A study of the historical evolution of accountability, set against the ever-changing socio-political backdrop, provides a rich texture to understand the origin of our angst.

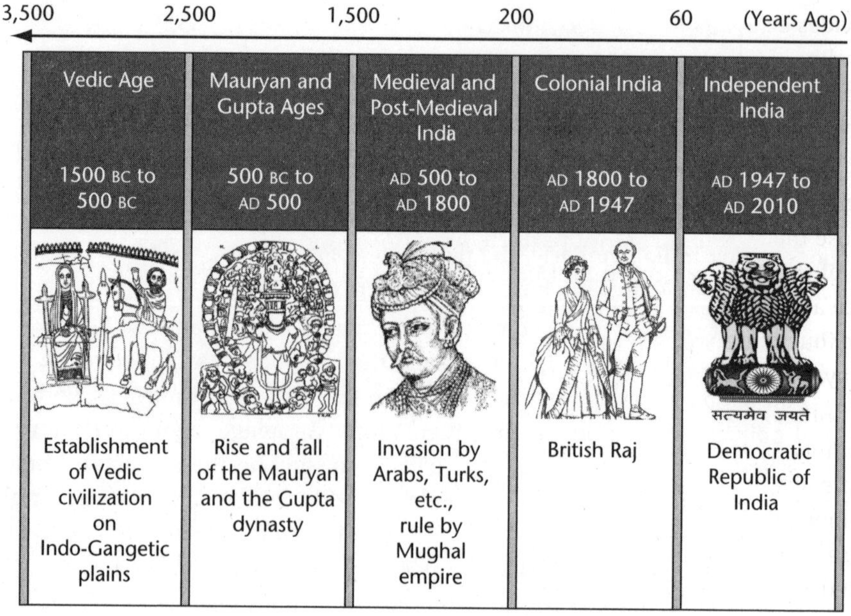

Figure 1.1   Five Historical Eras of India

::: The Vedic Age—1500 BC to 500 BC

The early invaders of India were the Aryans, who arrived around 1500 BC. This era saw the birth of the caste system and of religion, weaving the warp and weft of Indian society, still firmly enmeshed in the fabric of the Indian mind. This caste-based stratification divided society into four main varnas, or castes: the Brahmins, the Kshatriyas, the Vaishyas and the Shudras (*Encyclopædia Britannica* 2010). The Brahmins were the spiritual guides, teachers and promoters of law; the Kshatriyas were the warriors and rulers; the Vaishyas worked in agriculture or trade; and the Shudras served society as manual or agricultural labourers, artisans and masons. The original scheme of the varnas, based solely on the occupation of a person, was intended to provide a functional division of society, to improve productivity. Interestingly, interchange and intermixing of people belonging to different castes was liberally permitted (Sarma 2006).

The Vedic civilization laid down the foundations of Hinduism as well as the associated literature, which outlined the norms of social, political and religious life. Ancient Hindu scriptures illustrated the importance of duty and responsibility towards the family and society. Rulers were guided by this principle of duty towards the people. This responsibility was deemed so important that sometimes even 'questionable actions' were justified in the name of duty. The *Mahabharata* provides examples where decisions were taken for the sake of duty, ignoring the morality of those actions. The Vedic era thus allowed for a flexible approach to accomplishing one's duty (Varma 2004; Brown 2008).

This era also saw the introduction of accountability checks on the administration. The king was the ultimate authority, in charge of the management of the kingdoms and the administration of justice. There were provisions, however, to depose the king if he did not perform his duties appropriately, and for the election of the king by the general public. In practice, elections were a rare occurrence and dynastic rule was common. For instance, the Vedic period witnessed over four generations of rule by the Purus and 10 generations of rule by the Srnjayas (Pruthi 2004).

Another external check on the supreme authority of the king was the assembly—the *Sabha* and the *Samiti*. The *Sabha* was a permanent body of select people like the Brahmins and other rich patrons, while the *Samiti* was a body of common people, irrespective of class or wealth, equivalent to our modern Lower House or the Lok Sabha (Tiwari 2008). Matters of importance were always discussed with people through these public forums, providing citizens with an opportunity to participate in governance. It is truly remarkable that these provisions existed 3,500 years ago.

::: The Mauryan and Gupta Ages—500 BC to AD 500

In the beginning of this era, the Persians and Greeks invaded India, but their impact was marginal since they ruled for a brief period of time. They were defeated by the Mauryans, who went on to conquer and consolidate the entire subcontinent. Monarchy continued in this era; the king was the supreme ruler, the head of the army and the chief justice of the kingdom. As the kingdom grew, administration was decentralized to facilitate effective functioning and provide better supervision. The administrative machinery of the state developed, with numerous departments regulating and controlling state activities (Singh 1998). With expanding kingdoms and decentralized functioning of the government, it became increasingly difficult to organize *Sabhas* and *Samitis*. These were eventually discontinued, and so the opportunity for the common man to participate in the governance process diminished (Sharma 1996).

During this period, the *Arthashastra*, a comprehensive treatise on statecraft, economic policy and military strategy, was written by Kautilya, chief mentor of the emperor Chandragupta Maurya. The *Arthashastra* was adopted as the de facto guide to state administration and accountability in the Mauryan age. It emphasized the importance of institutional mechanisms, assuming that people behaved appropriately, only with the judicious application of restraint, punishment and incentives. The *Arthashastra* also suggested built-in checks and balances to contain malpractices (Adhikari 2010). Emphasis was placed on a network of spies and informers, who functioned as the surveillance arm of the king. These spies reported the malpractices and misconduct that officials engaged in (Prakash 1993). In the larger interest of expanding or protecting the State, however, rulers were allowed to compromise on morality and ethics (Boesche 2003; Chandrasekaran 2006). Since the welfare and development of the State were the main objectives of the king, it was justifiable to defeat an enemy using bribery or fraud as long as the kingdom benefited from it. Yet again in India's history, it appears that it was acceptable for morality to be sacrificed on the altar of duty.

Then appeared a book called *Manusmriti*, written by Manu, which prescribed the rules and responsibilities of people belonging to the four castes. Here, the duties of an individual belonging to a particular caste, or sub-caste, were set out. All facets of life were covered: rules related to dining, goods to be consumed, gods to be worshipped, and even marriage and relationships with other castes. The once flexible and vertical caste system designed in the Vedic times to enhance societal productivity became a horizontal, rigid and stratified structure with strong restrictions on inter-dining, inter-marriage and socialization. A strong social hierarchy was established, since the rules defined in the *Manusmriti* favoured first the Brahmins, then the Kshatriyas, followed by the Vaishyas and, lastly, the

Shudras. Equality before law did not exist, as social and religious restraints were imposed on the lower castes (Jaishankar and Haldar 2004). These Mauryan and Gupta traditions would forever seal the fate of countless millions for hundreds of generations to come, trapping them under the leaden weight of a 'caste-iron blanket'. As we will discover later in this book, the hierarchical nature of our present-day society, perhaps a product of the age-old caste system, does have some bearing on our ability to extract accountability from public officials.

⠿ Medieval and Post-Medieval India—AD 500 to AD 1800

Towards the end of the Mauryan and Gupta empires, the riches of India were plundered by Arab traders, Mongols, Turks, Iranian and Afghan rulers. In the early sixteenth century, the Mughals invaded India under the leadership of Babur. This laid the foundation of the Mughal dynasty, whose emperors became the most influential of all Muslim rulers in India. Poor governance, unfortunately, was one of the greatest weaknesses in the Mughal Empire's armoury. The King appointed and promoted civil and military officials based on references, introducing sub-jectivity and favouritism into the process. Administrative graft was rampant in the bureaucracy, as bribes became a common and acceptable practice to get work done. The judicial system too was plagued by mal-practices, as the *kazis* (judges) accepted bribes and amassed large fortunes as a result. For example, the chief *kazi* during Aurangzeb's reign amassed millions of rupees, jewellery, and other valuables (Bakshi 2003). The level of misgovernance increased in spite of the practice of using spies and agents to gather intelligence and report these malpractices.

The Mughal era also saw religious tolerance being reduced as most of the rulers discriminated against practitioners of other religions. The Emperor Akbar, though, tried to propagate religious harmony through initiatives like abolishing the discriminatory taxes levied on Hindus and including non-Mus-lims in his group of advisors (Thorpe and Thorpe 2009). Akbar's successors, however, did not sustain his efforts to encourage religious tolerance. Remnants of this religious disharmony occasionally surface in our society, shattering the silence of our peace.

⠿ Colonial India—AD 1800 to AD 1947

The British presence in India dates back to the early seventeenth century, with their early activities limited merely to business and trading. The Mughal Empire was disin-tegrating at this time, allowing the British a toe-hold from which to gain political and economic control over India. The British government, consequent to the Government of India Act 1858, assumed the task of directly administering India. A formal administrative and governance infrastructure was gradually established.

The blueprint of India's government and bureaucratic architecture was influenced by this British model of governance. A Legislative Council was responsible for enacting laws, while an Executive Council managed the government departments. The head of the administration (Governor-General or Viceroy) was assisted by the Legislative and the Executive Councils. For the first time, an organized system of justice was also created.

The foundation of a formal framework of accountability was also established during this era. The British set out policies to control the functioning of public officials and to curb misappropriation. An Auditor General was appointed to exercise control over the administration of public finances, and a Central Public Accounts Committee was created to monitor the reports of the Auditor General (Arora and Goyal 2005).

Another important development was the growing role of citizens and the media in demanding accountability from outside the government. A number of citizens' movements were held to highlight unfair government practices and injustices. The protest against the imposition of a heavy tax on salt (Mahatma Gandhi's Dandi March, or the Salt Satyagraha of 1930) avidly illustrates the power of these movements. Mahatma Gandhi and Bal Gangadhar Tilak started their newspapers, *Young India* and *Kesari*, respectively, as vehicles for communicating their ideas to citizens (Chaturvedi, www.congress.org.in).

There was also a darker side to the British Raj. Several provisions to curb transparency and public representation in government functioning were introduced. The Official Secrets Act 1923 was drafted to serve the interests of the colonial government and to control the flow of information on matters of public interest (Tiwari 2004). This created a culture of secrecy and information hoarding. Another provision introduced by the British in 1926 was called 'Contempt of Court' (Shah 2002; Chauhan 2010). The courts were considered to be representatives of the monarch, so any disregard shown for a court order, interference with administration of justice or insult to a court was a punishable offence. Citizens feared challenging the conduct of the Judiciary in case they invoked the 'contempt of court' provision.

Rather sadly, the religious disharmony between Hindus and Muslims, the seeds of which were sown in the earlier Mughal era, was deftly exploited by the British through their divide-and-rule policy. The partition of Bengal in 1905 divided the Hindus and Muslims, weakening the political protests against the British (Biswas 2005). Similarly, the encouragement provided by the British to the formation of the Muslim League of India and the granting of separate electorates to Muslims in

1909 were attempts to create a further divide, by playing up already simmering religious differences (Ouedraogo 2009).

The divergences between various castes also sharpened during the British era. Brahmins were endowed with privileges like differential access to Western education and positions in government services under the East India Company (Deane 2009). The British Raj further formalized the caste system by introducing caste-based records in a country-wide census in 1931 (Sanne, http://blog. designs-for-automotion.de). Differentiation between castes deepened even further, with the reservation of seats for certain castes in the provincial and central legislatures, through the Government of India Act 1935 (Lee 2008).

::: Independent India—AD 1947 to AD 2010

As India took its first giant step towards freedom and democracy, the Constitution granted all citizens certain fundamental rights: equality, freedom of speech, and recourse to constitutional remedies for the enforcement of these rights. From the first general elections in 1952, all adult citizens, irrespective of caste, religion, income, gender and geography, were provided with voting rights.

In the early post-independence years, the government established governance institutions like the Central Vigilance Commission and the Central Bureau of Investigation. With the passage of time, several mechanisms like the Public Interest Litigation (1980), Lokayukta (1984), Prevention of Corruption Act (1988) and, more recently, the Right to Information Act (2005), were also introduced to enforce accountability and allow citizens to proactively participate in the process of governance.

The relative timing of the introduction of these accountability mechanisms broadly mirrors the pattern seen in developed democracies like the US and the UK. India was not unduly late in introducing most key accountability mechanisms (Figure 1.2).

On paper, these accountability mechanisms and institutions have strengthened the capacity of citizens to register complaints and seek accountability for the conduct and performance of public officials. In practice, a lot more work is required.

A large number of Civil Society Organizations (CSOs) have also emerged in India, in the interests of the common good. They include organizations like NGOs, community groups, professional associations, parts of the media and academia (Essia and Yearoo 2009). More recently, citizens, CSOs and the media have played a catalysing role in increasing accountability in India by exposing acts of the corrupt and advocating more transparent policies in the interests of society.

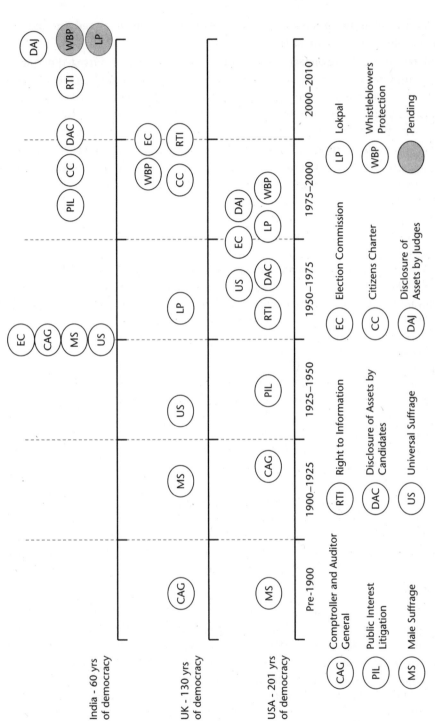

Figure 1.2 Introduction of Key Accountability Mechanisms

This brief study of the evolution of accountability in India partly explains the origin of our angst with the present. We are now better prepared to embark on the next phase of our journey: to witness the current deficit in accountability.

References

Adhikari, Gautam. 2010. 'Rediscovering Emperor Ashoka'. *The Times of India*, 9 October.

Arora, Ramesh Kumar and Rajni Goyal. 2005. 'Integrity in the Civil Service'. *Indian Public Administration: Institutions and Issues*. New Delhi: Wishwa Prakashan, p. 596.

Bakshi, S. R. 2003. *Advanced History of Medieval India*. New Delhi: Anmol Publications.

Biswas, Kumud. 2005. 'Lord Curzon and the Partition of Bengal'. Available at www.boloji. com (accessed on 5 April 2010).

Boesche, Roger. 2003. 'Kautilya's Arthashastra on War and Diplomacy in Ancient India', *The Journal of Military History*. Available at http://muse.jhu.edu (accessed on 6 April 2010).

Brown, Larry A. 2008. '*Mahabharata*: the Great Epic of India'. http://larryavisbrown. homestead.com (accessed on 4 February 2010).

'Caste—Social Differentiation'. 2010. *Encyclopædia Britannica*. Available at www. britannica.com (accessed on 3 February 2010).

Chandrasekaran, Pravin. 2006. 'Kautilya: Politics, Ethics and Statecraft'. Available at http://mpra.ub.uni-muenchen.de (accessed on 5 April 2010).

Chaturvedi, Jagdish Prasad. 'Role of Press in India's Struggle for Freedom'. Available at www.congress.org.in (accessed on 3 February 2010).

Chauhan, Meenakshi. 2010. 'Contempt Power of Court'. Available at www.legalserviceindia. com (accessed on 14 February 2011).

Deane, T. 2009. 'A Brief History of Discrimination in India'. Available at http://uir.unisa. ac.za (accessed on 3 February 2010).

Essia, Uwem and Afzal Yearoo. 2009. 'Strengthening civil society organizations/government partnership in Nigeria', *International NGO Journal*, 4(9), pp. 368–74. Available at www. academicjournals.org (accessed on 12 April 2010).

Jaishankar, K. and Debarati Haldar. 2004. '*Manusmriti*: A Critique of the Criminal Justice Tenets in the Ancient Indian Hindu Code'. Available at www.erces.com (accessed on 6 April 2010).

Lee, Yeonhwa. 2008. 'A Social History of Hindustan: The Indian Caste System and non-Hindu Influences'. Available at www.zum.de (accessed on 6 April 2010).

Ouedraogo, Dawn. 2009. 'Imperialist British India—Divide and Rule Tactic'. Available at http://indian-history.suite101.com (accessed on 5 April 2010).

Prakash, Aseem. 1993. 'State and Statecraft in Kautilya's *Arthashastra*'. Paper presented at the Fall Semester Mini-Conference organized by the Workshop in Political Theory and Policy Analysis, 11–13 December. Bloomington: Indiana University. Available at http://dlc.dlib.indiana.edu/dlc/ (accessed on 5 April 2010).

Pruthi, R. K. 2004. 'Vedic Society'. *Vedic Civilization*. New Delhi: Discovery Publishing House, pp. 107–08. Available at http://books.google.co.in (accessed on 12 February 2010).

Reichenbach, Bruce. 1988. 'The Law of Karma and the Principle of Causation', *Philosophy East and West*, 38 (4): 399-410. Available at http://ccbs.ntu.edu.tw (accessed on 4 February 2010).

Sanne, Sebastian. 'British colonialism in India and its influence on the Indian society'. Available at http://blog.designs-for-automotion.de (accessed on 2 February 2010).

Sarma, Manashi. 2006. 'Caste system and democracy in India'. Available at www.hvk.org (accessed on 2 February 2010).

Shah, Parth. 2002. 'We the people of free India'. Available at www.ccsindia.org (accessed on 22 July 2009).

Sharma, Ram Sharan. 1996. 'Stages in Polity: Vedic and Post-Vedic'. *Aspects of Political Ideas and Institutions in Ancient India*. New Delhi: MB Publishers Pvt. Ltd, p. 367.

Thorpe, Edgar and Showick Thorpe. 2009. 'History of India: Medieval India', in *The Pearson General Studies Manual*. New Delhi: Dorling Kindersley India Pvt. Ltd, pp. 2.77–2.78.

Tiwari, A. N. 2004. 'Transparency and Accountability in Administration'. *Orissa Review*, pp. 27–31. Available at www.orissa.gov.in (accessed on 23 July 2009).

Tiwari, Shashi. 2008. 'Democratic Assemblies in Vedic Era.' Available at www.scribd.com. (accessed on 2 February 2010).

Varma, Pavan. 2004. *Being Indian*. New Delhi: Penguin Books.

2   The Accountability Deficit

The hardest thing to see is what is in front of your eyes.

Goethe, 1749–1832

The word 'deficit' conjures up an image of an economy that is mismanaged, with significant trade imbalances and large-scale fiscal profligacy. The most worrisome 'deficit' that India faces, however, is not of a macro-economic nature; rather, it is the substantial deficit of accountability in our country's governance. Discuss the morning newspaper with your family, attend a business conference, chat with your office colleagues or friends, and you will find that the conversation invariably turns to the misgovernance in India. The mind-space that governance issues occupy in the Indian conversation is large, especially after the recent public agitation that exploded in the final months of this book going to print. In one 2010 survey, corruption was voted as the second-most serious global issue by 66 per cent of the respondents in India, next only to terrorism (Globescan 2010). Accountability is often discussed in the same breath, but is less well understood. This chapter reveals the shroud that wraps accountability, characterizes the idea it represents, examines its relationship with governance, and the economic and social performance of a country. Our first stop will be at the basic concept of governance and accountability.

Governance can be broadly defined as 'the manner in which political, economic and social power is exercised to manage a country's affairs for development' (McCawley 2005). Governance includes all the processes, the people and the public institutions that create and implement policies to enhance a country's economic growth, infrastructure, employment, environment, fiscal health, rule of law and more. Good governance provides the life-blood that courses through a country's socio-political and economic system. There is no principle more sacrosanct to good governance than ensuring that those who lead and manage governments are always accountable to their citizens. Governance is the heart of a pulsating democracy, and accountability is its heartbeat.

Accountability is the process that counter-checks the policies, people and institutions responsible for governance, to ensure that their performance is legitimate and transparent, and that the citizens' interests are protected. For example, if a Ministry has been granted funds to build roads and highways, accountability mechanisms should check whether the Ministry used the funds legitimately, whether the contract for road construction was granted through a fair and transparent process, and if the target outcome was met. Similarly, if a scheme guaranteeing employment has been introduced by the government, accountability mechanisms should monitor and assess the implementation status of the scheme; whether employment targets were met, whether the citizens received the salaries promised, and if their grievances were addressed.

Accountability involves holding public officials *answerable* for their performance, though some scholars argue that *answerability* alone does not result in accountability. *Answerability* allows only for the monitoring and questioning of these officials to judge their performance. Any assessment, however, needs to be followed by action, so that public officials are punished for any performance that does not meet expectations. Andreas Schedler (Schedler et al. 1999), a professor of political science at CIDE (Centro de Investigación y Docencia Económicas), suggests that *enforcement*—imposing penalties or sanctions on power-holders who have violated their public duties—is a key aspect of accountability. Mark Bovens (2006), a professor of public administration at Utrecht University, argues that penalties or sanctions are the key elements that distinguish accountability from mere justifications of poor performance. Accountability, therefore, is best defined as the process of *monitoring* and *assessing* action plans and performance of public officials, as well as *sanctioning* them accordingly (Ackerman 2005; Bovens 2006; Malena et al. 2004). By that definition, public officials in India may be answerable for their actions, but are less accountable, given the endemic delays in delivering justice.

Accountability is a two-way process, a dialogue between the *objects* of accountability and the *agents* of accountability (Ackerman 2005; UNDP 2006). Public officials, or other power-holders, are the *objects* of accountability since they are entrusted with the authority to take decisions on behalf of all citizens. They are obligated to provide justifications for their actions. Ordinary citizens, civil society organizations (CSOs), the media and independent government agencies act as the balancing *agents* of accountability. These *agents* monitor the actions of public officials and reward or punish them, when necessary (Figure 2.1).

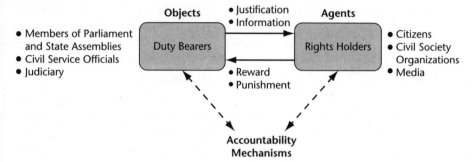

Figure 2.1 The Actors of Accountability

Source: United Nations Development Programme. 2006. 'Mutual Accountability Mechanisms: Accountability, Voice and Responsiveness', Diagram 1, www.undp.org.

An important aspect of the relationship between the *objects* and *agents* of accountability is the tension that exists at the surface where they interact. While it is the duty of public officials to explain their conduct and performance, it is also the responsibility of the *agents* of accountability, including ordinary citizens, to question these public officials. This is the cornerstone of a truly robust democracy, one where a constructive dialogue between the *objects* and *agents* of accountability keeps the system in a state of perpetual improvement.

Both the *objects* and the *agents* of accountability have various *accountability mechanisms* at their disposal; laws, policies, independent agencies and public campaigns, to enhance accountability. Public officials (*objects*) can use these mechanisms to provide information about their conduct and performance, so that citizens are aware that officials are obeying the law and serving the public interest in an effective manner. Citizens, CSOs and the media (*agents*) can leverage these accountability mechanisms to seek justification from public officials for their actions.

Accountability should not be restricted to merely a reactive analysis of past actions taken by public officials, though this helps to detect transgressions in conduct. True democracy flowers only when there is proactive participation in policy-making and execution by citizens, CSOs and the media, to prevent misgovernance and incompetence. Accountability, therefore, should be both *proactive* (ex-ante) and *reactive* (ex-post), as stated by John Ackerman (2005) of the Latin American Faculty of Social Sciences.

A key element of *proactive* or *ex-ante* accountability involves citizens selecting competent individuals to represent them in public office, so as to reduce the probability of misgovernance. We call this element *Appropriate Representation*.

Another key element of proactive accountability is when citizens continuously participate in the process of decision-making and execution of public policies. This *Participative Conduct* helps to reduce the potential for misconduct during the implementation of policies. Proactive accountability thus improves the quality of public representation and the efficacy of decision-making by public officials.

On the other hand, *reactive* or *ex-post* accountability examines the actions of public officials to check their legitimacy. We call this element *Legitimate Conduct*. Reactive accountability also includes enforcing a liability on public officials to make them responsible for their conduct. We call this element *Liability Enforcement*. *Legitimate Conduct* and *Liability Enforcement* are the two key elements of reactive accountability, designed to check the actions of public officials and hold them responsible.

The *house of accountability* thus rests on the strength of four foundations: *Appropriate Representation, Participative Conduct, Legitimate Conduct* and *Liability Enforcement*. The first two foundations are the key elements of proactive accountability, while the latter two are the key elements of reactive accountability (Figure 2.2).

These four foundations stabilize and reinforce each other, providing a firm base on which the house of accountability can be built. We will now closely examine each of these four foundations, to better understand what each one stands for.

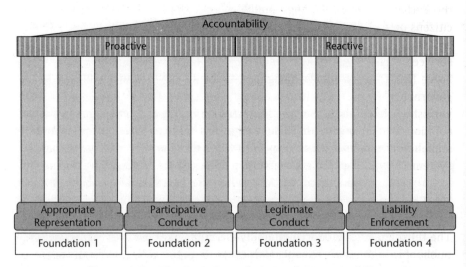

Figure 2.2 The Four Foundations of Accountability

::: Foundation 1—Appropriate Representation

The first foundation of accountability is the appropriate representation of citizens by capable and reliable officials in public administration. The key to having a responsive and transparent government is ensuring that the right individuals occupy public office. Accountability mechanisms strengthen this foundation by ensuring free and fair elections, a competitive selection process for public officials, a transparent process for the transfer of officials, and objective assessment and promotion of officials.

The Union Public Service Commission (UPSC), for example, conducts competitive examinations for the appointment of officials in public administration. Similarly, the Judicial Collegium is an independent body that is supposed to evaluate judges based on merit, and recommend deserving candidates for appointment to the Supreme Court and the High Court.

::: Foundation 2—Participative Conduct

The second foundation of accountability implies that the government proactively invites the participation of citizens, CSOs and the media to assist in effective governance on a continuous basis. This process increases trust and transparency between public officials and citizens, reducing the frictional tension between the *objects* and the *agents* of accountability. Several mechanisms exist to engage citizens in the process of governance.

Public hearings, for example, held by some ministries, are platforms where citizens are invited to share their views while policies are being formulated in the Parliament. The Planning Commission, for example, invited opinions from citizens on the creation of the 12th Five-Year Plan. State governments like Delhi and Bangalore have involved citizens in the planning and delivery of public services, through joint initiatives like Bhagidari and the Bangalore Agenda Task Force (BATF), respectively. Bhagidari, in Delhi, is an example of participatory governance, where both citizens and city administration officials jointly conduct workshops to discuss the civic issues commonly faced in Delhi, suggest probable solutions and implement them. Similarly, BATF is an initiative in Bangalore where stakeholders jointly define projects to improve the city's infrastructure and systems, and support the government in its implementation.

::: Foundation 3—Legitimate Conduct

The third foundation of accountability is the transparent and honest conduct of public officials, living up to the standards expected from those in public life. Public officials should act fairly, operate within their legal boundaries, and perform their duties in the interests of the citizens. One of the key objectives of most account-ability mechanisms is monitoring and assessing the performance of these public officials.

The Annual Performance Appraisal Reports, for example, is a mechanism to assess whether the performance targets of public officials have been met. Similarly, agencies like the Central Vigilance Commission (CVC) and the Central Bureau of Investigation (CBI) monitor and investigate cases of misappropria-tion and fraud committed by public officials. Citizens, through Report Cards and Audits, can assess the quality of public services delivered by local officials.

∷ Foundation 4—Liability Enforcement

The fourth foundation of accountability is the application of sanctions against errant public officials. Mere evaluation of an individual's actions does not nec-essarily result in better accountability. Punitive actions such as legal proceed-ings, penalty fees, resignation or public justification are needed to enforce accountability.

For example, the Constitution provides for dismissal or reduction in rank of civil service officials as a penalty for misconduct. Citizens can also use the Public Inter-est Litigation mechanism to legally challenge suspect practices of public officials.

Accountability mechanisms and institutions should be designed with the objective of stabilizing and reinforcing these four foundations. When these foun-dations are truly stable, the beat of accountability rhythmically powers the heart of governance.

How stable are these four foundations of accountability? To gauge the level of accountability in a country, one can look at a measure of governance, since the quality of governance is ultimately a reflection of the level of accountability in a country. The general perception among citizens is that accountability in India is abysmally low, based on the poor quality of governance in our country. Even a casual glance at the state of governance in India reveals innumerable instances of apathy, liberal abuse of power, the pathetic state of public services, and ram-pant corruption that invades the life of an ordinary citizen. Cases of misappro-priation of public funds regularly make headlines. Grants or subsidies allocated by ministries fail to reach the beneficiaries. The reputation of law enforcement agencies has also been checkered by instances of bribes, injustice and political interference.

How do we quantify this poor quality of governance? On a relative basis, how do we fare against other countries? Fortunately, a whole range of comprehensive indicators is available, which allows us to view India's position on multiple dimensions of governance. Some indicators are straight-forward measures of the quality of governance institutions, while others derive the quality of governance by measuring contributing factors like the extent of bribes paid, or the quality of bureaucracy in a country. A survey of these comparative indicators of governance firmly anchors our fears about India's poor performance in many critical areas needed to build a sound democracy.

India is perceived to be one of the world's greatest democracies, largely due to the miracle of our regular and efficient elections, a free media and significant civil liberties. We take great pride in the knowledge that we are the world's largest democracy. In reality, India is far from being the perfect democracy that we would like to imagine. 'The Democracy Index 2010', compiled by the Economist Intelligence Unit, measures the quality of democracy around the world, and categorizes countries into *full* democracies (the top 26 countries), *flawed* democracies (middle 53 countries), *hybrid* regimes (the next 33 countries), and *authoritarian* countries (bottom 55 countries). Disappointingly, India is classified as a flawed democracy, ranked 40th out of the 167 countries evaluated by the 2010 index (Figure 2.3).

Country	India	USA	UK	China	Brazil	Russia
Rank (167 Countries)	40	17	19	136	47	107

Figure 2.3   Democracy Index, 2010

Note: The numbers indicate the ranks of the countries on the index; a lower rank (1) is a better functioning democracy.
Source: The Economist Intelligence Unit. 2010. 'Democracy Index 2010: Democracy in Retreat', Table 2, www.eiu.com.

To join the elite club of *full* democracies, citizens need to actively and constructively engage in the political process, not just momentarily at the time of elections, in order to create a more favourable democratic culture in the country. Governance and accountability are important pillars of democracy, just as much as individual rights and civil liberties. India's score on this index is low due to corruption and poor accountability in the government.

India's poor performance on governance has been well-established by other international studies over the years. With a score of 3.3 on 10 in Transparency International's 'Corruption Perceptions Index 2010', India was ranked a lowly 87th among the 178 countries evaluated, on perceived corruption in the public sector (Figure 2.4).

India has had a consistently poor score on this indicator, in the range of 2.5–3.5 on 10, across the last decade. We continue to be perceived as a corrupt nation. Given the recent outbreak of corruption scandals, it is unlikely that we will see

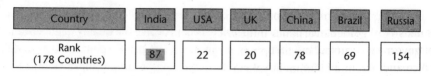

Country	India	USA	UK	China	Brazil	Russia
Rank (178 Countries)	87	22	20	78	69	154

Figure 2.4   Corruption Perceptions Index, 2010

Note: The numbers indicate the ranks of the countries on the index; lower rank (1) means lower corruption.
Source: Transparency International. 2010. Reprinted from *Corruption Perceptions Index*. Copyright 2010. Transparency International: The Global Coalition Against Corruption. Used with permission. For more information, visit http://www.transparency.org.

any change in this position over the next few years. Another study conducted by Transparency International, the 'Bribe Payers Index' (2008), measures the likelihood of firms from 22 of the world's industrialized countries having to pay bribes abroad. India was ranked 19th of the 22 countries in 2008, indicating a higher likelihood of Indian companies paying bribes abroad (Figure 2.5).

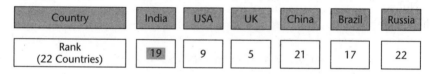

Country	India	USA	UK	China	Brazil	Russia
Rank (22 Countries)	19	9	5	21	17	22

Figure 2.5   Bribe Payers Index, 2008

Note: The numbers indicate the ranks of the countries on the index; lower rank (1) means lower incidence of bribes.
Source: Transparency International. 2008. Reprinted from *Bribe Payers Index*. Copyright 2008. Transparency International: The Global Coalition Against Corruption. Used with permission. For more information, visit http://www.transparency.org.

Another survey conducted by Transparency International, called 'Global Corruption Barometer 2010', interviewed members of the general public in 86 countries to understand their views on corruption. This study found that 74 per cent of Indian respondents felt that corruption in India had increased in the previous three years (Transparency International 2010). India came in the top tier of countries, where more than 50 per cent of the respondents reported paying a bribe to access public services over the previous year. This high level of bribery in India is widely perceived as a major obstacle for the country. A study by the Political and Economic Risk Consultancy in 2010 evaluated 12 Asian countries on the efficiency of their bureaucracy, and ranked them on the basis of the performance of their civil servants and public administration. India was ranked last. The study said that civil services in India are 'power-centres who have resisted reforms' (Press Trust of India 2010).

India's poor performance on governance is powerfully highlighted by the World Bank's Worldwide Governance Indicators, which ranks countries on six dimensions of governance: control of corruption, government effectiveness, regulatory quality, voice and accountability, political stability and rule of law. In 2009, India ranked way down at 112 of the 213 countries evaluated, scoring poorly on dimensions like political stability, control of corruption and regulatory quality (Figure 2.6).

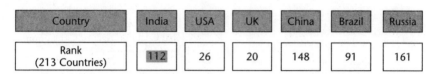

Country	India	USA	UK	China	Brazil	Russia
Rank (213 Countries)	112	26	20	148	91	161

Figure 2.6   Worldwide Governance Indicators, 2009

Note: The numbers indicate the ranks of the countries on the index; lower rank (1) means better governance.
Source: Kaufmann et al. 2010. *The Worldwide Governance Indicators 2009*. The International Bank for Reconstruction and Development. The World Bank. www.data.worldbank.org.

Not surprisingly, the quality of governance in India has remained dismal over the last decade, with scores ranging between −0.11 and −0.26 (Figure 2.7).

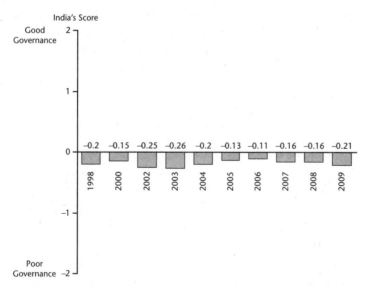

Figure 2.7   Worldwide Governance Indicators, 1998–2009

Note: The numbers indicate the average score on the six dimensions; a lower score means poor governance.
Source: Kaufmann et al. 2010. *The Worldwide Governance Indicators 1998–2009*. The International Bank for Reconstruction and Development. The World Bank. www.worldbank.org.

While many surveys measure and reiterate India's poor performance on governance, a study by Global Integrity, an independent organization, attempts to assess India's performance on accountability. Global Integrity conducted an assessment of the effectiveness of key accountability and anti-corruption mechanisms across countries (Global Integrity 2009). India is rated between weak to moderate (Figure 2.8).

Country	India	USA	China	Brazil	Russia
Score (Out of 100)	70	85	60	76	69

Figure 2.8   Global Integrity Index, 2009

Note: The numbers indicate the scores of the countries. The latest data available for Russia is for the year 2008.

| < 60 | Very weak | 60–69 | Weak | 70–79 | Moderate | 80–89 | Strong | 90–100 | Very Strong |

Source: Global Integrity. 2009. 'Global Integrity Report 2009'. www.globalintegrity.org.

This survey gave India high scores on the existence of accountability mechanisms, but low scores on their implementation. For example, while India has a strong rating on the existence of an anti-corruption law, it has a weak rating on its implementation. This implementation gap results in India scoring poorly on the survey parameters of 'government accountability' and 'administration and civil service' (Figure 2.9).

Over the years, India's performance has remained in the weak to moderate range on the Global Integrity Index (Figure 2.10).

India's low ranking on all these governance and accountability indicators clearly and unequivocally indicates that the quality of our governance is poor, compared to most countries. What is the impact of poor governance on the economic and social performance of our country? Does poor governance drag India down in other spheres? In a globalized world with cross-border flows of financial and intellectual capital, the quality of governance in a country is likely to have a bearing on its economic performance. If this is true, then a country's economic performance also points towards the efficiency of its governance institutions.

India's relatively poor economic performance, notwithstanding the euphoria around 'emerging India', is plainly visible in the World Bank's 'Doing Business Index 2010'. India ranks all the way down at 133 out of the 183 countries on this index, scoring low on most parameters like ease of starting a business, employing workforce, enforcing contracts and securing permits (Figure 2.11).

Parameter	Description	India's Score (out of 100)	Rating
Civil Society, Public Information, Media	Freedom of functioning to Civil Society Organizations, free media and information availability	72	Moderate
Elections	Conduct of free and fair elections at the national and local level	70	Moderate
Government Accountability	Existence and effectiveness of accountability mechanisms for Legislature, Executive and Judiciary, budget process	59	Very weak
Administration and Civil Service	Existence and effectiveness of civil service regulations, whistle-blowing measures, e-procurement provisions	66	Weak
Oversight and Regulation	Existence and effectiveness of National Ombudsmen, Supreme Audit Institution, business regulations	80	Strong
Anti-Corruption and Rule of Law	Existence and effectiveness of anti-corruption laws and agencies	71	Moderate
	Overall Score	70	Moderate

Figure 2.9   India's Scorecard on Global Integrity Index, 2009

Note: The numbers indicate the score of the country on the parameters

| < 60 | Very weak | 60–69 | Weak | 70–79 | Moderate | 80–89 | Strong | 90–100 | Very Strong |

Source: Global Integrity. 2009. 'Global Integrity Report 2009'. www.globalintegrity.org.

Our lethargic bureaucracy makes India a difficult country to do business in. For instance, it takes 30 days and 13 procedures to start a business in India, six days and six procedures in the United States, and just three days and three procedures in Singapore. Registering a property in India takes 44 days, while it takes 12 days in the United States and just five days in Singapore. Other administrative hurdles in the payment of taxes and enforcing contracts have made India one of the poorest performing countries on this global index (World Bank et al. 2009). India's performance on this index has been consistently poor; India scored a low rank of 132 on the index in 2009 as well.

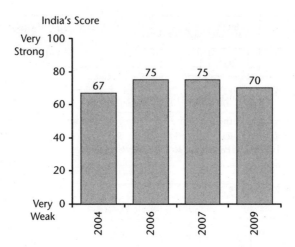

India's Score

Figure 2.10   Global Integrity Index, 2004–09

Note: The numbers indicate the overall score of India on the index
Source: Global Integrity. 'Global Integrity Report: 2004–2009'.
www.globalintegrity.org.

Country	India	USA	UK	China	Brazil	Russia
Rank (183 Countries)	133	4	5	89	129	120

Figure 2.11   Doing Business Index, 2010

Note: The numbers indicate the ranks of the countries on the index; lower rank (1) indicates greater ease of doing business.
Source: IBRD. The World Bank. 2010. 'Doing Business 2010: Reforming Through Difficult Times'. Table 1.3. www.data.worldbank.org.

India's relatively poor competitive position from an economic standpoint is also visible in the World Economic Forum's 'Global Competitiveness Index' rankings. This index measures competitiveness in countries based on the performance of institutions, policies and factors that determine the level of productivity of a country. In 2010–11, India ranked 51st among the 139 countries evaluated, with inadequate infrastructure, corruption and an inefficient government bureaucracy being the top reasons for its poor score (World Economic Forum 2010). The detrimental impact of poor governance and accountability on India's economic performance is again highlighted (Figure 2.12). What is worse is that India's ranking on this indicator has seen no substantial improvement since 2004 (Figure 2.13).

A correlation analysis that we conducted between the World Bank's Worldwide Governance Indicators (governance performance) and the World Economic Forum's Global Competitiveness Index (economic performance) across 96

Country	India	USA	UK	China	Brazil	Russia
Rank (139 Countries)	51	4	12	27	58	63

Figure 2.12 Global Competitiveness Index, 2010–11

Note: The numbers indicate the ranks of the countries; lower rank (1) indicates better economic competitiveness.
Source: World Economic Forum. *The Global Competitiveness Report 2010–11*. Table 4. www.weforum.org.

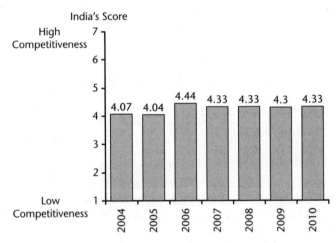

Figure 2.13 Global Competitiveness Index, 2004–10

Note: The numbers indicate the overall scores of the country, between 1 and 7; lower score indicates lower economic competitiveness.
Source: World Economic Forum. *The Global Competitiveness Report: 2004–2010*. www.weforum.org.

countries clearly shows the strong positive relationship (r = 0.86) between governance and economic competitiveness (Figure 2.14).

Some scholars have established a statistically significant link between corruption (Transparency International's Corruption Perceptions Index) and Foreign Direct Investment (FDI) inflows, showing that the more corrupt a country is, the lower is the inflow of FDI. By discouraging FDI, corruption impacts the revenues available for development (Ketkar et al. 2005). Another study indicated that countries with higher corruption and lower public transparency receive larger equity inflows, which are flighty and not as sustainable as FDI (Kose et al. 2006; Prasad 2011). While there has been a steady increase in FDI since India liberalized in 1991, in the more recent past FDI flow to India has dwindled. With the continuous onslaught of corruption scandals that occupy great mind-share among investors, it will become even more difficult to obtain sustainable investments from overseas.

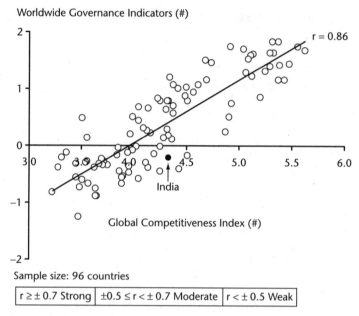

Worldwide Governance Indicators (#)

Figure 2.14   Correlation between Governance and Economic Competitiveness

Note: Author's own analysis.
Source: Data from the World Economic Forum, *Global Competitiveness Report 2010–2011* (www.weforum.org); and the World Bank, Worldwide Governance Indicators 2009 (www.worldbank.org).

Researchers at the Stanford University Graduate School of Business studied the relationship between the level of corruption in a country and the valuation of its corporations. The research shows that firms in more corrupt countries pay a price in terms of their market value, since they trade at much lower market multiples, than firms in less corrupt countries. The perception that corrupt countries are riskier to operate in, translates into investors demanding higher rates of return (Lee and Ng 2004). Furthermore, corruption deters long-term investors, who prefer well-regulated, easily accessible equity markets.

Clearly, good governance and economic development are strongly inter-linked.

The social impact of poor governance is a cause for even greater worry. India's poor performance on social indicators is highlighted by the United Nations Development Programme's (UNDP) 'Human Development Index 2010'. This index evaluated 169 countries on three basic dimensions of human development: access to knowledge (actual and expected years of schooling), long and healthy life (life expectancy at birth), and decent standard of living (Gross National Income per capita). India ranks a dismal 119th out of 169 countries on overall human development (Figure 2.15).

On the important social indicator of Infant Mortality Rate (deaths per 1,000 live births), India fares badly again, compared to other countries (Figure 2.16).

Figure 2.15   Human Development Index, 2010

Note: The numbers indicate the ranks of the countries on the index; lower rank (1) indicates better human development.
Source: United Nations Development Programme. 2010. *Human Development Report 2010*. Statistical Annex -Table 1. www.undp.org.

Figure 2.16   Infant Mortality Rate, 2009

Note: The numbers indicate the values of the countries on the index; lower value (1) indicates lower infant mortality.
Source: The World Bank. 2009. www.data.worldbank.org.

Yet another social indicator that brings to the surface our poor social performance is the 'Global Hunger Index 2010' (International Food Policy Research Institute 2010). This index ranks developing countries on three components of hunger—proportion of the population that is under-nourished, proportion of children under five who are underweight and the child mortality rate. India ranks right at the bottom, at 67th out of 84 countries.

Gender inequality is also a key social issue in India. The 'Global Gender Gap Index 2010' (World Economic Forum 2010) measures the level of gender inequality in 134 countries. India is among the lowest ranked countries at 112, mainly due to poor education, poor health conditions of women, and poor participation in the economic growth of the country (Figure 2.17).

A strong association between governance and human development is clearly visible when we do a correlation analysis between the World Bank's Worldwide

Figure 2.17   Global Gender Gap Index, 2010

Note: The numbers indicate the ranks of the countries on the index; lower rank (1) indicates lower gender gap.
Source: World Economic Forum. 2010. *The Global Gender Gap Report 2010*. Table 3a. www.weforum.org.

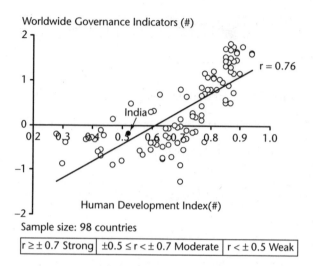

Figure 2.18   Correlation between Governance and Human Development

Note: Author's own analysis.
Sources: United Nations Development Programme, 2010, *Human Development Report 2010* (www. undp.org); and International Bank for Reconstruction and Development, the World Bank, 2009, Worldwide Governance Indicators (databank.worldbank.org).

Governance Indicators (governance performance) and the UNDP's Human Development Index (social performance). The graph shows a strong positive correlation coefficient (r) of 0.76, which means that both governance and human development tend to move in the same direction (Figure 2.18).

The last few pages bring alive the almost coordinated manner in which India's poor performance on governance indicators, economic indicators and social indicators, perhaps acting in concert, unceremoniously place us near the bottom of most country rankings.

Central to this disappointing performance is the lack of accountability in public office, plainly visible in all facets of our life. The consistently mediocre governance is symptomatic of a deeply embedded inability to hold the corrupt accountable for their actions. Governance, economic and social performance are tightly coupled to accountability, the absence of which creates a vicious circle that constantly gathers momentum (Figure 2.19). We cannot afford to neglect any more the creeping danger of weak accountability, so critical to the economic, social and political development of India.

Imagine for a moment that we are able to improve the level of accountability by pushing the right levers. Gradually, you would see the vicious wheel grind to a halt and start to reverse its directional spin, till it transforms into a virtuous circle of improved economic, social and governance performance. This leads us to the next question and one of the central issues that this book seeks to address—Why is accountability so low in India? Is it the poor implementation of accountability mechanisms, or does our socio-economic environment play a role in weakening

Figure 2.19   The Vicious Circle of Accountability

accountability? Is poor accountability an outcome of the inertial attitude of public officials; or is it a product of the lack of participation by citizens in the process of demanding accountability? Perhaps this attitude to accountability is deeply entrenched in our socio-cultural fabric, but there might also be yawning gaps in the institutional mechanisms of accountability that were originally set out.

In the next part of the book, the socio-economic and political fabric of India is evaluated to understand its potential influence on accountability.

References

Ackerman, John. 2005. 'Social Accountability for the Public Sector: A Conceptual Discussion', *Social Development Papers*. The World Bank. Available at www.uam.es (accessed on 12 December 2008).

Bovens, Mark. 2006. 'Analysing and Assessing Public Accountability: A Conceptual Framework', *European Governance Papers* (EUROGOV) No. C-06-01. Available at www.connex-network.org (accessed on 5 January 2009).

'Bribe Payers Index'. 2008. Transparency International: The global coalition against corruption. For more information, visit http://www.transparency.org (accessed on 28 May 2009).

'Corruption Is World's Most Talked About Problem'. 2010. Available at http://www.globescan.com/news_archives/bbc_corruption/ (accessed on 10 December 2010).

'Corruption Perceptions Index'. 2010. Transparency International: The global coalition against corruption. Used with permission. Available at http://www.transparency.org (accessed on 18 November 2009).

'Democracy Index 2010: Democracy in Retreat'. 2010. Economist Intelligence Unit. Available at www.eiu.com (accessed on 25 February 2011).

'Doing Business 2010: Reforming Through Difficult Times'. 2009. Palgrave Macmillan, IFC and The World Bank. Available at www.doingbusiness.org (accessed on 26 March 2010).

'The Global Competitiveness Report 2010–2011'. 2010. Switzerland: World Economic Forum. Available at www.weforum.org (accessed on 12 November 2010).

'Global Corruption Barometer'. 2010. Transparency International: The global coalition against corruption. Available at http://www.transparency.org (accessed on 28 October 2010).

'The Global Gender Gap Report 2010'. 2010. World Economic Forum. Available at http://www3.weforum.org/docs/WEF_GenderGap_Report_2010.pdf (accessed on 4 February 2011).

'Global Hunger Index 2010'. 2010. International Food Policy Research Institute. Available at http://www.ifpri.org/sites/default/files/publications/ghi10.pdf (accessed on 4 February 2011).

'Global Integrity Report'. 2009. Available at www.globalintegrity.org/ (accessed on 6 April 2009).

'Human Development Report 2010'. 2010. United Nations Development Programme. Available at http://hdr.undp.org (accessed on 8 November 2010).

'Indian bureaucracy the worst in Asia: Survey'. 2010. Press Trust of India, 3 June.

'Infant Mortality Rate'. World Development Indicators, International Bank for Reconstruction and Development, The World Bank. Available at http://data.worldbank.org/ (accessed on 24 January 2011).

Kaufmann Daniel, Art Kraay and Massimo Mastruzzi. 2010. 'The Worldwide Governance Indicators, 1996-2009'. The World Bank. Available at www.worldbank.org (accessed on 9 July 2009).

Ketkar, Kusum, Athar Murtuza and Suhas L. Ketkar. 2005. 'Impact of Corruption on Foreign Direct Investment and Tax Revenues'. Available at www.allbusiness.com (accessed on 16 February 2011).

Kose, Ayhan M., Eswar Prasad, Kenneth Rogoff and Shang-Jin Wei. 2006. 'Financial Globalization: A Reappraisal'. Available at www.imf.org/ (accessed on 10 January 2011).

Lee, Charles M. C. and David Ng. 2004. 'Corruption and International Valuation: Does Virtue Pay'. Available at www.socialinvest.org/ (accessed on 10 January 2011).

Malena, Carmen, Reiner Foster and Janmejay Singh. 2004. 'Social Accountability: An Introduction to the Concept and Emerging Practice', Social Development Papers. Available at www.worldbank.org (accessed on 12 December 2008).

McCawley, Peter. 2005. Governance in Indonesia: Some Comments. Tokyo: Asian Development Bank Institute. Available at www.adbi.org/ (accessed on 17 February 2010).

'Mutual Accountability Mechanisms: Accountability, Voice and Responsiveness'. 2006. UNDP Development Group. Available at www.undp.org/ (accessed on 9 December 2008).

Prasad, Eswar. 2011. 'How India Can Cope With Plenty', The Wall Street Journal, 7 January.

Schedler, A., et al. 2009. The Self-Restraining State: Power and Accountability in New Democracies. London: Lynne Reinner.

PART II

Awareness

3 Unveiling the Shroud

... The success of democracy is not merely a matter of having
the most perfect institutional structure that we can think of.
It depends inescapably on our actual behaviour patterns and
the working of political and social interactions ....

Amartya Sen, The Idea of Justice

The emotive Indian unwittingly carries within a weighty baggage of tradition, superstition, cultural biases and societal norms on life's travels. Our ancient lineage is a two-faced coin, at one moment anchoring us, at another, immobilizing us. This blend of emotions, churned in the centuries-old cauldron of hope and helplessness, creates a flavour of accountability that is quintessentially Indian. How does our complex socio-economic milieu influence accountability? Can we conveniently label the present state of accountability as an artefact from the crypt of history?

This chapter attempts to unveil the potential impact that a number of common socio-economic factors could have on accountability in India. Intuitively, one would assume that low income, low literacy, high social diversity and a large population are likely to weaken accountability. Countries with more favourable socio-economic conditions would naturally be expected to have better governance and accountability.

How do we test this hypothesis? To assess the relationship between common socio-economic factors and the quality of accountability and governance, a cross-country correlation analysis needs to be conducted. First, we need a solid measure of accountability and governance. While there is no stand-alone measure of accountability that provides a comparative view across countries, there exists a robust index of governance, which incorporates accountability and other factors that are directly or indirectly linked to accountability.

This index is the World Bank's Worldwide Governance Indicators (Kaufmann et al. 2009), which comprehensively measures the quality of governance in 213 developing and developed nations. This index measures governance on six parameters:

1. *Voice and Accountability*: Citizens' participation in selecting their government, freedom of expression, freedom of association and a free media
2. *Government Effectiveness*: Quality of public services, the quality of civil service, the degree of its independence from political pressures, quality of policy formulation and implementation, credibility of the government's commitment to such policies
3. *Control of Corruption*: The extent to which public power is exercised for private gain, including both petty and grand forms of corruption, as well as the capture of the state by elites and private interests
4. *Political Stability and Absence of Violence*: Perceptions of the likelihood that the government will be destabilized or overthrown by unconstitutional or violent means, including domestic violence and terrorism
5. *Regulatory Quality*: The ability of the government to formulate and implement sound policies and regulations that permit and promote the private sector
6. *Rule of Law*: The extent to which citizens have confidence in and abide by the rules of society, the quality of contract enforcement, the police and the courts, as well as the likelihood of crime and violence

These six parameters of the World Bank's Worldwide Governance Indicators closely map onto our four foundations of accountability that I referred to earlier in the book (Figure 3.1). This mapping implies that our four foundations of accountability are more likely to be stable in those countries that have high scores on the six parameters that comprise the Worldwide Governance Indicators. An average of the scores on these six governance indicators was used in our analysis, as the measure of governance for a country.

The next step in our correlation analysis is to develop a cross-country comparison, on the socio-economic factors that we thought would have the most impact on accountability. These are set out below:

1. *Income Per Capita*: Measured by GDP per capita (on Purchasing Power Parity), it indicates the degree of economic prosperity of a nation
2. *Social Hierarchy*: Measured by Hofstede's Power Distance Index, it indicates the degree of inequality or disparity in wealth and power distribution in a country

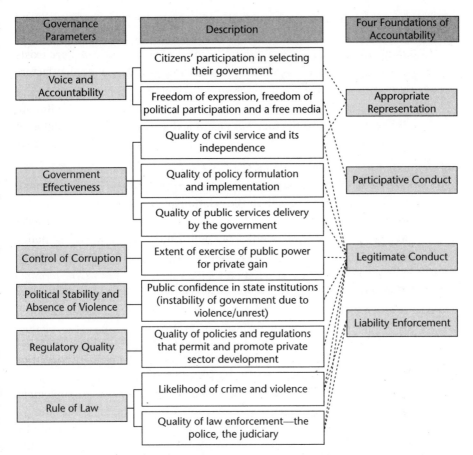

Figure 3.1 Worldwide Governance Indicators (WGI) and Accountability

Source: The World Bank. 2009. Worldwide Governance Indicators. www.databank.worldbank.org.

3. *Individualism*: Measured by Hofstede's Individualism Index, it assesses the degree to which individuals are integrated or dis-integrated into groups in a society. It indicates the degree of independence, assertiveness and self-responsibility for actions and outcomes in a society

4. *Democratic Lineage*: Measured by the number of years since a country attained democracy, it is an indication of the age and experience of a democracy

5. *Urbanization*: Measured by the share of the total population residing in urban areas, it is an indication of economic development and industrialization of a country

6. *Adult Literacy*: Measured by the share of the population over 15 years of age who can read and write simple statements, it is an indication of the ability of individuals to interpret information

7. *Voter Turnout*: Measured by the number of registered voters who cast their votes in general elections, it is an indicator of citizens' participation in the governance of a country

8. *Social Diversity*: Measured by the degree of racial, ethnic, linguistic and religious diversity present in a country, it indicates the level of social fragmentation in a country

9. *Population*: Measured as the total number of people who are the inhabitants of a country

We then conduct a correlation analysis between these socio-economic factors and the average of the Worldwide Governance Indicator scores for all countries, in order to determine the strength of the relationship between governance and socio-economic conditions.

The correlation between two variables is measured by the coefficient of correlation (r). The value of 'r' can lie somewhere between 1 (positive correlation) and -1 (negative correlation). The closer the correlation coefficient (r) is to 1 or -1, the stronger is the relationship between the two variables, while an 'r' value closer to 0 signifies a weak relationship. The coefficient of correlation (r) between each socio-economic factor and governance provides interesting insights into the strength of the relationship between the two variables, for the countries that we examined. This correlation exercise does not attempt to tease out the direction of the causality between the socio-economic factors and governance. The focus here is to understand the strength of the correlation, and not causality. Other researchers have conducted some causality analysis, and we refer to them where appropriate.

We now proceed to examine each of the socio-economic factors that could have a bearing on accountability, to understand which factors are correlated with governance.

::: Income Per Capita

Income Per Capita is a broad indicator of a country's economic prosperity, measured by GDP per capita (GDP/population) on a purchasing power parity basis. It indicates the average standard of living of individuals residing in that country.

Intuitively, it would appear that countries with low income per capita would not have the resources to create, develop and maintain robust governance and accountability institutions, since the monetary, physical and knowledge resources needed to build them are enormous. The government would need to spend public money to set up agencies involved in monitoring and investigating government functioning. Adequate funds would have to be provided for the acquisition and training of personnel and upgrading information technology in these institutions. Capacity building is critical, but costly. For the developing economies, allocation of their scarce resources towards governance and institution-building would perhaps be perceived as less critical than focusing their effort on economic and social development (Khan 1999). The economically underdeveloped countries grapple with a vast range of worries—lower literacy rates, higher incidence of disease, higher mortality rates and fewer employment opportunities. The attention of the government should naturally be on providing essentials like shelter, clothing, food, electricity, roads, education and healthcare. The trade-off between satisfying basic needs and providing good governance seems clear at this nascent stage of a country's economic development, or so it appears.

Over time, the economic and social development of a nation would give rise to a segment of population that has higher educational levels, greater awareness and a greater need for self-expression (Inglehart and Welzel 2005; Vega-Gordillo and Alvarez-Arce 2003). This would lead to a rise in demand-driven accountability, in which ordinary citizens exact accountability for government actions. This external force then acts as a trigger for the development of accountability institutions. Accountability might need to wait in queue in developing countries, while economic and social development takes the lead.

We compared the income per capita of a large set of countries from the World Development Indicators (World Bank 2009). India's income per capita (on a purchasing power parity basis) was USD 3,275 in 2009, much lower than the world average of USD 12,542 (Figure 3.2).

The questions we ask are: Is India's relatively low income per capita a barrier to achieving a higher level of governance and accountability? Are lower-income countries destined to have a poor quality of governance until they rise out of the quagmire of poverty?

A correlation between *governance* and *income per capita* provides a thought-provoking perspective (Figure 3.3).

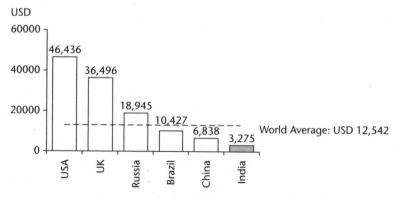

Figure 3.2   Income Per Capita (PPP), 2009

Source: International Bank for Reconstruction and Development, the World Bank. 2009. *World Development Indicators*. www.data.worldbank.org.

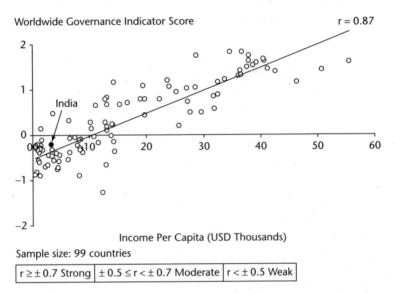

Figure 3.3 Correlation between Governance and Income Per Capita

Note: Author's own analysis.
Source: IBRD, the World Bank. 2009. Worldwide Governance Indicators 2009 and
World Development Indicators 2009. http://data.worldbank.org.

This graph compares the income per capita for 99 countries on the X axis and their corresponding scores on the Worldwide Governance Indicators on the Y axis. The line shows the trend of the relationship between these two variables. The upward slope of the line in the graph indicates a positive relationship between income per capita and governance, implying that income per capita and governance levels of a country move in the same direction. The correlation between these two variables is very strong, with a correlation co-efficient 'r' of 0.87, which means that in general, there is a very high probability that countries with lower income per capita will have poor governance scores as well.

Does this relationship between income per capita and governance hold up across a long temporal span? To answer this question, we also conducted a correlation analysis between income per capita and governance scores, across a 10-year period. The analysis indicates that there is a consistently high correlation (r = 0.85 to 0.88) between income per capita and governance across the 10-year period (Figure 3.4). The conclusion we can draw is that we are likely to find higher governance scores for countries with higher income per capita, just as lower governance scores are more likely for lower-income per capita countries. This analysis does not mean, of course, that higher income per capita *results* in greater accountability and better governance, or that better governance will directly *translate* into higher income per capita. The arrow of causality just cannot be established with this simple correlation analysis.

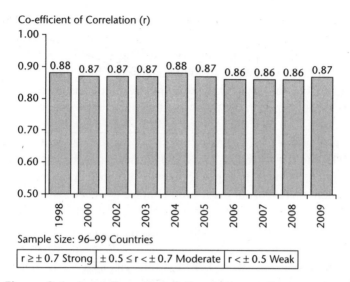

Sample Size: 96–99 Countries

| r ≥ ± 0.7 Strong | ± 0.5 ≤ r < ± 0.7 Moderate | r < ± 0.5 Weak |

Figure 3.4   Long-Term Correlation between Governance
and Income Per Capita

Note: Author's own analysis.
Source: IBRD, the World Bank. 1998–2009. Worldwide Governance Indicators
and *World Development Indicators.* http://data.worldbank.org.

In a classic re-play of the timeless question, 'which came first, the chicken or the egg?', the query that immediately springs to mind is in the same vein: 'which comes first, economic prosperity or good governance?' Academic literature seems to suggest that it is crucial to improve governance in order to improve economic performance. A global economics paper by Goldman Sachs, titled 'Ten things for India to achieve its 2050 potential', lists the 10 action areas that need to be addressed by India to achieve its forecasted potential by 2050. One of these areas is governance, and the report suggests that it is the overarching problem the country faces. Improving governance would not just result in more effective delivery systems, but will also facilitate progress in areas like education, agriculture and infrastructure (O'Neil and Poddar 2008).

Research by World Bank experts Daniel Kaufmann and Aart Kraay also seems to confirm that there is a strong positive causal effect directionally running from governance to income per capita. They say that improvement in governance is unlikely to occur as a consequence of economic development. A plausible explanation for this is the phenomenon of 'state capture', defined as the undue and illicit influence of the elite in shaping the laws, policies and regulations of the state. As long as the established elite within a country reap private benefits from low-quality public institutions, there is little reason to expect that higher incomes will lead to better governance (Kaufmann and Kraay 2002).

Ilian Mihov and Antonio Fatás, Professors of Economics at INSEAD, show that a country's economic growth hits a 'wall' if the country's institutional quality does not improve. According to their study, a country can have high growth rates in the early stages of its development, despite having poor institutions, because institutional quality is relatively less important in developing economies. As income per capita reaches closer to the USD 12,000 mark, countries appear not to progress much further, till they reform their institutions. The authors of this research claim that no country has become rich with poor quality institutions (Fatas and Mihov 2009). The 'Great Wall' of USD 12,000 in per capita income is still a distant mirage for India. We have managed to sustain high growth rates in recent years, despite the poor quality of our institutions, but we will need institutional reforms to ultimately scale the great wall that lies out in the future.

The criticality of governance in driving economic growth has thus been widely acknowledged. Without good governance, India is destined to drift in the seas of inequitable economic growth and deep-seated corruption. The long march forward will be shackled to the drumbeat of good governance.

::: Social Hierarchy

Social hierarchy measures the distribution of power and wealth in a country and is an indication of the degree of social inequity that exists among people. Does this social inequity influence the quality of governance? Is social hierarchy an important determinant of accountability?

In countries with greater social hierarchy, the rich and powerful are in a position to abuse the institutions of accountability to suit their needs. They could influence the bureaucratic framework, or may even attempt to buy favourable interpretations of the law. Research conducted by Joris Lammers and Adam Galinsky suggests that people with power think it is justifiable to break the rules, as they know they can get away with it (*The Economist* 2010). Other research also suggests that political, regulatory and legal institutions might favour wealthier and more powerful individuals, and be less likely to hold them accountable for their actions (Licht et al. 2003).

This bias towards the rich and the powerful often leads people on the lower rungs of the social hierarchy to believe that they are helpless, as they fall victim to the skewed distribution of economic and social power. The less fortunate are then convinced that they just cannot progress through fair means, thus allowing them to justify their own involvement in unethical practices. The torque of this downward spiral spins off even more favouritism and poor governance. A society with greater social hierarchy is therefore sandwiched between the haves and the have-nots, both of whom have equal incentive to bypass the institutions of accountability to serve their selfish needs.

The social hierarchy in India is not only a function of inequity in power and wealth, but also of vast differences in literacy, opportunity and beliefs. The horizontal petrifaction of the caste system sealed the impermeable stratigraphy that defined the life of the ordinary Indian, transfixing the individual in a web of hierarchy. Even public officials in the institutions of governance are perhaps trapped in these sediments. Decision-making is largely top-down, with implementation being the responsibility of junior officials. These juniors are unlikely to provide critical feedback to senior officials who create policy, resulting in a gap between policy design and implementation (Mehta 2009). Social inequality results in fear of authority and the inability to demand accountability. The power differential in a hierarchical society is therefore likely to predispose a country to lower levels of accountability and poor governance.

To measure the degree of social inequality in India and other countries, we referred to Geert Hofstede's Power Distance Index, a quantified measure of social hierarchy. Hofstede's book *Cultures and Organizations, Software of the Mind* (2010) examines five different cultural dimensions across countries: Power Distance, Individualism, Masculinity, Uncertainty Avoidance and Long-Term Orientation. The Power Distance Index effectively measures social hierarchy in a society. It specifically measures the extent to which less powerful members of institutions or societies accept that power is distributed unequally. A higher score on this index signifies greater inequality of wealth and power, as perceived and accepted in a society.

India has a rather worrisome score of 77 on Hofstede's Power Distance Index (Figure 3.5), much higher than the world average of 55, indicating that there is high inequality of wealth and power in India.

Does the social hierarchy and power inequality in India act as a significant barrier to achieving higher accountability and better governance? To understand this relationship more closely, we studied the correlation between the *Worldwide Governance Indicators* and *Social Hierarchy* (Hofstede's Power Distance Index) across 63 countries (Figure 3.6).

The downward slope of the graph shows a negative relationship between social hierarchy and governance, implying that social hierarchy and governance levels of a country move in opposite directions. A correlation coefficient (r) of −0.65 indicates that there is a moderate to strong probability that countries with higher levels of social hierarchy will have lower levels of accountability and governance.

Research conducted by Licht et al. also studied the relationship between Hofstede's cultural dimensions and three of the six Worldwide Governance Indicators—Rule of Law, Control of Corruption, and Voice and Accountability. They also found a moderate to strong correlation between Power Distance and the three Worldwide Governance Indicators, with 'r' values in the range of −0.61 and −0.67 (Licht et al. 2003).

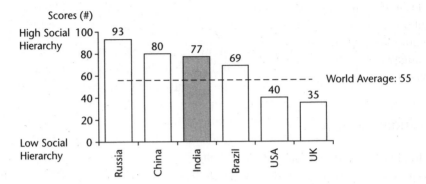

Figure 3.5 Social Hierarchy (Hofstede's Power Distance Index)

Source: Hofstede, Geert, Gert Jan Hofstede and Michael Minkov. 2010. *Culture and Organizations, Software of the Mind*. Third Revised Edition. New York, NY: McGraw-Hill. www.geert-hofstede.com.

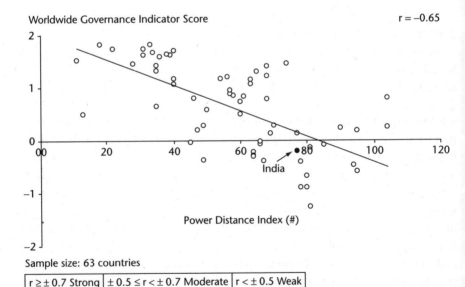

Figure 3.6 Correlation between Governance and Social Hierarchy (Power Distance)

Note: Author's own analysis.
Source: Data from Hofstede, Geert, Gert Jan Hofstede and Michael Minkov. 2010. *Cultures and Organizations, Software of the Mind*. Third Revised Edition. New York, NY: McGraw-Hill. www.geert.hofstede.com; and Worldwide Governance Indicators 2009. The World Bank. www.worldbank.org.

From this analysis, it appears that social hierarchy could be one of the significant obstacles on the path to better governance and greater accountability. If we do not make extraordinary efforts to improve our governance, there will never be adequate institutionalized pressure to demolish this dangerous demon of our divisive society.

::: Individualism

Individualism can be described as the degree to which individuals are integrated or dis-integrated into groups (Hofstede et al. 2010). Depending on the affinity between individuals and their social groups, country cultures can be broadly classified as either individualistic or collectivist. For instance, Asians are known to have very strong social networks that act as a support system in times of need. Western cultures, on the other hand, are commonly known to be more nuclear family-oriented and less reliant on outsiders for social support.

How does the degree of individualism or collectivism impact the quality of governance and accountability in a country?

In countries where people are more individualistic, social relationships are loosely knit and often kept at arm's length. Individuals are expected to take care of themselves and their immediate families. Assertiveness and confrontation are dominant behavioural norms in an individualistic society (Gelfand and Realo 1999). People are more likely to express opinions and take initiatives uninhibited by any societal barriers (Greif 1994; Leake and Black 2005). Individualistic populations are characterized by values like independence, self-determination and self-responsibility.

Countries that have strong collectivist, high-affinity cultures, on the other hand, value tightly knit relationships in which people see themselves as part of a larger extended social group. Interpersonal relationships are of prime importance and social behaviour is strongly guided by group norms, family and societal obligations. Decision-making is often done in a group, and by people higher up in the group hierarchy (Leake and Black 2005). As a result, the group, or a sub-group, assumes a nebulous and diffused responsibility for its actions, spreading accountability around the table. There are also greater instances of nepotism or favouritism, as emphasis is always placed on promoting the interests of one's group members. In collectivist societies, it is often considered disrespectful for younger people, or those with less experience or power, to express their opinions or ask questions of individuals higher up in the social chain. In the larger interest of their group or community, these juniors may choose to ignore the negative actions of seniors, resulting in lower expectations of accountability.

People in individualistic environments are more likely to obey formal rules and use formal institutions to raise their concerns (Licht et al. 2003). A study by an economics professor at Stanford University on the structures of two distinct traders groups operating between the fourteenth and fifteenth centuries showed that individualistic societies founded elaborate formal institutions much before collectivist societies did. This is because collectivist societies could rely on strong personal networks, reducing the need for formal enforcement mechanisms (Klasing 2008). Individualistic societies thus encourage stricter law enforcement.

To quantify and compare the level of individualism across countries, we referred to Hofstede's research on cultural dimensions. A higher score on the *Individualism Index* signifies that a country is more individualistic in nature, while a lower score indicates that the country is more collectivist in nature. India has a score of 48, marginally more than the world average of 43, and is a relatively more collectivist society than countries like the UK and the US (Figure 3.7).

Is the culture of collectivism in India a significant barrier in holding public officials responsible for their actions? To test the strength of the relationship between *governance* and *individualism*, a correlation analysis was conducted across 63 countries (Figure 3.8).

The results indicate a strongly positive relationship ($r = 0.69$) between individualism and governance. So there is a strong probability that countries with higher levels of individualism would also have higher scores on governance, and therefore better accountability levels. A similar study conducted by a professor of economics at Carleton University also found that individualism is strongly correlated to institutional performance (Klasing 2008). This could imply that a

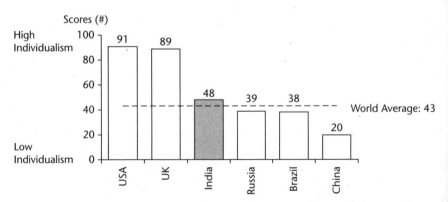

Figure 3.7   Individualism (Hofstede's Individualism Index)

Source: Hofstede, Geert, Gert Jan Hofstede and Michael Minkov. 2010. *Culture and Organizations, Software of the Mind.* Third Revised Edition. New York, NY: McGraw-Hill. www.geert-hofstede.com

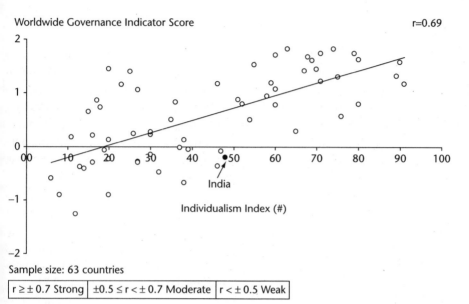

Figure 3.8   Correlation between Governance and Individualism

Note: Author's own analysis.
Source: Data from Hofstede, Geert, Gert Jan Hofstede and Michael Minkov. 2010. *Cultures and Organizations, Software of the Mind.* Third Revised Edition. New York, NY: McGraw-Hill. www.geert-hofstede.com; and Worldwide Governance Indicators 2009. The World Bank. www.worldbank.org.

collectivist culture may inherently present a barrier to India achieving higher levels of accountability and a better order of governance.

I am not suggesting here that Indian society should become more self-centred and individualistic. There are tremendous benefits of being a collectivist society. A strong social fabric that is taut and allows individuals to lean back on it for support is an excellent brace in the absence of government-sponsored social and institutional infrastructure. Accountability, unfortunately, appears not to be one of collectivism's beneficiaries.

::: Democratic Lineage

Abraham Lincoln, the 16th President of the United States, famously said in 1863, '... a government of the people, by the people and for the people ...', to describe the proposed functioning of a democratic nation. Since then, democracy appears to have become the aspirational model of government for many of the world's people. The term *democratic lineage* used here refers to the number of years that a country has been democratic.

Would it be reasonable to assume that the passage of democratic time gradually forces the hand of governance? Does governance wisdom travel in the same direction and at the same speed as democratic age? With decades of experience, democratic institutions would take shape, evolve and adapt. The electoral process would improve, resulting in better public representation. Mature democracies would also have developed robust mechanisms to enforce accountability. Citizens would be more willing to participate in political debates and engage in the political process. Active and involved citizens would imply closer monitoring of public institutions, and ultimately greater accountability.

To determine the democratic lineage of countries, we referred to *The Polity IV Project*, which sets out the number of years since a country adopted democracy (Center for Systemic Peace 2007). In chronological terms, India is a moderately mature democracy (Figure 3.9).

We studied the correlation between the quality of *governance* and *democratic lineage* across 98 countries (Figure 3.10).

The correlation analysis indicates a moderate relationship between democratic lineage and governance (r = 0.63), indicating a moderate probability that older democracies would have better governance. More than 30 democracies, clustered within the 15–25 year range, have governance scores that vary widely between −0.7 and +1.5. This suggests that governance does not depend solely on democratic lineage and that young democracies are equally capable of demonstrating good governance. What is worrisome for India is that many democracies below the age of 60 (India's age), to the left of the vertical line (in Figure 3.10), have substantially better governance scores than India. Similarly, virtually all democracies at or above the age of 60 have significantly better governance scores than India, as seen in the graph to the right of the vertical line. India is clearly a poor performer on this measure. Even at the ripe old age of 60, governance wisdom lags behind our six decade-old democratic heritage.

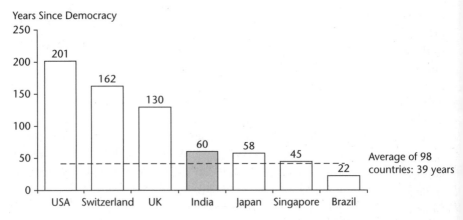

Figure 3.9   Democratic Lineage (as of 2010)

Source: Center for Systemic Peace. 2007. *The Polity IV Project.* www.systemicpeace.org/polity/polity4.htm.

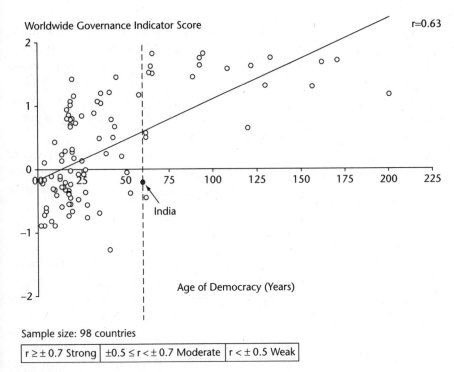

Figure 3.10 Correlation between Governance and Democratic Lineage

Note: Author's own analysis.
Source: Data from Center for Systemic Peace, 2007, www.systemicpeace.org; and Worldwide Governance Indicators 2009, the World Bank, http://databank.worldbank.org.

⠿ Urbanization

Urbanization is the process of transformation of a rural society to one that resides primarily in large urban clusters. It is the most visible sign of economic prosperity. In the early twentieth century, Mahatma Gandhi famously said, 'India lives in its villages'. Nearly 100 years later, the 638,365 villages in India are a living testament to his words (Census of India 2001). The question for governance is this: does the largely rural setting of India, in any way, pose a constraint to achieving higher accountability?

A majority of the population living in the rural areas lags behind the urban population economically. Many rural areas struggle for access to even basic services like education, clean water, sanitation and healthcare. Vast tracts of rural India are trapped in traditional social structures detrimental to the weaker sections of society, with fewer opportunities for women and people belonging to lower castes. The struggle for survival leaves little time and energy to fight misgovernance and those in power who flout accountability.

Even where accountability mechanisms exist to protect rural populations, villagers are not particularly well-informed about their rights. This leaves them vulnerable to exploitation by powerful officials. Surveys evaluating the implementation of the RTI Act in India highlight that the most glaring deficiency is the lack of awareness, particularly in rural areas. A study published in 2009 suggests that only about 13 per cent of the rural population, compared to 33 per cent of the urban population, is aware of the RTI Act (www.rtiindia.org). Low literacy levels and poor access to information are big barriers to better governance in rural areas.

Urbanization, with all its ills, fosters greater awareness among citizens and provides for greater resources to implement accountability mechanisms and, therefore, better governance. Accountability is apparently easier to enforce in urban areas.

A good measure of urbanization is the World Development Indicators (World Bank 2009), which measures urban population as a percentage of the total population of a country. According to this data, only 30 per cent of India's population is urban, which is significantly lower than the world average of 57 per cent (Figure 3.11).

Do urbanization and good governance really move in tandem? A correlation between *governance* and *urbanization* for 100 countries is shown in Figure 3.12.

The graph shows a positive relationship between urbanization and governance, indicating that countries with higher urbanization levels tend to have better governance. The strength of the relationship is moderate ($r = 0.55$). Does this finding hold up over long periods of time? To test this, we conducted this correlation analysis between urbanization and governance scores for a period of 10 years (Figure 3.13).

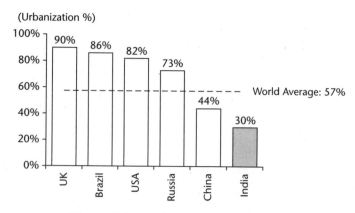

Figure 3.11   Urbanization, 2009

Source: The World Bank. 2009. *World Development Indicators*. http://databank.worldbank.org.

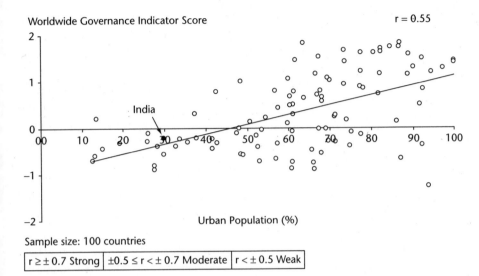

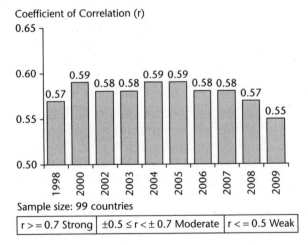

Figure 3.12   Correlation between Governance and Urbanization

Note: Author's own analysis.
Source: International Bank for Reconstruction and Development, the World Bank. 2009. World-wide Governance Indicators and *World Development Indicators*. http://databank.worldbank.org.

Figure 3.13   Long-term Correlation between Governance and Urbanization

Note: Author's own analysis.
Source: International Bank for Reconstruction and Development, the World Bank. 1998–2009. World-wide Governance Indicators and *World Development Indicators*. http://databank.worldbank.org.

The correlation is consistent across the 10-year period ($r = 0.55$ to 0.59), reinforcing the view that there is a moderate probability that countries with lower urbanization will have poorer governance. It appears, then, that as long as

India remains largely rural, governance may remain a challenge, unless effort is invested to raise the awareness of accountability among citizens in rural areas.

India, though, is rapidly urbanizing. A recent study by a consulting firm suggests that by 2030, India will have 590 million people living in cities, which will be 40 per cent of the projected 2030 population of 1.47 billion. This great migration from the rural heartlands of India to the mesmerizing din of our metropolises, may just provide one of the pressure points that could force better governance (*DNA*, 20 December 2010). According to a study by World Bank, the most rapid growth in urbanization happens as countries move from low-income to middle-income levels (The World Bank 1997). This increasing middle-income population could indirectly have a positive impact on the quality of governance in India through urbanization.

::: Adult Literacy

India has a large population of adults who are illiterate. Adult literacy, by definition, is the percentage of the population over 15 years of age that can both read and write a short simple statement on everyday life (UNESCO 2010). Does illiteracy compound the problem of inadequate accountability?

One could postulate that countries with higher adult literacy may have better accountability and governance, since literacy empowers people to interpret information to make better decisions related to economics, politics and society. Literacy confers on citizens the ability to comprehend general and political news, resulting in a population that is both well-informed and aware of their rights and duties. These citizens are more likely to participate in the political process. A literate society also supports stricter law enforcement, protection of citizens' rights, and increased social and community participation. Literacy also helps to bridge the economic gap between rural and urban populations, between gender, caste and income groups, by providing equal opportunities to all segments of society. The increase in adult literacy levels would possibly create more egalitarian societies over time.

A measure of adult literacy levels across countries can be found in the UNESCO Institute for Statistics. According to them, the adult literacy of 66 per cent (2008) in India is much lower than the world average of 89 per cent (Figure 3.14). This means that India has a staggering 388 million adult population that is illiterate (2008). Gender disparity in literacy rates is high, with 77 per cent of adult males and only 55 per cent of adult females being literate (National Sample Survey Office 2010).

How significant is the relationship between adult literacy and the quality of governance? Will India continue to stumble on the cobblestoned pathway to better governance, burdened by the baggage of illiteracy?

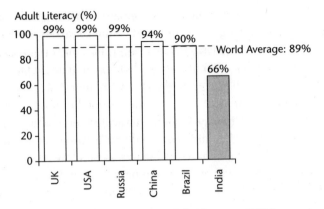

Figure 3.14   Adult Literacy, 2008

Source: Statistics and other related data produced by the UNESCO Institute for Statistics. 2008. Adult Literacy, www.uis.unesco.org.

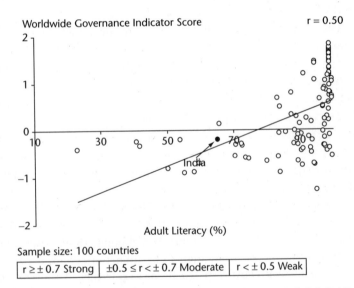

Figure 3.15   Correlation between Governance and Adult Literacy

Note: Author's own analysis.
Source: Statistics and other related data produced by the UNESCO Institute for Statistics 2008, www.uis.unesco.org; and Worldwide Governance Indicators 2009, the World Bank. http://databank.worldbank.org.

A correlation between *governance* and *adult literacy* was conducted to understand the relationship between them (Figure 3.15).

A correlation coefficient (r) of 0.50 indicates a weak-moderate correlation between adult literacy levels and the quality of governance. Although most countries have literacy rates between 80–100 per cent, there are wide variations in the governance scores among these countries. Many countries like Argentina, Mongolia, Paraguay, Philippines, Thailand and Venezuela have negative scores on governance, in spite of having adult literacy rates of more than 90 per cent. This seems to suggest that higher literacy among a nation's people does not necessarily translate into better governance.

For India, our low levels of literacy might not be a significant barrier to improving governance, as we feared. The ability of the illiterate to extract accountability from local public officials is well-known in India. The poor and the illiterate are often the ones who turn up to vote in large numbers. Good governance is not just the preserve of the well-read.

::: Voter Turnout

The ancient Greeks, who were the inventors of democracy, referred to citizens who did not vote as 'idiots'. The simple act of voting is symbolic of the power of citizens residing in a democracy. Voter turnout is defined as the percentage of registered voters in a country who cast their vote in a particular election (Institute for Democracy and Electoral Assistance, www.idea.int). It is an indication of the level of engagement of citizens in selecting the public officials of the country, and is seen as an essential prerequisite for a democracy.

A higher voter turnout is more likely to result in a government representative of all citizens across geography, age group, income and community, reflecting an inclusive and participative democracy. Citizens hold the government responsible for their performance by re-electing and rewarding them for results, or by deposing and punishing them for their failure to meet expectations. This provides the government an incentive to be more responsive to citizens' demands. The government takes a keen interest in the concerns of the electorate and translates their preferences into policies, in the hope of earning more votes. If voting participation declines, however, government actions may be less likely to mirror the needs of the citizens. Can we therefore assume that countries with higher voter turnouts have better accountability and governance?

The Institute for Democracy and Electoral Assistance (IDEA) measures the level of citizens' participation in elections around the world. The average voter turnout in India is 59.3 per cent, lower than the world average of 69.5 per cent (Figure 3.16). Voter turnout in general elections in India has in fact remained stagnant over the last 60 years (Figure 3.17).

This low voter turnout possibly points to a general indifference among citizens towards the political process. The oft-repeated reason is that no matter who comes to power, basic necessities and infrastructure hardly improve. One would

Voter Turnout (%)

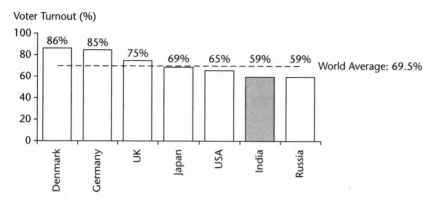

Figure 3.16 Average Voter Turnout

Source: Institute for Democracy and Electoral Assistance. 2009. Voter Turnout, www.idea. int. Reproduced by permission of International IDEA from 'Voter Turnout' © International Institute for Democracy and Electoral Assistance 2009.

Voter Turnout (%)

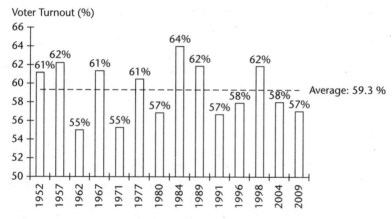

Figure 3.17 Voter Turnout in General Elections (India), 1952–2009

Source: Election Commission of India, www.eci.nic.in.

think that 60 years of being denied basic services and good governance would drive citizens to exercise their right to elect competent leaders. The segment of people who do not vote, however, are the upper-income groups, sufficiently insulated from the indignity of living in poorly-governed corners of India, to bother with the drive to the nearest poll booth.

Does the consistently low voter participation in India act as a roadblock to achieving higher levels of accountability and better governance? How significant is the relationship between voter turnout and governance levels? A correlation between *governance* and *voter turnout* was conducted to understand the strength of the relationship between them (Figure 3.18).

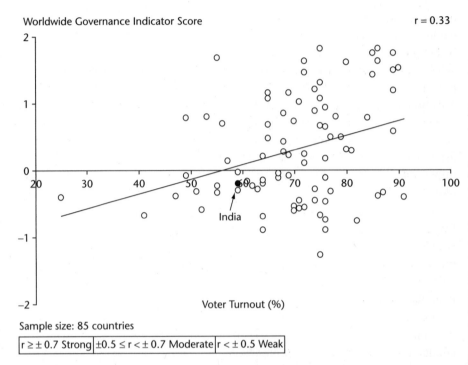

Figure 3.18 Correlation between Governance and Voter Turnout

Note: Author's own analysis.
Source: Data from Institute for Democracy and Electoral Assistance 2009, www.idea.int; and
Worldwide Governance Indicators 2009, the World Bank. http://databank.worldbank.org.

To our astonishment, the graph shows a weak correlation (r = 0.33) between
the two variables. We observe that most of the countries fall in the 60–80 per
cent voter turnout range, yet their governance scores vary significantly from
around −1.2 to +1.8. A possible explanation could be that voter turnout, while
necessary, is not sufficient to address the issue of poor governance. Voting is just
the starting point. Continuous engagement in the political process between elections, through bargaining, discussion and negotiation between the polity and the
public officials, is the hallmark of a great democracy.

::: Social Diversity

Pandit Jawaharlal Nehru often said, India's strength lies in its 'Unity in Diversity'.
India is a land of great social diversity with a high degree of racial, ethnic, linguistic
and religious fragmentation.

This social diversity provides a vibrant environment where the multitude of
divergences can converge to create the alchemy of growth and progress. Equally,

diversity can lead to a cacophony of views, a chaotic environment ripe for exploitation by those in power. The latter is more representative of India. Identity-based politics is rampant, as individuals attempt to promote their own groups. While representation of all sections of society is important, when performance and competence are ignored, voting as an accountability mechanism is compromised. This breeds nepotism, with inappropriate individuals nominated to positions of power, weakening governance. Social diversity, coupled with weak institutions, could foster an ethnically divided society, where misgovernance and violence are more likely. Studies find that ethnic divisions make it difficult, although not impossible, to develop the social cohesion necessary to achieve common goals, like demanding transparency or accountability (Ritzen et al. 2001).

To measure the degree of social diversity in a country, we referred to the Social Diversity Index, published in *The American Journal of Economics and Sociology* (Okediji 2005). The index measures the social fragmentation in a country, based on the number of linguistic, racial and religious groups. India scores 0.98 out of 1 on the Social Diversity Index, much higher than the worldwide average of 0.77, making it one of the most socially diverse countries on the planet (Figure 3.19).

Does diversity truly divide us in our fight for better governance and higher accountability? To understand this relationship more closely, a correlation was conducted between *governance* and *social diversity* (Figure 3.20).

Surprisingly, the graph indicates a weak negative correlation (r = −0.28) between social diversity and governance. There are more than 25 countries with high governance scores of more than 1, but their scores on social diversity are spread across the spectrum, from a low of 0.20 to a high of 1. This suggests that countries can have relatively good governance in spite of differing levels

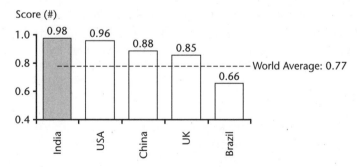

Figure 3.19   Social Diversity Index, 2005

Note: The scores on the index range from 0 to 1, lower score (0) means less social diversity
Source: Okediji. 2005. 'The Dynamics of Ethnic Fragmentation', *The American Journal of Economics and Sociology*, 64 (2).

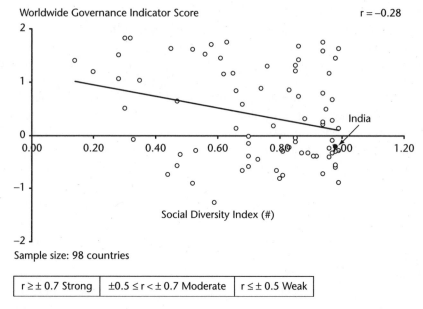

Figure 3.20   Correlation between Governance and Social Diversity

Note: Author's own analysis.
Source: Data from Okediji, 2005, 'The Dynamics of Ethnic Fragmentation', *The American Journal of Economics and Sociology* 64 (2); and The World Bank, 2009, Worldwide Governance Indicators, http://databank.worldbank.org.

of social diversity. Similarly, there are a large number of countries with high social diversity scores around 1.0, but with wide-ranging governance scores from –0.9 to 1.7.

We therefore surmise that India's great diversity across regions, culture, language and religion is not argument enough to justify the poor quality of governance, nor is it likely to be a significant barrier to better governance. Good governance and social diversity can coexist in harmony.

::: Population

India is now the second-most populous country on earth. Can we assume that the large populations of countries like India, relegate them to the basket of poor governance?

A large population can often prove favourable for a country, an advantage termed the *demographic dividend*, where manpower resources are available in abundance. This window of opportunity, however, can fast turn into a demographic disaster, especially in poorer and developing countries, as the limited fiscal resources are unable to fulfil the needs of so many people. The British economist Thomas Malthus, in his famous 'Essay on the Principle of Population' in 1798, interpreted overpopulation as an evil that would reduce the amount of food available per person, since population would grow at a faster rate than food supply. The overall quality of life for people would then drop, as the demand for basic goods and services would out-run supply, particularly in economically less developed nations. This lack of adequate resources and opportunities for all citizens could force them to resort to any means, in order to fulfil their basic needs. Governance would then become a serious challenge.

According to the World Bank's World Development Indicators (2009), India has a population of over 1.1 billion people (Figure 3.21).

Does governance become a greater challenge with a larger population? To understand this relationship more closely, a correlation was conducted between *governance* and *population* (Figure 3.22).

The graph shows that there is no meaningful relationship ($r = -0.078$) between these two variables. Most of the 100 democracies in this dataset had a population of less than 200 million, but their governance scores varied substantially. A correlation analysis between population and governance scores across a 10-year period also shows a consistently negligible correlation between the two variables (Figure 3.23).

What this means is that there is a low probability that countries with large populations would necessarily have poor governance, although India does lie at one end of the spectrum. We cannot blame a billion people for the absence of good governance.

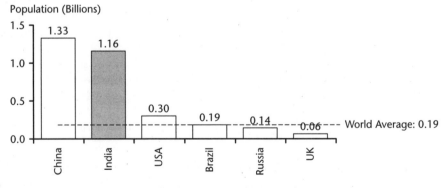

Figure 3.21 Population, 2009

Source: International Bank for Reconstruction and Development, The World Bank. 2009. *World Development Indicators*, http://databank.worldbank.org/ddp/home.do.

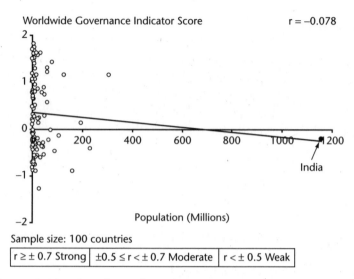

Figure 3.22   Correlation between Governance and Population

Note: Author's own analysis.
Source: International Bank for Reconstruction and Development, the
World Bank. 2009. Worldwide Governance Indicators 2009 and *World
Development Indicators 2009*. www.databank.worldbank.org.

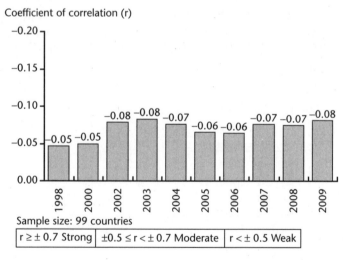

Figure 3.23   Long-Term Correlation between Governance and Population

Note: Author's own analysis.
Source: International Bank for Reconstruction and Development, the World
Bank. 1998–2009. Worldwide Governance Indicators and *World Develop-
ment Indicators*. http://databank.worldbank.org.

::: Conclusion

The correlation analyses we conducted in this chapter reveal that socio-economic factors such as income per capita, individualism, social hierarchy and democratic lineage tend to have a strong-to-moderate correlation with governance, while factors such as voter turnout, social diversity and population tend to have a weak correlation with governance. The summary of these correlations are presented in Figure 3.24.

This analysis appears to challenge some common myths about governance and accountability in India. Lower adult literacy levels, higher social diversity and a large population are often perceived to contribute significantly to weak governance and poor accountability. That these factors show a weaker correlation with governance indicates that they do not have a significant bearing, by themselves, on the levels of governance and accountability.

A note of caution is in order at this stage. The correlation analysis conducted here, as mentioned earlier, cannot be assumed to infer *causality* (Levin and Rubin 1991). If a variable A is strongly correlated with another variable B, it does not

Socio-Economic Factors	Correlation with Governance	r
Income Per Capita	Strong	0.87
Individualism		0.69
Social Hierarchy		(0.65)
Democratic Lineage	Moderate	0.63
Urbanization		0.55
Adult Literacy		0.50
Voter Turnout		0.33
Social Diversity	Weak	(0.28)
Population		(0.07)

Figure 3.24 Summary of Correlations

mean that A *causes* B, or that B *causes* A. For example, since individualism has a high degree of correlation with governance, it cannot be concluded that an increase in individualism will automatically result in an increase in the quality of governance, or the converse. Individualism could directly, indirectly, independently, or in conjunction with another factor, impact a nation's quality of governance. What is clear, though, is that countries with higher levels of individualism are more likely to have better governance quality. Apart from the obvious effort needed to improve governance directly, by implementing appropriate accountability mechanisms, it would perhaps be beneficial to attempt to improve a country's position on those socio-economic factors that tend to have a strong-to-moderate correlation with governance. How feasible would it be, to attempt to improve India's rating on those socio-economic factors that have a moderate-to-high correlation with governance? To understand the magnitude of this challenge, let us look again at India's position on these socio-economic factors, relative to other countries (Figure 3.25).

The report card corroborates that India's relative ranking on many of these socio-economic factors is not favourable. Strong social and economic reforms,

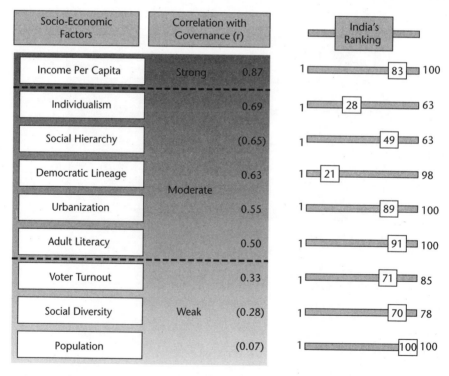

Figure 3.25   India's Ranking on Socio-Economic Factors

in addition to governance reforms, are required to tilt the scales in our favour and transport us out of our current position. Effective implementation of reforms will positively influence the relative position of India on several of these socio-economic factors, albeit in fits and starts, over the next two decades.

Our current ratings on governance and the related socio-economic factors leave me with the sobering realization that a swift improvement in accountability is unreasonable to expect and impossible to realize. The pattern of evolution of accountability in India will not be a planned, gradual, linear process, since the forces of change exert sporadic pressure from the outside, rather than emanating from an ongoing internal desire to improve. This change is likely to follow the principle of 'punctuated equilibrium', the theory from the science of evolutionary biology that suggests that species evolve through sudden periods of rapid change in response to external disruptions, followed by prolonged periods of stability and incremental change. Similarly, in the world of accountability and governance, there will be short periods of angst, then increased awareness, followed by action, resulting in change for the better. Most of this change will be triggered by forces from outside the government, namely citizens, civil society and media. This will be interspersed with long periods of gradual and incremental improvements in accountability.

We now turn our attention to the other important factor that drives governance in a country—the accountability institutional structure. The three-dimensional framework developed in the next chapter will help explain the role and effectiveness of all the mechanisms and institutions that support accountability.

References

Bose, Debopriya. 'Thomas Malthus: Theory of Population'. Available at www.buzzle.com (accessed on 23 April 2010).

Fatas, Antonio and Ilian Mihov. 2009. 'Another challenge to China's growth'. *Harvard Business Review*, March.

Gelfand, M. J. and A. Realo. 1999. 'Individualism-collectivism and accountability in inter-group negotiations', *Journal of Applied Psychology*.

'Global Rankings—Adult Literacy Rate (Total)'. 2008. Available at www.uis.unesco.org (accessed on 8 April 2009).

'Glossary'. 2010. *Education for All: Global Monitoring Report*. Available at www.unesco.org (accessed on 23 April 2010).

Greif, Avner. 1994. 'Cultural Beliefs and the Organization of Society: A Historical and Theoretical Reflection on Collectivist and Individualist Societies', *The Journal of Political Economy*, 102 (5).

'Gross domestic product, PPP (at current international $)'. 1996–2009. World Development Indicators, The World Bank: International Bank for Reconstruction and Development. Available at http://data.worldbank.org/ (accessed on 7 June 2010).

Hofstede, Geert, Gert Jan Hofstede and Michael Minkov. 2010. *Cultures and Organizations, Software of the Mind.* New York: McGraw-Hill, 3rd rev. edn.

'How to build inclusive cities and sustain economic growth'. 2010. *DNA*, 20 December.

Inglehart, R. and Christian Welzel. 2005. *Modernisation, Cultural Change and Democracy.* New York: Cambridge University Press.

Ingram Gregory. 1997. 'Patterns of Metropolitan Development: What Have We Learned'. The World Bank. Available at www.worldbank.org (accessed on 29 August 2011).

Kaufmann, Daniel and Art Kraay. 2002. 'Growth without governance'. The World Bank. Available at www.worldbank.org (accessed on 18 November 2010).

Kaufmann, Daniel, Art Kraay and Massimo Mastruzzi. 2010. *The Worldwide Governance Indicators, 1996–2009.* The World Bank. Available at www.worldbank.org (accessed on 9 July 2009).

Khan, Mushtaq Husain. 1999. 'Governance and Anti-Corruption Reforms in Developing Countries: Policies, Evidence and Ways Forward'. Available at www.g24.org (accessed on 20 August 2009).

Klasing, Mariko J. 2008. 'The Cultural Roots of Institutions'. Available at http://www.vwa.unisg.ch/ (accessed on 30 December 2010).

Leake, David and Rhonda Black. 2005. *Cultural and Linguistic Diversity: Implications for Transition Personnel.* University of Minnesota: National Center on Secondary Education and Transition. Available at www.ncset.org (accessed on 6 May 2010).

Levin, Richard and David Rubin. 1991. 'Simple Regression and Correlation', *Statistics for Management.* New Jersey: Prentice Hall.

Licht, A., Chanan Goldschmidt and Shalom H. Schwartz. 2003. 'Culture Rules: The Foundations of the Rule of Law and Other Norms of Governance'. Working Paper No. 605, William Davidson Institute. Available at http://wdi.umich.edu (accessed on 5 March 2010).

Mehta, Pratap Bhanu. 2009. 'Creating a credible state'. *Mint*, 9 March.

National Sample Survey Office. 2010. 'Press Note: Education in India, 2007–08: Participation and Expenditure'. Available at http://mospi.gov.in/press_note_NSS_%20Report_no_532_19may10.pdf (accessed on 19 October 2010).

'No. of villages by states & union territories in 2001 and 1991 censuses'. Available at http://censusindia.gov.in/Data_Products/Library/Post_Enumeration_link/No_of_Villages_link/no_villages.html (accessed on 25 January 2011).

O'Neil, Jim and Tushar Poddar. 2008. 'Ten things for India to achieve its 2050 potential'. Available at www2.goldmansachs.com (accessed on 9 April 2009).

Okediji, T. 2005. 'The dynamics of ethnic fragmentation: A proposal for an expanded measurement index', *American Journal of Economics and Sociology.* Available at http://findarticles.com (accessed on 8 April 2009).

'Polity IV report'. 2007. Center for Systemic Peace. Available at www.systemicpeace.org/polity/polity4.htm (accessed on 6 April 2009).

'Population, total'. 1996–2009. World Development Indicators, International Bank for Reconstruction and Development. Washington, D.C.: The World Bank. Available at http://data.worldbank.org/ (accessed on 7 June 2010).

'The psychology of power: Absolutely'. 2010. *The Economist*, 23 January, pp. 74–75.

Ritzen, J., William Easterly and Michael Woolcock. 2001. 'On Good Politicians and Bad Policies: Social Cohesion, Institutions, and Growth'. Available at www.worldbank.org (accessed on 21 May 2010).

'Understanding the key issues and constraints in implementing the RTI Act'. 2009. Available at http://rti.gov.in (accessed on 11 January 2010).

'Urban population (% of total)'. 1996–2009. World Development Indicators, International Bank for Reconstruction and Development. Washington, D. C.: The World Bank. Available at http://data.worldbank.org/ (accessed on 7 June 2010).

Vega-Gordillo, M. and L. Alvarez-Arce. 2003. 'Economic Growth and Freedom: A Causality Study'. Available on the freetheworld.com (accessed on 15 February 2011).

'Voter Turnout'. Reproduced by permission of International IDEA © International Institute for Democracy and Electoral Assistance. Available at www.idea.int (accessed on 30 March 2010).

4   Three-Dimensional Accountability

> *The real voyage of discovery consists not in seeking new lands, but in seeing with new eyes.*
>
> Marcel Proust, 1871–1922

This chapter creates the scaffold on which we can evaluate the quality of our existing *accountability systems* and understand the role they play in enforcing accountability in India.

Accountability is best viewed in three dimensions (3D). The first dimension is the *mechanisms of accountability* (Internal, Horizontal and External); the second dimension is the four *foundations of accountability* (Appropriate Representation, Participative Conduct, Legitimate Conduct and Liability Enforcement); and the third dimension is the three *institutions of government* (Legislature, Executive and Judiciary). Let us look at each of these dimensions in greater detail, to understand how they create the structure of the *accountability scaffold.*

⋮⋮ The Mechanisms of Accountability (First Dimension)

Accountability is not just a fuzzy word that describes the act of being responsible to your constituents. Accountability embodies tangible mechanisms that are laid down to create an architecture for governance. The government is subjected to accountability that it 'imposes upon itself', as well as accountability

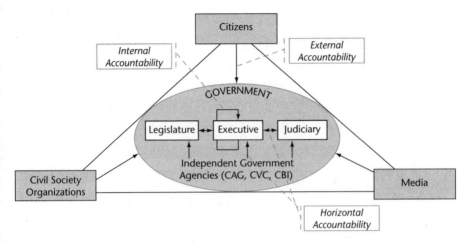

Figure 4.1   Mechanisms of Accountability

that is 'imposed upon it by others'. Based on who imposes this accountability, the mechanisms can be categorized into three types: *internal* accountability mechanisms—imposed within a government institution; *horizontal* accountability mechanisms—imposed by adjacent, independent government institutions; and *external* accountability mechanisms—imposed from outside, by citizens, civil society organizations (CSOs) and the media (Figure 4.1).

These three types of mechanisms—internal, horizontal and external—which exist to hold the government accountable, are explained in the next section.

Internal Accountability

Internal accountability mechanisms are imposed from within the government, on itself, through self-monitoring. They include mechanisms through which a government department can monitor the performance of its staff internally, for example:

- *Judicial Collegium,* an internal mechanism for selection of judges for the Supreme Court and the High Court
- *Annual Performance Appraisal Reports,* to evaluate the performance of public officials by their seniors
- *Whistleblowers Protection,* to encourage employees to highlight misappropriation or fraud by co-employees
- *Dismissal or reduction in the rank of officials,* to penalize them for misconduct.

Horizontal Accountability

Horizontal accountability mechanisms are imposed by independent institutions on the government through peer monitoring. They include mechanisms through which one government department scrutinizes the activities of another government department, for example:

- The *Election Commission* monitors and facilitates the election of officials in the Legislature

- The *Central Bureau of Investigation* investigates corruption charges against officials in the Legislature, the Executive and the Judiciary
- The *Legislature* scrutinizes acts of the Executive through debates in Parliament
- The *Judiciary* questions the policies passed by the Legislature, if they are in conflict with the Constitution

External Accountability

External accountability mechanisms are imposed upon the government from the outside, by citizens, CSOs and the media. In recent times, these external entities, especially the media, have begun to exert tremendous pressure on the government to drive accountability. Citizens can use both formal and informal mechanisms to enforce accountability (Malena et al. 2004).

Formal mechanisms have been introduced by the government to encourage citizens' participation in demanding accountability from the government, for example:

- *Elections* to select appropriate candidates to run public administration
- *Public hearings* to provide feedback and public opinion on policies formulated by public officials
- *Right to Information Act* to seek information about the plans and actions of public officials
- *Citizens Charters* to demand the quality of public services promised by the government departments
- *Public Interest Litigations* to seek legal remedy against errant public officials in the larger interest of citizens

Informal mechanisms are developed by citizens and CSOs to monitor the performance of the government and seek accountability, for example:

- *Policy Advocacy* to seek modifications in policies for the benefit of citizens
- *Budget Advocacy* to evaluate allocation and utilization of funds by officials

- *Citizen Report Cards* to assess the quality of public services
- *Public meetings* (*Jansunwais*) to question government officials publicly about discrepancies in funds allocation.

These internal, horizontal and external accountability mechanisms form a critical and important dimension of the accountability scaffold, since these mechanisms help to extract accountability from public officials.

::: The Foundations of Accountability (Second Dimension)

The second dimension of the accountability scaffold is the four foundations of accountability we discussed in Chapter 2—*Appropriate Representation, Participative Conduct, Legitimate Conduct* and *Liability Enforcement* (Figure 4.2). Under ideal conditions, the three accountability mechanisms discussed earlier are designed to directly or indirectly support and strengthen these four foundations. In later chapters, we will evaluate the effectiveness of these existing accountability mechanisms in reinforcing these four foundations.

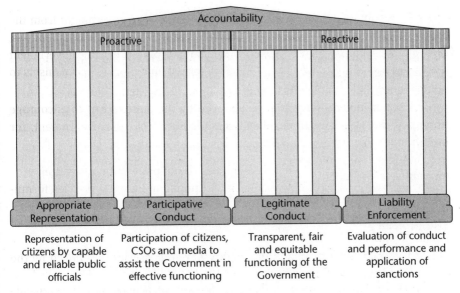

Figure 4.2 The Foundations of Accountability

::: The Institutions of Government (Third Dimension)

The three key institutions of government in the country—the *Legislature,* the *Executive* and the *Judiciary,* form the third and final dimension of the accountability scaffold. The internal, horizontal and external accountability mechanisms mentioned previously enforce accountability across all three branches of the government. A brief description of these three branches of government and the role they play in enforcing accountability is important at this stage.

The Legislature

The Legislature is a bi-cameral Parliament which consists of the *Lok Sabha* (House of People) and the *Rajya Sabha* (Council of States). The Legislature is regarded as the law-making body, as its primary function includes debating legislations proposed in the Parliament, approving budget and economic policies, as well as discussing and amending the Constitution when needed. This branch of government formulates and amends policies that impact the rights, responsibilities and benefits that citizens can hope to receive. Accountability mechanisms are therefore critical, within the Legislature, to ensure that policies are indeed in the interest of citizens.

The Executive

The Executive consists of the *Political Executive* (the Council of Ministers), responsible for policy formulation, and the *Administrative Executive* (civil servants), involved in the implementation of policies. The Executive, through Ministries, public-sector units and public officials, is responsible for managing the country's resources and delivering public services to the citizens. Monitoring the functioning of the Executive to ensure high quality of public services is of utmost importance to every citizen. This book discusses accountability in the Political and Administrative Executive, but does not delve into details of accountability for public-sector units.

The Judiciary

The Judiciary is a single integrated hierarchy of courts, with the *Supreme Court* as the apex court, the *High Courts* and the *District Courts*. The Judiciary's primary function is administering justice. It also reviews legislations passed by the Parliament and revokes them, if found unconstitutional. While the Judiciary holds the government accountable by penalizing it for misconduct, monitoring accountability within the Judiciary is equally important. There are various accountability mechanisms to ensure the transparent functioning of the Judiciary.

These three institutions of the government span a majority of the administrative functions performed by public officials.

::: 3D Accountability

The scaffold of accountability that we develop here is a lattice of these three dimensions—the *mechanisms of accountability,* the *foundations of accountability* and the *institutions of government.* First, the internal, horizontal and external accountability mechanisms that exist for the Legislature, the Executive and the Judiciary are enumerated. Second, these mechanisms are mapped onto the four foundations of accountability they are intended to support. Finally, we evaluate the efficacy of these accountability mechanisms in supporting the four foundations of accountability (Figure 4.3).

Before we dive into studying this 3D lattice, let me point out those accountability mechanisms not covered in this study. This book is restricted to examining accountability mechanisms that exist currently. In some areas, we have highlighted the absence of accountability mechanisms. We are unable to comment on those mechanisms that are under discussion but have not yet been implemented, as it is difficult to forecast their effectiveness. While we broadly evaluate the effectiveness of accountability mechanisms like the Election Commission, Comptroller and Auditor General of India and the Central Vigilance Commission, which exist to hold the government accountable, we do not evaluate accountability mechanisms that may exist to cross-check the functioning of these agencies.

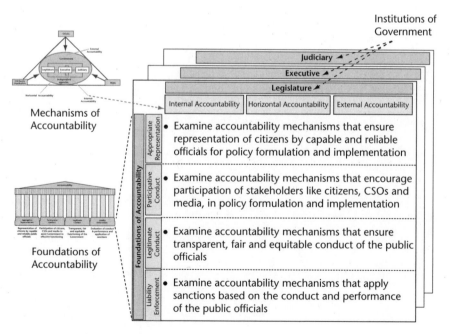

Figure 4.3 3D Accountability

We also do not delve into location-specific or period-specific variations that may differentially impact the effectiveness of these accountability mechanisms across geographies and time. An accountability mechanism might function effectively at one location or at one point in time, but not at others, for several qualitative reasons like strength of political support, the presence of CSOs, and the quality of media support.

We now begin our all-important journey into the three-dimensional world of accountability, with the three institutions of government, the Legislature, the Executive and the Judiciary, as our key destinations. As you walk through each of these three worlds, we will provide guiding lights with the help of the four foundations of accountability (*Appropriate Representation, Participative Conduct, Legitimate Conduct* and *Liability Enforcement*) and the three mechanisms of accountability (*Internal, Horizontal* and *External*), to lead the way.

Reference

Malena, Carmen, Reiner Foster and Janmejay Singh. 2004. 'Social Accountability: An Introduction to the Concept and Emerging Practice', *Social Development Papers*. Available at www.worldbank.org (accessed on 12 December 2008).

5 Legislative Accountability

*No man is good enough to govern another man
without that other's consent.*

Abraham Lincoln, 1809–1865

This chapter examines the functioning and effectiveness of the key mechanisms enforcing accountability in the Legislature. The matrix in Figure 5.1 lists the key internal, horizontal and external accountability mechanisms in the Legislature and assesses their ability to reinforce the four foundations of accountability—Appropriate Representation, Participative Conduct, Legitimate Conduct and Liability Enforcement.

Let us take each foundation and closely examine the mechanisms of accountability that positively or negatively impact it.

::: Foundation 1—Appropriate Representation

The Legislature comprises the Lok Sabha and the Rajya Sabha at the Centre, and the Legislative Assemblies at the State level, where the majority of members are elected by citizens. Appropriate Representation in the Legislature can only be possible if capable and responsible Members of Parliament (MPs) and Members of Legislative Assemblies (MLAs) are elected through a robust election process. Accountability mechanisms therefore need to first ensure that these elections are conducted freely and fairly. For this foundation, we evaluate the efficiency

Mechanisms of Accountability-Legislature		
Internal Accountability	**Horizontal Accountability**	**External Accountability**
Not Applicable	**Election Commission**	**Elections**
MPs/MLAs are elected by citizens, and not internally	*Independent agency to monitor election and appointment of MPs/MLAs*	*Citizens to elect MPs/MLAs based on their performance*
Participative Policy Formulation	**Participative Policy Formulation**	**Citizen's Feedback and Advocacy**
Internal check to ensure Ministries implement public participation mechanisms	*Independent check to ensure Ministries implement public participation mechanisms*	*Citizens to provide opinions on policies and advocate for changes*
Internal Evaluation of Performance	**Judicial Review**	**Citizen's Evaluation of Performance**
Internal check to monitor the conduct and performance of the MPs/MLAs in Parliament	*Independent check to monitor the conduct and performance of the MPs/MLAs in Parliament*	*Citizens to monitor the conduct and performance of MPs/MLAs in Parliament*
Expulsion of MPs	**Police, Judiciary**	**Public Interest Litigation**
Expel MPs to penalize them for mis-conduct	*Independent authority to prosecute MPs involved in cases of corruption*	*Citizens to challenge MPs and legislations in court of law*
		Right To Recall
		Citizens to recall the elected representatives before the end of their term

The left side of the table is labelled **Foundations of Accountability**, with rows grouped as **Appropriate Representation**, **Participative Conduct**, **Legitimate Conduct**, and **Liability Enforcement**.

Legend: ▇ Mechanism not applicable   ▢ Mechanism does not exist

Figure 5.1   Mechanisms in the Legislature

of accountability mechanisms in appointing appropriate MPs/MLAs through a transparent process.

Internal Accountability Mechanisms

The MPs/MLAs are elected by citizens through an election process conducted by the Election Commission. There is no other internal process for the selection of these officials and therefore internal accountability mechanisms are not applicable.

Horizontal Accountability Mechanisms

Election Commission   The Election Commission (EC) is a permanent, independent agency responsible for conducting elections for the Lok Sabha (Centre) and the Legislative Assemblies (State). It is a neutral and autonomous mechanism that checks the election process. The Election Commission (EC) performs the following functions to ensure that the electoral process is robust, free and fair:

- Checks unethical practices during elections, like bogus voting, use of force, or monetary incentives, and ensures that candidates follow the election code
- Facilitates the entire electoral process to increase voters' participation. It prepares and revises electoral rolls, provides voters with information about candidates, and decides the location and number of polling stations
- Regulates candidates and their campaigning during the voting process. It scrutinizes nomination papers and the election expenses of candidates
- Acts as a quasi-judicial body to resolve electoral disputes and monitor election conduct

Since its inception in 1950, the EC has successfully conducted 15 general elections for the Lok Sabha and more than 300 elections for the State Legislative Assemblies, while fiercely safeguarding its independence (*The Times of India*, 7 July 2010). The role played by the EC is commendable, given the immense scale of activities that have to be undertaken to cover all the constituencies spread across India. For the 2009 general elections, 830,000 polling stations, 1.18 million electronic voting machines, eight million polling personnel and three million police personnel were deployed to support 714 million electorates participating in the elections (Chawla 2009). The EC has also taken various initiatives over the past decades to improve the electoral process and check unethical practices; introduced electronic voting machines, voter ID cards and photo electoral rolls; videographed the electoral process at sensitive polling booths; and made proactive efforts to increase voter participation.

The Election Commission, however, lacks the authority to enforce the election code that checks malpractices related to elections. Currently, if the EC finds a candidate involved in any unethical or illegal practice during elections, it files a petition with the High Court. The High Court then conducts proceedings and pronounces a judgement. If the person is ultimately found guilty, the case then goes up to the President, who takes the final decision on the period of disqualification of the candidate. The EC suggests the period of disqualification based on the gravity of the offence, but it can only provide its opinion in this regard to the President. Unfortunately, no immediate disqualification follows any alleged violation of the election code, since the entire judicial process takes years. The inadequate authority of the EC prompts candidates to blatantly violate the code of electoral conduct in a variety of ways. It is well-known that the expenses incurred by candidates while campaigning for elections often exceed the electoral funding limits. The official limit for spending is Rs 2.5 million for a Lok Sabha candidate and Rs 1 million for a State Assembly candidate. In the 2009 Lok Sabha elections, 85 per cent of the candidates claimed to have spent less than 50 per cent of the prescribed expenditure limit. In reality, candidates spend much more than the eligible limit (Yadav 2009). Candidates sometimes also tamper with the voters' list or create fictitious voters and use these votes to favour their party. In Hyderabad, seven million names, over and above the eligible voters, were found after the second revision of the voters' list in 2008 (*The Times of India*, 6 January 2009). Candidates sometimes use force to capture polling booths while the voting process is on, to garner votes for their party. In the 2008 Rajasthan elections, re-polling was conducted in 130 polling booths since they had been captured by a political party to force voting in their favour (*The Tribune*, 6 December 2008). In the 2009 Lok Sabha elections, widespread violence occurred in nearly 25 polling booths in Chhattisgarh, which affected polling in these areas (IBN Live, 25 April 2009).

There are also a number of obstacles in the voter registration process, often due to the non-cooperative attitude of election officers. This results in citizens facing difficulties in getting their voter ID cards, or even registering their names on the voter rolls. Prior to the general elections in 2009, some new voters in Mumbai were turned away by officers at the election registration office, citing reasons such as 'backlog of forms to be processed', 'understaffing issues', 'hectic schedule', 'lack of adequate supporting documents', 'half-day work' and 'strike' (Sen 2009). While the registration form is simple and can be completed in 10 minutes, it may take weeks for this document to reach the desk of the election registration office. The problems faced by citizens continue even after their names are registered on the electoral rolls. Often, their names do not appear on the electoral list. Those citizens relocating residences are required to re-register, which is a tedious process. For example, a citizen who moved residence from one area of Mumbai to another had to make more than four visits and wait several days to cancel his name at the old location and enrol himself on the voters' list in his new location (ibid. 2009). Similarly, a senior citizen of Bangalore did not receive his electoral photo identity card for several years, even though he had enrolled in the electoral list (Faiza 2009). It is no surprise that the time and effort required by citizens to register and vote dissuades them from participating in the electoral process by further stoking the widespread electoral inertia.

External Accountability Mechanisms

Elections   The elections are a powerful mechanism that citizens use to select appropriate representatives and reject those who have not delivered on their promises. When citizens make informed and unbiased voting decisions based on the capabilities and track records of candidates, it ensures high quality of public representation in the corridors of political power.

In reality, there is low participation of citizens in the electoral process, as we saw in earlier chapters. The percentage of eligible citizens voting has remained stagnant in spite of increasing literacy levels. On an average, around 60 per cent of those registered have voted in the general elections in the last 60 years, in spite of the fact that literacy rates have increased from 18 per cent to 66 per cent in the same period (Census of India 2001; www.uis.unesco.org 2008). The urban and the more affluent citizens have shown even less electoral interest. Urban voting in general elections between 1977 and 2004 fell from 61.4 per cent to 53.1 per cent (Datta 2008). To counter this apathy, civil society organizations (CSOs) like the Association for Democratic Reforms, Janaagraha, AGNI and MKSS, among others, ran media campaigns to encourage citizens to vote prior to the 2009 general elections. Voter turnout, however, remained stagnant at 59 per cent (indiaenews.com, 13 May 2009).

Citizens also find it difficult to evaluate candidates, due to the paucity of information about their past performance. Through relentless advocacy by a CSO, Association of Democratic Reforms, the Supreme Court passed an order in 2002, making it mandatory for all candidates standing for elections to file an affidavit with information on their education, financial status and criminal record. A network of 1,200 CSOs, National Election Watch, ran country-wide campaigns in 2009 to disseminate this information to the public, with the help of pamphlets, posters, print media and SMS services. Some candidates conceal controversial information by leaving certain columns blank in their election affidavits. A study conducted by Resurgence India, a CSO, found that during the 2007 elections in Punjab, 369 of the 388 candidates belonging to the six major political parties had left some columns blank on their affidavits (*Zee News*, 15 April 2008). Timely availability and accessibility of information on candidates is also an issue, as updated details of candidates' affidavits are available only two weeks before elections. Further, these affidavits only provide information about the backgrounds of the candidates and do not comment on their past performance. Ideally, records of development in the candidate's constituency, measured in terms of quantifiable output, should be made available to the electorates before elections. A few CSOs have worked to make citizens more aware of the past performances of candidates. Satark Nagrik Sangathan, a CSO based in New Delhi, assessed the performance of 70 MLAs prior to the Delhi Assembly elections in 2008, on parameters like attendance, number of questions asked in Parliament, and an account of the money spent through the MLA Local Development Scheme. Report cards were published in newspapers to disseminate this information to citizens (www.snsindia.org 2008). Candidates themselves, have taken little initiative, however, to provide more detailed information about the progress of their constituencies.

Perhaps the biggest area of worry is that electorates make biased and influenced voting decisions. According to a study conducted by the Centre for Media Studies, 22 per cent of the total electorate and 37 per cent of the below-poverty-line electorate has been bribed in India over the last decade. In one assembly election in 2008, it is believed that one out of two votes was bought and Rs 455 million was spent on bribes (Mathew 2008). Identity politics is also very common. Caste and religion are unscrupulously used by some candidates to influence voters. Fortunately, the recent elections in Bihar were a positive sign. Citizens voted for development and not caste; there were no incidents of booth capturing or violence reported; and the incumbent returned, riding on the saddle of good governance and development (*The Economist*, 25 November 2010; Mrug 2010). A shift in the mindset of voters has possibly started, and hopefully this will set the trend for all future elections.

To summarize, the first foundation of accountability, Appropriate Representation, can be fortified if the inadequacies in the above-mentioned horizontal and external accountability mechanisms are addressed, ultimately ensuring the triumph of democracy.

::: Foundation 2—Participative Conduct

The Legislature is involved in debating and formulating policies in the interest of the citizens. The Participative Conduct foundation of accountability, in the context of the Legislature, implies seeking citizens' participation in the policymaking process by inviting their feedback and comments on policies, while they are being formulated. This is an important aspect of policy creation, as it strengthens the law-making process by increasing its legitimacy and credibility.

Internal Accountability Mechanisms

Participative Policy Formulation   Ministers can invite public opinion and feedback on policies through many platforms. Official public hearings are held by some ministries, where citizens are invited to post their views through a website, or via e-mail, within a limited time frame. For instance, the Ministry of Women and Child Development had prepared a Bill intended to provide protection to women, against sexual harassment at the workplace. A draft of the Bill was put up on its website and comments were invited from citizens (PRS Legislative Research). The Planning Commission also invited opinions from citizens for the development of the 12th Five-Year Plan. Citizens were provided with the broad issues being discussed in the Plan, and were asked to mail their suggestions to the Planning Commission (*IBNlive*, 21 December 2010). Standing Committees that facilitate the Legislature in policy-making, also invite citizens to submit research relevant to a proposed policy. For example, The Maintenance and Welfare of Parents and Senior Citizens Bill 2007 seeks to make it a legal obligation for children and heirs to provide maintenance to senior family members. In response to their invitation, the Standing Committee received written submissions and oral testimony from several groups like the All India Senior Citizens Confederation, the Senior Citizens Service Forum and Age Care India (PRS Legislative Research).

Ministries are not obligated, however, to seek citizens' feedback on policy formulation, resulting in scarce use of this important mechanism. Further, Ministries, or Standing Committees that invite citizens' participation, can choose to ignore the views of the public without evaluation and without any explanation. A formal acknowledgement of receipt of these public opinions is not mandated, nor do the Ministries need to respond to the suggestions. A formal response and feedback mechanism would help ensure that public opinion is considered while formulating policies, and that citizens do not lose interest in providing their opinions. For instance, in the United States, the Administrative Procedures Act (APA) provides that citizens have to be given a formal response within 30 days, to any queries on proposed government policies (Nylander 2006). A similar accountability mechanism is needed in India, to ensure that Ministries encourage citizens' opinions and respond to them in a timely manner.

Horizontal Accountability Mechanisms

Participative Policy Formulation   As highlighted in the earlier section, there is no compulsion on the part of Ministries to seek citizens' feedback and respond to their views. An independent, horizontal check or a legal compulsion for the government to consult citizens within a limited time frame, will encourage public participation in the policy formulation process (Caddy 2001).

Without this check by an adjacent authority, the government might not pay serious attention to the public participation process. For example, one citizen filed a complaint with the Central Information Commission (CIC) against the city Police and the Home Department, for not making the draft Police (Amendment) Bill available in the public domain. The CIC issued an order to the city's Government to publish all draft policies in the public domain, for citizens to debate, as these policy changes affect public lives (Chauhan 2010). Horizontal checks by independent agencies are therefore required, in addition to the internal checks, to ensure that the government seeks citizens' participation in policy formulation.

External Accountability Mechanisms

Citizens' Feedback and Advocacy   The ideal political process should be a two-way street, with information exchanged on a continuous basis between citizens and the government. Citizens need to make the effort to provide their opinions on public policies, in response to invitations from Ministries and Standing Committees. Citizens can also participate in this process by working with CSOs. The CSOs and think-tanks play a major role in generating and sustaining public opinion on policies and issues related to government functioning. They conduct research on public policy and advise the government based on their findings.

Currently, participation by citizens in the policy formulation process is low. One of the key reasons for low participation, not surprisingly, is low aware-ness about participation mechanisms. Ad-hoc usage of these mechanisms by the Ministries, coupled with limited publicity, exacerbates the problem. A low liter-acy rate of 66 per cent and a low Internet penetration of 7 per cent results in a limited number of people being able to access these participatory mechanisms (www.uis.unesco.org 2008; internetworldstats.com 2009). Most citizens are also unaware of the existence and role of think-tanks and CSOs, actively advocating for policy changes. The biggest cause for concern lies with the indifferent attitude and apathy of citizens, vis-à-vis engaging in the process of political dialogue. Sub-stantive, frequent and high-intensity campaigns need to be run by CSOs and the media, to cajole and coax citizens to engage with the government.

The second foundation of accountability, Participative Conduct, is weak, not only due to a lack of both internal and horizontal mechanisms, but also due to a lack of external participation by citizens in policy formulation. Without this valu-able feedback loop, the critical and continuous engagement between citizens and government, the keystone of a robust democratic process cannot be sustained.

::: Foundation 3—Legitimate Conduct

The main function of the Legislature is to debate and formulate policies in the Parliament, in the interest of the citizens. The Legislature also scrutinizes and questions the functioning of the government (the Executive) on behalf of the citizens. The third foundation of accountability, Legitimate Conduct, results in a transparent and healthy process of debate in Parliament, leading to policies that nudge us towards a path of economic and social prosperity.

Internal Accountability Mechanisms

Internal Evaluation of Performance   Members of Parliament are supposed to regularly attend parliament sessions, raise relevant issues, engage in healthy de-bate, and provide constructive comments on the policies proposed in Parliament. Ideally, internal accountability mechanisms should exist, to keep a check on MPs' participation and behaviour in Parliament. In reality, there is barely any check.

First, there are no stringent criteria for minimum attendance of an MP in the Parliament; MPs only need to inform the Parliament of their absence. While there is a Committee that examines the attendance of members, it can prescribe an action only in those cases where an MP is absent for a period of 60 days or more, without permission. Of those MPs who attend, only a few actually sit through a complete session of Parliament. For instance, attendance in the first half of a session is 65–70 per cent, but falls to 15–20 per cent after lunch (Ramesh 2005). A study by the National Social Watch Coalition found that MPs with celebrity status, like actors or cricketers, had abysmally low attendance. This study tracked the attendance of MPs in the Lok Sabha (10th and 11th sessions) and the Rajya Sabha (210th and 211th sessions) in 2009. None of the 12 celebrity MPs who were tracked attended more than 20 per cent of the days in each session of Parliament (*The Times of India*, 7 April 2009).

Second, there are no mechanisms to check an MP's participation in parliamentary proceedings. A study by PRS Legislative Research shows that during the five-year term of the 14th Lok Sabha (2004–09), 56 MPs did not ask a single question and 67 MPs asked less than 10 questions (headlinesindia.mapsofindia.com, 13 March 2009). The study conducted by the National Social Watch Coalition on celebrity MPs found that of the approximately 80,000 questions raised in both the Lok Sabha and the Rajya Sabha, not even 1 per cent was raised by the 12 celebrity MPs studied (*The Times of India*, 7 April 2009).

Third, the MPs often boycott parliamentary proceedings instead of engaging in healthy and constructive debates. The time lost due to parliamentary pandemonium has increased from 5.28 per cent in the 11th Lok Sabha (1996–98), to 22 per cent in the 14th Lok Sabha (2004–09) (IBN Live, 6 April 2009). The winter session of the 15th Lok Sabha, which concluded in 2010, saw the Parliament sit for only seven of the scheduled 114 business hours due to the disruption caused by the 2G telecom spectrum scam (Nichenametla 2010). These disruptions result in minimal time being spent on discussing important Bills. In 2008, eight Bills were passed in about 20 minutes without any debate. In 2009, of the 15 non-financial Bills passed by the Lok Sabha in the winter session, eight were passed without any discussion (Madhavan 2009).

Lack of an internal accountability mechanism within the Legislature, that oversees the performance and conduct of MPs in Parliament, sometimes undermines the sanctity of our democracy.

Horizontal Accountability Mechanisms

Judicial Review   The Judiciary, as an independent arm of the government, has the power to interpret the Constitution and determine the legality of a Bill passed by Parliament. The Judiciary exercises 'Judicial Review' on the Legislature by interpreting provisions of the laws enacted by the Parliament, and by declaring a law unconstitutional if it does not conform to the tenets of the Constitution of India.

The Judiciary does not have the power to review the proceedings within the Parliament. It has attempted to monitor these proceedings in some cases, but its attempts have been accused of 'judicial over-reach', or interference in the internal proceedings of the Legislature. One state assembly case in 2005 is an example of this. To improve the functioning of the assembly, the Supreme Court issued detailed directives, such as the day and the process of convening the assembly to ascertain majority in the House. Since the Indian Constitution bars judicial scrutiny of in-house proceedings, the directives were cast aside as 'judicial over-reach' (*The Indian Express*, 3 May 2007).

No other independent authority exists, which can review the functioning of the Legislature and minimize disruptions in Parliament.

External Accountability Mechanisms

Citizens' Evaluation of Performance   Citizens, CSOs and the media need to exert external pressure on MPs/MLAs by closely tracking parliamentary debates, attendance and participation records, and by challenging their actions and performance.

The information required to track parliamentary proceedings and MPs' perfor-mances is provided by the Legislature in detail. The government broadcasts the Lok Sabha sessions through a dedicated TV channel called Lok Sabha TV, and pub-lishes a copy of debates and questions asked by MPs on the Lok Sabha website, and in the Parliament and State Assembly libraries. A number of CSOs like PRS Legis-lative Research and Democracy Connect collate information about parliamentary proceedings and translate them into an easy-to-read format for citizens. The media regularly updates citizens about parliamentary proceedings through TV channels and newspapers. PRS Legislative Research also conducts workshops to train jour-nalists to understand parliamentary debates on policy and the passage of impor-tant laws. More importantly, the indifferent attitude of citizens and their declining faith in the government prevents them from playing the role that they should in monitoring the performance of MPs/MLAs.

In summary, there are inadequate internal and horizontal accountability mechanisms that can keep a check on the functioning of the Legislature. The external accountability mechanisms also need to be strengthened to ensure that the third foundation of accountability, Legitimate Conduct, is always on display in the Legislature.

::: Foundation 4—Liability Enforcement

The ability to hold public officials responsible for their actions is an important aspect of accountability, but even more critical is the ability to penalize them for their misconduct. Ideally, MPs should be held accountable for misconduct in the Parliament. The power to enforce a liability could be a strong deterrent to unparliamentary conduct.

Internal Accountability Mechanisms

Expulsion of MPs   There is a Constitutional provision that allows MPs to be expelled from the Parliament for misconduct, based on a unanimous decision by all other MPs.

Expelling MPs for misconduct is a tool that has been used only in extreme cases. In 2005, the Parliament expelled 11 MPs involved in the 'cash-for-query' scandal, where they accepted cash and in-lieu consented to 'sell' their question time (Sharma 2007). In 2009, a State Legislative Assembly suspended four MLAs of a political party for four years, on charges of assaulting another MLA in the Assembly. The resolution for their suspension was adopted by a voice vote of members (*Rediff News,* November 9 2009). Such examples of liability enforcement, however, are very rare.

Sanctions are not applied to MPs boycotting or disrupting sessions. There is no system of awarding penalties to control participation or attendance of MPs in Parliament. A scaled system of penalties, from minor to major, could help the smooth functioning of the Parliament, and perhaps result in better utilization of time.

Horizontal Accountability Mechanisms

Police   The Police is an independent authority that can conduct investigations into any corrupt practices engaged in by parliamentarians, or their involvement in fuelling identity-based conflicts, based on complaints filed by citizens.

The Police, however, cannot function as independently as needed, due to the random and frequent transfers of police officials. Appointments and promotions of police officers, especially at higher levels, are sometimes driven by political compulsions. One RTI query filed by an individual revealed that between January–April 2008, a State Police headquarters had received 2,700 political recommendations for transfers of police officers (www.pcrf.in 2009). Reform commissions like the National Police Commission and the Padmanabhaiah Committee have recommended fixed tenures of officers and independent boards to monitor transfers and promotions (Salve 2009). These reforms, however, have faced resistance from state governments, and no action has been taken so far.

The Police are sometimes influenced by public officials to help protect their associates, or harass their opponents. Investigations against corrupt public officials are often stalled, or influenced, due to this nexus. One citizen faced difficulties in getting a police complaint filed against the ruling MLA and his supporters.

He alleged that the MLA and his associates had threatened him over a land dispute. The police, however, refused to entertain the complaint. The citizen then approached the court and managed to get a court order, to lodge a complaint against the MLA. Here, the citizen, who was also an advocate, was aware that he could use the services of the court to get his case registered (Singh 2008). The vast majority of citizens, especially in villages and smaller districts, find it cumbersome to file their complaints and seek redressal for the injustices committed against them.

The inadequate number of police personnel also contributes to the poor quality of law enforcement and the significant workload on the police. In India, there are only 130 police for every 100,000 people, which is way below the United Nations norm of 220 police for every 100,000 people (Phadnis 2010). This is also lower than many other countries, with 315 police per 100,000 people in the USA, 300 police per 100,000 people in Germany, 290 police per 100,000 people in Australia and 200 police per 100,000 people in the UK (*India Today*, 9 January 2009). Disturbingly, this ratio for states like Bihar and Uttar Pradesh is as low as 75 and 115 police per 100,000 people, respectively (www.pib.nic.in 2010).

A study conducted by the Centre for Media Studies and Transparency International (2007) showed that about 50 per cent of the respondents who used the police service paid bribes to the police (cmsindia.org 2008). Apart from the direct acts of misconduct, citizens sometimes have to suffer the indifferent attitude of the police in dealing with criminals. Moreover, inadequate objectivity during the evaluation of complaints against fellow police officers can result in an inability to pinpoint blame for misconduct.

The Police are a key instrument to enforce the rule of law, but are sometimes used as a pliable tool in the hands of unscrupulous public officials.

Judiciary The Judiciary is most critical in enforcing accountability within the Legislature, as it can prosecute MPs involved in acts of misconduct or misappropriation, based on investigations conducted against them.

The Judiciary has its own limitations, since it lacks adequate infrastructure to conduct swift trials. Currently, India has only 12–13 judges per one million people, compared to 107 in the United States and 51 in the United Kingdom (www.transparency.org 2007). In 2009, there was a shortage of seven judges in the Supreme Court, 234 judges in the High Courts and 2,998 judges in the lower courts. Inadequate infrastructure and a lengthy judicial process has resulted in 26 million pending cases in subordinate courts, about four million pending cases in the High Court, and close to 50,000 pending cases in the Supreme Court, as of March 2009 (Rahman 2009). Insufficient funds are allocated to the Judiciary, further compounding the problem. The Judiciary has no financial autonomy, as budgetary allocations for its operations are decided by the Legislature and the funds utilization is decided by the Executive. In 2007, just 0.04 per cent of the annual budget in India was allocated to the Judiciary, as compared to 1.8 per cent in the United Kingdom and 1.6 per cent in the United States (Transparency International 2007; GPO Access). Moreover, allocated funds are sometimes not completely utilized for the development of the Judiciary and there have been cases of misappropriation of funds. One High Court judge was even recommended for impeachment due to the misappropriation of Rs 5 million of the Judiciary's funds (*The Times of India*, 9 September 2008).

The prospect of receiving delayed justice clouds the performance of the Judiciary and prompts citizens to use illegal methods to expedite their cases. A 2005 study conducted by Transparency International India and the Centre for Media Studies showed that about 60 per cent of the survey respondents paid bribes to lawyers, 5 per cent to judges and 30 per cent to court officials (*Mint*, 3 May 2007).

We have seen that two key horizontal organizations, the Police and the Judiciary, that are supposed to reinforce one of the foundations of accountability, Liability Enforcement, are themselves compromised. The lack of punitive action against corrupt public officials dramatically lowers the citizens' confidence in the government, the Police and the Judiciary. This compromised condition of the law-keepers, serves to encourage the actions of the law-breakers.

External Accountability Mechanisms

Public Interest Litigation   The external role of citizens in demanding accountability from the Legislature, given the weaknesses in the internal and horizontal accountability mechanisms identified earlier, cannot be over-emphasized. Citizens should pressurize the government and law enforcement agencies to act against the corrupt. Citizens can challenge the functioning of MPs and the legislations passed by them by using a powerful tool called the Public Interest Litigation (PIL). The PIL is a litigation mechanism that can be introduced by the court, or by any private party, to seek legal remedy for the protection of public interest. The PIL can be used to challenge legislations and policies passed in the Parliament, or constitutional amendments made by the Parliament.

There are several examples of the usage of PILs. A CSO, Youth for Equality, filed a PIL with the Supreme Court in 2007 to stay 'The Central Educational Institutions (Reservation in Admission) Bill, 2006', which provides 27 per cent reservation for 'Other Backward Classes' in centrally funded educational institutions. The CSO complained that the issued notification violated the basic structure of the Constitution and infringed on an individual's fundamental rights (*IBN Live*,

19 February 2007; Youth for Equality). In response, the Supreme Court stayed the implementation of the quota till the litigation was evaluated. In another example, People's Union for Civil Liberties, a CSO, successfully petitioned the Supreme Court in 2001, seeking the enforcement of the 'Right to Food Act'. The main argument of the petition was that Central and State governments have neglected the serious issue of malnutrition in India. While the final ruling is still pending, the Supreme Court has issued several interim rulings; directing all states to convert the benefits of nutrition programmes into legal entitlements, mandating awareness and transparency in its implementation, and expanding the coverage of the Mid-Day Meal scheme in public primary schools (Chopra 2009). For instance, under the Mid-Day Meal scheme, the states were instructed to provide mid-day meals to all children in government and government-assisted primary schools for at least 200 days in a year.

Citizens lack knowledge and understanding, however, on the scope and applicability of the PIL, as seen by the number of PILs that are ruled against. For instance, a PIL was filed by a CSO, challenging the appointment of a senior police officer allegedly involved in communal riots. The Judiciary ruled against the PIL on the grounds that the appointment of public officials is a prerogative of the government and it cannot be interfered with (Sharma 2009). The Judiciary ruled against another PIL on similar grounds, where the CSO was requesting for a cut in the salaries of MPs and MLAs who do not attend Parliament sessions and frequently resort to walkouts (janhitmanch.org).

By and large, the PIL is a powerful and successful mechanism that can be used to enforce liability and external accountability on the government.

Right to Recall   Citizens elect candidates they deem appropriate for a public position. One school of thought is that they should also have the right to remove or recall elected candidates, if they are found ineffective or fraudulent. Based on this principle, citizens have the 'right to recall' an elected representative before the end of their term in office, for non-performance or misuse of position. The right to recall is currently implemented only in Chhattisgarh and Madhya Pradesh. In June 2008, the first successful recall elections were held in Chhattisgarh, where the majority of the electorate voted for the removal of three elected Presidents of local urban bodies (Bhanu 2008).

This provision, however, exists only for municipal bodies, where citizens have the right to demand the removal of an elected President of the Municipal Council for non-performance. The recall process can be initiated only after a request is made by a minimum number of electorates and after the elected President has served for a minimum period in office. Internationally, in states like California (USA), recall elections can be held for legislators at both the state and local levels. The process of recall and of conducting fresh polls results in extensive costs to a functioning democracy. This is a tool that is used with discretion even in other countries. A study estimated that there had been around 40 attempts to recall state officials in California (Civitas Website). Even if recall is not successfully held, the very fact that people can use this tool sends a message to public officials to not abuse their positions.

To conclude, Liability Enforcement, the fourth foundation of accountability, is fragile, weakened by internal, horizontal and external accountability mechanisms that are not implemented effectively. The overall constraints in the implementation of accountability mechanisms in the Legislature are set out in Figure 5.2.

Weaknesses in Mechanisms of Accountability-Legislature		
Internal Accountability	Horizontal Accountability	External Accountability
Appropriate Representation — Not Applicable	**Election Commission** • *Lack of authority with the Election Commission in controlling unethical voting practices* • *Lack of cooperation from election officers in the voter registration process*	**Elections** • *Low participation by citizens in elections, biased voting decisions*
Participative Conduct — **Participative Policy Formulation** • *No internal check on implementation of citizens' participation mechanisms*	**Participative Policy Formulation** • *No independent check to ensure implementation of citizens' participation mechanisms*	**Citizens' Feedback and Advocacy** • *Low awareness about feedback mechanisms and advocacy organizations* • *Indifferent attitude of citizens*
Legitimate Conduct — **Internal Evaluation of Performance** • *Lack of checks on parliamentary proceedings and behaviour of MPs*	**Judicial Review** • *Judiciary cannot question the functioning of Legislature* • *No independent check to review parliamentary proceedings exists*	**Citizens' Evaluation of Performance** • *Poor access to information about MPs' performance* • *Indifferent attitude of citizens*
Liability Enforcement — **Expulsion of MPs** • *Expelling MPs is rare* • *No minor penalties for poor participation in Parliament*	**Police, Judiciary** • *Political interference in appointments and transfers* • *Lack of accountability* • *Inadequate infrastructure*	**Public Interest Litigation** • *Difficulty in using PILs due to lack of understanding of its scope and application* **Right to Recall** • *Inadequate implementation*

(Left axis: Foundations of Accountability)

Mechanism not applicable   Mechanism does not exist

Figure 5.2 Assessment of Mechanisms in the Legislature

We now turn our attention to the Executive and examine the accountability mechanisms that exist to strengthen accountability in this all-important arm of the government.

References

'56 MPs asked no questions in last Lok Sabha: study'. 2009. Available at http:// headlinesindia.mapsofindia.com/ (accessed on 20 January 2010).

'59–60 percent voter turnout in Election 2009'. 2009. Available at www.indiaenews.com (accessed on 6 January 2010).

'Asia View—A triumph in Bihar'. 2010. *The Economist*, 25 November.

Bhanu, Vinod. 2008. 'Right to Recall Legislators: The Chhattisgarh Experiment'. *Economic and Political Weekly*, 4 October.

'Bogus votes beef up voters' list by 71 lakh'. 2009. *The Times of India*, 6 January.

Caddy, J. 2001. 'Why citizens are central to good governance'. Available on www. oecdobserver.org (Accessed on 11 December 2010).

'Celebrity MPs among top absentees from Parliament'. 2009. *The Times of India*, 7 April.

'Chapter 7—State of Literacy'. Census of India. Available on censusindia.gov.in (accessed on 18 February 2011).

Chauhan, Chetan. 2010. 'CIC to Delhi Govt: put all draft bills in public domain'. *Hindustan Times*, 11 July.

Chawla, Navin. 2009. 'India's General Elections 2009—Some Insights'. Available at http:// eci.nic.in (accessed on 22 November 2010).

'Chidambaram Calls for Doubling Capacity of Police Training Institutes and Recruitment in States'. 2010. Available at www.pib.nic.in (accessed on 8 October 2010).

Chopra, Surabhi. 2009. 'Holding the State Accountable for Hunger'. *Economic and Political Weekly*, 15 August.

'Citizen Selection Procedure (Nominee: Ajay Dubey)'. RTI Awards 2009 Section. Available at www.pcrf.in (accessed on 6 January 2010).

'Corruption in Judiciary'. 2007. *Mint*, 3 May.

'Country reports on judicial corruption (India and UK)'. 2007. *Global Corruption Report*. Available at www.transparency.org (accessed on 19 May 2009).

'Current Services Budget Authority by Function, Category, and Program'. Budget of the United States Government for fiscal year 2007. Available at www.gpoaccess.gov (accessed on 28 May 2009).

Datta, Kanika. 2008. 'A vote is more than worth the candle'. *Business Standard*, 11 December.

'Direct Democracy could help clean up Parliament'. 2009. Available on www.civitas.org.uk (accessed on 16 December 2010).

'Evolution of a Commission'. 2010. *The Times of India*, 7 July.

'Four MNS legislators suspended for 4 years for assaulting Azmi'. 2009. Rediff News, 9 November. Available at http://news.rediff.com (accessed on 18 December 2009).

'Global Rankings—Adult Literacy Rate (Total)'. 2008. Available at www.uis.unesco.org (accessed on 8 April 2009).

Haneef, Faiza. 2009. 'Bangalorean's EPIC struggle for a voter ID card'. *The New Indian Express*, 11 October.

'Judicial activism is like an unruly horse'. 2007. *The Indian Express*, 3 May.

'Kolkata judge's case adds to judiciary woes'. 2008. *The Times of India*, 9 September.

Madhavan, M. R. 2009. 'Asleep in the House'. *Financial Express*, 28 December.

Mathew, Liz. 2008. 'Politicians buy a fifth of votes, shows study'. *Mint*, 22 October.

'Milestones: 29 Mar 2007—SC Stayed the OBC Reservation Bill, 10 Apr 2008—Supreme Court Verdict on OBC quota is out'. Available at www.youthforequality.com/ (accessed on 17 December 2009).

Mrug, Jay. 2010. 'What worked for Nitish? Social coalition'. *DNA*, 25 November.

Nichenametla, Prasad. 2010. 'Winter dud at House'. *Hindustan Times*, 13 December.

Nylander, Jill. 2006. 'Administrative Procedure Act', *Michigan Bar Journal*, November.

'Overhauling the police'. 2009. *India Today*, 9 January.

Phadnis, Aditi. 2010. 'Our police will be effective in 7–8 years'. *Business Standard*, 14 February.

'Plan Panel set targets for 12th Plan'. 2010. Available at www.ibnlive.in.com (accessed on 4 January 2011).

'Police Services'. 2007. *TII-CMS India Corruption Study 2007—With Focus on BPL House-holds.* Available at http://cmsindia.org (accessed on 19 May 2009).

'Primer: Engaging with Policy Makers'. Available at www.prsindia.org/ (accessed on 7 January 2010).

'Public Interest Litigations (PILs)'. Available at www.janhitmanch.org (accessed on 2 March 2009).

'Quota PIL: SC grants time to Centre'. 19 February 2007. Available at http://ibnlive.in.com (accessed on 25 January 2009).

Rahman, Shafi. 2009. 'Lords on Trial'. *India Today*, 7 September.

Ramesh, Jairam. 2005. 'Will Parliament Live mean more accountability?'. *The Times of India*, 2 January.

'Repoll in 130 stations today'. 2008. *The Tribune*, 6 December.

'Repoll in parts of Bihar, Chhattisgarh'. 2009. Available at http://ibnlive.in.com (accessed on 25 July 2009).

'Report cards on the performance of Delhi MLAs'. 2008. Available at www.snsindia.org (accessed on 19 January 2010).

Salve, Harish. 2009. 'A case for prosecution'. *India Today*, 1 May.

'SC notice to Govt, EC on candidates not revealing info'. 2008. *Zee News*, 15 April (accessed on 20 January 2010).

Sen, Somit. 2009. 'Getting name on voter rolls no easy task'. *The Times of India*, 17 March.

Sharma, Tanu. 2007. 'Parliament right to expel errant MPs but its actions open to scrutiny, says SC'. *The Indian Express*, 11 January.

_____. 2009. 'SC upholds Pande's appointment, says it is govt's will'. *The Indian Express*, 14 January.

Singh, Sanjay. 2008. 'Engineer murdered by MLA for Mayawati's birthday hafta'. *The Indian Express*, 25 December.

'Top 20 Countries with the Highest Number of Internet Users'. 2009. Available at www. internetworldstats.com (accessed on 28 April 2010).

'Unruly MPs wasted 22 pc of Parliament's time, money'. 2009. Available at http://ibnlive. in.com/ (accessed on 6 April 2010).

Yadav, Puneet Nicholas. 2009. 'Candidates campaign funds under a cloud'. *DNA*, 15 December.

6 Executive Accountability

Bureaucracy is not an obstacle to democracy but an
inevitable complement to it.

Joseph A. Schumpeter, 1883–1950

This chapter examines the functioning and effectiveness of the key mechanisms enforcing accountability in the Executive. Here is where India's famed bureaucracy resides and operates from. We will find a wide range of accountability mechanisms, all attempting to bolster the quality of governance, but in some cases failing to do so. The matrix in Figure 6.1 lists the key internal, horizontal and external accountability mechanisms in the Executive. We assess these mechanisms to determine their ability to reinforce the four foundations of accountability.

Let us take each foundation of accountability and closely examine the mechanisms of accountability that positively or negatively impact it.

::: Foundation 1—Appropriate Representation

The Executive includes the *Political Executive* (Council of Ministers) at the Centre and the State, which formulates policies, and the *Administrative Executive* (Civil Servants), which assists the Political Executive in formulating and implementing these policies. Since the Executive plays a major role in designing and executing

Mechanisms of Accountability–Executive		
Internal Accountability	**Horizontal Accountability**	**External Accountability**

<table>
<tr>
<td rowspan="5" style="writing-mode:vertical-lr">Foundations of Accountability</td>
<td>Appropriate Representation</td>
<td>**Objective and Transparent Process**

Internal check to monitor appointment and transfer of public officials</td>
<td>**Objective and Transparent Process**

Independent check to monitor appointment and transfer of public officials</td>
<td>**Public Disclosure of Appointments**

Citizens to monitor appointment and transfer of public officials</td>
</tr>
<tr>
<td>Participative Conduct</td>
<td>**Participative Policy Implementation**

Internal check to ensure executive implements public participation mechanisms</td>
<td>**Participative Policy Implementation**

Independent check to ensure executive implements public participation mechanisms</td>
<td>**Advocacy and Government Citizen Initiatives**

Citizens to participate in governance through advocacy and government citizen initiatives</td>
</tr>
<tr>
<td>Legitimate Conduct</td>
<td>**Annual Performance Assessment Reports, Results Framework Document**

Internal mechanism to evaluate performance of public officials/depts
Whistleblowers Protection
Internal mechanism for employees to expose internal misgovernance</td>
<td>**Legislature, Parliamentary Committees, Delivery Monitoring Unit, Planning Commission, CAG, CBI, CVC, Lokayukta**

Independent agencies to monitor functioning of public officials</td>
<td>**RTI Act, Citizens Charter, Budget Advocacy, Social Audits, PETS, Report Cards and Community Scorecards**

Citizens to monitor the performance of public officials</td>
</tr>
<tr>
<td>Liability Enforcement</td>
<td>**Dismissal, Removal or Reduction in Rank**

Internal provisions to penalize public officials for misconduct</td>
<td>**Police, Judiciary**

Independent authority to prosecute public officials for misconduct</td>
<td>**Public Interest Litigation**

Citizens to challenge public officials for their misconduct in the court of law</td>
</tr>
</table>

☐ Mechanism does not exist

Figure 6.1   Mechanisms in the Executive

policies that help govern the country, selecting the appropriate public officials is most critical. We therefore evaluate the effectiveness of accountability mechanisms in ensuring that the process to select these public officials is well-defined and transparent.

Internal Accountability Mechanisms

Objective and Transparent Process   The Council of Ministers is directly selected by the Prime Minister, the head of the ruling government. The Prime Minister recommends the names of the MPs who are to form part of the Council of Ministers to the President, who then approves the list recommended. Based on the political party's strategy, coalition dynamics and the profile of the candidates, the Prime Minister handpicks the Council of Ministers for his government. Since the Ministers are chosen without any transparent process, their selection could be subjective. Regional allies often lobby for cabinet positions and important portfolios, based on the bargaining power they have. Following the 2009 elections, the largest ally to the ruling party got the railways portfolio (Bhattacharya 2009). The second largest ally negotiated hard for nine ministerial berths, where all members of the family would be given a Ministry (*NDTV*, 22 May 2009). Deserving candidates for a portfolio could be overlooked to satisfy political interests. There is no consultative process adopted, or justification provided for these appointments.

Meanwhile, the process of selection and assignment of civil servants is conducted independently by the Union Public Service Commission, in a free and fair manner. There is no interference in the selection and assignment of these officials. The officials can, however, be re-assigned or transferred internally from one post to another by the heads of their departments. This provision of transfer, introduced for administrative benefit, is sadly misused for political reasons. For example, senior bureaucrats and police officers of a state were reshuffled after the 2009 general election results. More than 80 officers, including 51 Indian Police Service officers and 19 Indian Administrative Service officers, were transferred within a week of the poll results. Many of these officers had jurisdiction over those constituencies where the ruling party faced defeat in the polls (*The Indian Express*, 9 June 2009).

The report of the second Administrative Reforms Commission (ARC) reveals that over the years, 48–60 per cent of Indian Administrative Services (IAS) officers have spent less than a year in their postings, and only around 10 per cent have spent more than three years in their postings (Eshwar 2009). According to another study, the average tenure of IAS officers in a given post is merely 16 months. Frequent transfers of officials inhibit them from gaining domain expertise because of the limited time they spend in a post (Iyer and Anandi 2009). This adversely affects their job satisfaction, career progression and family life. Public officials then resort to unethical means to hold on to their postings. From time to time, the ARC has made recommendations to streamline civil services, but has met with limited success. A distinguished collective of 83 bureaucrats recently filed a petition in the Supreme Court, seeking to depoliticize transfers, promotions and disciplinary matters relating to the civil services (Mahapatra 2011).

Despite the attempt of our Constitution to insulate the bureaucracy from political pressures by appointing an independent selection commission, rampant and unreasonable transfers of public officials weaken the sanctity of the selection process.

Horizontal Accountability Mechanisms

Objective and Transparent Process   The President has the power to approve the Council of Ministers at the Centre, based on the advice of the Prime Minister. The Governor has the same powers at the state level, and acts based on the advice of the Chief Minister. The President and the Governor act as independent authorities, not representing any political party, in the selection of the Council of Ministers. In most cases, however, the President and the Governor do not disagree with the appointment of the Council of Ministers.

At another level, the Union Public Service Commission (UPSC) serves as an independent, horizontal check on the selection and appointment of public officials for the civil services. The UPSC autonomously evaluates candidates by testing them on three levels: a preliminary test, a main examination and an interview. It also objectively advises the government on the suitability of internal civil service officials for appointment to higher posts. The selection of civil service officials is fortunately conducted through an objective and independent process.

In addition to the absence of any internal check—as stated earlier—there is also no independent check on the transfer of civil service officials. The need for a watchful eye on transfers is critical to maintaining the dignity and pro-bity of public service. The Civil Services Performance Standards and Account-ability Bill 2010 proposes to set up an independent agency called the Central Public Services Authority, which will manage the transfers of public officials. The Bill also proposes a minimum fixed tenure for officials at different levels. If a bureaucrat is transferred before the minimum tenure, he or she will have to be compensated for the inconvenience caused due to such a move. The fundamental goal of the Bill is to check political interference in the bureaucracy (Phadnis 2009). The Department of Personnel and Training is still finalizing the draft bill (as of 31 March 2011), which will be presented to the Union Cabinet and then be tabled in the Parliament for approval (*Hindustan Times*, 7 June 2010).

External Accountability Mechanisms

Public Disclosure of Appointments   Details of appointments and transfers of public officials should also be available in the public domain to ensure transparency. Citizens, CSOs and the media should be able to access information regarding appointments and transfers and demand justifications, if necessary. This external pressure will ensure that the selection and transfer process is con-ducted in a legitimate manner.

Unfortunately, there is no public explanation available for the selection of indi-viduals for various Ministerial posts in the Political Executive. Citizens are not informed about the merits and profiles of candidates evaluated for a ministerial berth, and the reasons for selecting the Ministers who represent the Cabinet. What makes this problem even worse is the lack of transparency in the transfer process of civil service officials. The lack of any disclosure of reasons or justifications for these transfers adds opaqueness to the whole process.

Citizens, activists and the media have tried to obtain this information by filing RTI applications. In one instance, a query by an activist showed that from March to September 2006, a Director General of Police had received 99 recommendations for the transfer of police officials, of which 30 were directly sent by a Minister of that state (www.rtiindia.org 2006). These numbers, however, only indicate those cases in which a written recommendation was provided; there may also be several verbal recommendations, which are not captured through the RTI.

Civil service officials themselves have also tried getting information regarding transfers by filing RTI applications. For example, in October 2006, an officer with a public sector company was successful in stalling his transfer by using the RTI. When he was to be transferred to another state, his mother filed an RTI application seeking information related to his transfer. In their reply, the company admitted that the transfer was based on the request of an important public official and that they had no administrative ground for taking such an action. Acting on this information, the officer moved the state High Court and got a stay order on his transfer (Rajgadia 2007). In another instance, a citizen tried to probe the reason behind the transfer of her husband, a manager with another public company. She approached the Chief Information Commission, who ruled that every public authority is free to deploy its manpower resources in any manner for optimizing efficiency, and that the use of the RTI was uncalled for (Rajagopal 2009). These differing outcomes indicate that the RTI alone is not sufficient to solve the epidemic of transfers. Instead, upfront disclosure of transfer information by public officials is required.

In summary, in the Executive, the first foundation of accountability, Appropriate Representation, is supported by the objective selection process of the UPSC, but weakened by the constant, unexplained transfers of public officials.

::: Foundation 2—Participative Conduct

The Executive is tasked with the responsibility of implementing the policies enacted by the Legislature. The Executive is therefore directly responsible for the delivery of public services like food, healthcare and education, and should actively encourage citizens' participation in their delivery through the joint implementation of public schemes. This collaborative engagement increases buy-in for government actions among citizens, providing an ongoing feedback mechanism for the government.

Internal Accountability Mechanisms

Participative Policy Implementation   There are several examples of participative policy initiatives between the government and citizens. The Bangalore Agenda Task Force (BATF) is a government-citizen partnership, where citizens work with the Bangalore Municipal Corporation to improve the city's infrastructure and systems (Samuel 2004). Another example is *Bhagidari*, a scheme of the Delhi government, where citizens' groups discuss civic issues with local public officials, suggest solutions and jointly implement them (http://www.delhigovt. nic.in). For these partnerships to be successful, public officials need to respond to citizens' suggestions and actively work with them to implement solutions. An internal accountability mechanism to ensure responsiveness from these public officials is necessary, but non-existent.

A study conducted by the Centre for Civil Society on the *Bhagidari* scheme showed that non-participation of junior and mid-level public officials is one of the main reasons for the failure of government-citizen initiatives (Gaurav and Singhal 2003). Little attempt has been made to monitor the impact of these initiatives and duplicate them in other areas, resulting in few success stories of government-citizen partnerships. Strong efforts are needed to expand such initiatives to develop healthy partnerships between the government and citizens.

Horizontal Accountability Mechanisms

Participative Policy Implementation   There are currently no horizontal mechanisms to monitor the implementation of government-citizenship partnerships. At this early stage of their development, internal, rather than horizontal, mechanisms are needed to ensure the effective implementation of participatory initiatives.

External Accountability Mechanisms

Advocacy and Government-Citizen Initiatives   Citizens can participate in governance by initiating government-citizen partnerships where they feel the need for improvement is critical, such as education, healthcare or infrastructure. Working with public officials to prioritize local civic issues, identify solutions and implementing them improves the quality of service delivery and drives transparency and accountability. Citizens can also advocate for greater funds allocation in specific social areas.

A decentralized governance structure is necessary for citizens' participation at the local level. An accessible and responsive local government results in speedier resolution of disputes, better service delivery and greater transparency in the deployment of funds. Inadequate decentralization constrains the benefits of such government-citizen initiatives. Currently, states have achieved *political* decentralization by setting up a three-tier local government structure. For example, in the rural areas, the local government is devolved to a three-tier structure: the Zilla Parishad at the District level (the first tier), the Panchayat Samiti at the Block level (second tier), and the Gram Panchayat at the village level (third tier). *Administrative* decentralization, though, is less clear, since there is no demarcation of functions between the three tiers of governance. Besides, decision-making power has not been devolved to the lowest tier of local government, so these officials do not have adequate authority to take action on citizens' suggestions. *Fiscal* decentralization, too, is minimal, as local governments continue to depend on the states for finances. The local government therefore has limited capacity for service delivery. This weakens the partnership that local officials and citizens can build in the journey towards better governance. For the reasons stated above, the second foundation of accountability in the Executive, Participative Conduct, is weak.

::: Foundation 3—Legitimate Conduct

Indian newspapers are replete with examples of misappropriation of funds and misuse of power in some departments of the Executive. Hundreds of committees and commissions have been formed to investigate and prosecute fraudulent officials, but the scale and volume of scams have only increased with time. Conduct of public officials that is not legitimate erodes the confidence of citizens. Accountability mechanisms that support Legitimate Conduct are critical in monitoring the Executive's performance and restoring the citizen's faith in the Executive.

Internal Accountability Mechanisms

Annual Performance Appraisal Reports   The Annual Performance Appraisal Report is a mechanism to monitor the performance of government employees and incentivize them to perform better. Each government department conducts annual performance reviews of its employees, based on targets set at the beginning of the year. The whole evaluation process is objective and quantifiable, since employees are rated on a numerical scale ranging from 0–10. The results of the assessment are then discussed with the employee. In case employees are not satisfied with the assessment, they can discuss the ratings with the appraising officer and make a representation against the rating within 15 days.

The performance assessments, however, are not linked to the salaries of the officials. The salary of the public official is fixed by the Pay Commission based on hierarchy, not on performance. Public officials enjoy permanence of tenure and cannot be expelled for incompetence. They can be removed only if they are convicted of a criminal charge. A look at the performance-related incentives (PRIs) in the Executive branch of other countries highlights the weaknesses in our system. France implemented a PRI in the form of performance linked bonuses (up to 20 per cent of basic salary) at the senior level for its public officials in six Ministries in 2004. In Switzerland, merit increments are given to public employees; 4–6 per cent of the salary for outstanding performance, 3 per cent for good performance and no bonus for bad performance. In Singapore, the variable component of the remuneration of civil servants (up to 40 per cent of the total salary) is based on the performance of the employee, as well as on the economy. The 'annual incremental merit pay programme' of the Korean Government evaluates employees on a four-point scale, and links the variable component of the salary (8 per cent for excellent, 5 per cent for outstanding, 3 per cent for normal performance) and annual bonus (110 per cent for excellent, 80 per cent for outstanding, 40 per cent for normal performance) to their performance (Sixth Central Pay Commission Report 2008). The current performance assessment practices in the Executive in India fail to meet the objective of incentivizing better performance.

Results Framework Document (RFD)   While Annual Performance Appraisal Reports are used to monitor the performance of individuals, the Results Framework Document (RFD) has been introduced to monitor and evaluate the performance of government departments. Ministries and Departments are required to prepare RFDs, a document stating their planned objectives, action areas and success indicators. The Ministries/Departments assign targets for each success indicator at the beginning of the year. These targets are represented on a five-point scale and the performance of the departments is judged against them at the end of the year. For example, one of the objectives of the Department of School Education and Literacy is the expansion of quality school education. This objective is further broken down to action areas and success indicators (Figure 6.2). The performance of the department is then rated based on the number of schools opened by the end of the year.

This performance monitoring and evaluation process involves an initial appraisal of targets by an independent panel, a mid-term progress review, and an evaluation of year-end results. All the RFD documents prepared at the beginning of the year (planned objectives) and at the end of the year (actual outcome and performance scores) are to be published in the public domain. Ministries are also scored on the timely submission of all these documents, so that they adhere to the timelines.

Objective	Action Area	Success Indicator	Unit	Targets				
				Excellent	Very Good	Good	Fair	Poor
				100%	90%	80%	70%	60%
1. Expansion of quality school education	1.1 Opening of schools/ centres	1.1.1 Opening primary schools	Number	4000	3600	3200	2800	2400
		1.1.2 Opening upper primary schools	Number	12000	10800	9600	8400	7200
		1.1.3 Approval of secondary schools	Number	2250	2000	1800	1600	1400

Figure 6.2   Results Framework Document (RFD)—Sample Format

Source: Ministry of Human Resource Development, www.education.nic.in.

The Performance Management Division (PMD) of the Cabinet Secretariat acts as an agency that continuously coordinates, integrates and supports all Ministries/Departments to ensure that they adhere to this system. Training and capacity building support have also been provided by the PMD to the 62 Departments that have adopted the RFD process. The PMD has also invited feedback from thought leaders to improve this system. Going forward, the RFDs will be linked to the incentives of public officials, as proposed by the Civil Services Performance Standards and Accountability Bill. While the RFD initiative is new and it is too early to comment upon its effectiveness, it has the potential to strengthen accountability in the Executive, from within.

Whistleblowers Protection   Whistle-blowing is a mechanism to encourage employees to highlight frauds, or misappropriation of funds committed by other employees. To drive the reporting of internal mal-administration, whistleblowers should be protected from criminal or civil liability, demotion, harassment and discrimination in any form.

A bill to protect whistleblowers, *The Public Interest Disclosure and Protection to Persons Making the Disclosure Bill 2010*, has been proposed in Parliament. While this bill awaits the Parliament's nod, an interim arrangement, termed *Public Interest Disclosure and Protection of Informers Resolution*, was enacted back in 2004. The resolution empowers employees to file complaints with the Central Vigilance Commission (CVC) to seek protection from victimization by internal authorities. The CVC guarantees confidentiality to the whistleblower and provides protection to the complainant or the witnesses if they are convinced about the genuineness of the complaint (Central Vigilance Commission 2004).

Despite the assurance of confidentiality and protection, there have been several instances of whistleblowers not being adequately protected. They have been subjected to departmental enquiries and demotions, or were victimized after filing complaints. In one such instance, a divisional engineer of a public-sector company complained against the illegal routing of international calls by some of the employees to benefit a private telecom player. He complained about this illegitimate act to the CVC in 2005, under the whistleblower protection notification. A month after his filing the complaint, the authorities at the telecom company initiated departmental proceedings against him for certain operational shortcomings. Fearing victimization by the internal authorities, he filed a petition in the Supreme Court, alleging harassment by his supervisors (*The Times of India*, 1 September 2009).

In another case, a graduate working with a government department discovered rampant mismanagement and poor implementation of work in the area where he had been posted. He wrote directly to the highest authority, detailing the financial and contractual irregularities in the project and pointing out the companies and public officials responsible for it. Fearing retribution, he had requested that his name be kept secret, but this was not to be (*The Hindu*, 14 December 2003). Such incidents highlight the lack of systems to protect whistleblowers. Without adequate protection, one cannot expect the 'internal eye' to reveal all that it sees. For Legitimate Conduct in the Executive, we need the whistle to blow louder and more frequently.

Horizontal Accountability Mechanisms

Legislature   The Legislature (Parliament), as an independent and horizontal organization, monitors and questions the performance of the Executive. The Legislature can scrutinize the functioning of the Executive using the following methods:

- *Opposition Party*—The Opposition Party has the right to keep a check on the ruling government by monitoring and questioning their functioning and performance
- *Question Hour*—An hour in the Parliament dedicated to seeking clarifications from the Executive on the implementation of policies, the quality of public services and functioning of the PSUs
- *Debates*—The Legislature discusses and scrutinizes legislations, the budget and the finance bills proposed by the Political Executive in Parliament, and monitors the financial affairs of the Executive
- *Vote of No Confidence*—If the Legislature is not satisfied with the performance of the ruling government, they can pass a motion of no-confidence in the Parliament, which can result in the fall of the ruling government

The Legislature, however, is unable to function as effectively as needed, compromising its ability to extract accountability from the Executive. An article in the *Financial Express* (11 December 2008) stated that from 2004 to 2008, 40 per cent of the total time in question hour was lost due to disruptions. Further, the average number of Lok Sabha sittings in a year has halved from around 135 in the 1950s to about 65 in 2009 (PRS Legislative Research 2009). This has resulted in poor quality of deliberation on issues of national significance. As a result of this, many important bills are in Parliament for years before being enacted as laws. The Women's Reservation Bill was debated in Parliament for nearly 14 years, having met with resistance from regional parties and independent candidates. The bill was passed in the Rajya Sabha after years of deliberation; it still needs to be approved by the Lok Sabha before it sees the light of day (*The Times of India*, 9 March 2010). The Right to Information Act was formulated in 1996, first introduced in Parliament in 2002, and finally enacted as law only in 2005, after 10 years of deliberation and modifications (National Campaign for People's Right to Information, 2011).

The credibility of some of the MPs in Parliament is suspect, since candidates can contest elections even if they are charge-sheeted, as long as they are not convicted in the courts. Nearly 28 per cent of the elected MPs from the 2009 Lok Sabha elections have criminal cases pending against them (National Election Watch, 16 May 2009).

Parliamentary Committees   The Legislature is involved with the issues of the moment, has a considerable volume of work and pressing agendas that consume a large proportion of its time. Parliamentary Committees support and facilitate the functioning of the Legislature by working in the background on a significant number of legislative issues. These committees review and examine the legislative and budgetary proposals of the Executive in detail. Parliamentary Committees comprise members of different political parties, thus bringing in diverse perspectives. Some committees, like the financial committees, are headed by a member from the opposition to ensure that they function objectively. These Parliamentary Committees can be Standing Committees or Ad-hoc Committees. Standing Committees are those that are formed on a regular basis. Some of them oversee specific *departments*, for instance the Committee on Home Affairs or the Committee on Health and Family Welfare, while others oversee specific *functions*, like the Committee on Public Accounts or the Committee on Estimates, that looks into financial matters. These committees provide the focused attention required to research, scrutinize, discuss and report on the bills, grants and policies under their purview.

Ad-hoc Committees can be formed for a specific purpose and duration, like a Joint Parliamentary Committee (JPC). They are set up by a motion in

Parliament, where the membership and objectives are decided. For example, in early 2011, a JPC was constituted to investigate the multi-billion dollar 2G telecom spectrum scam after sustained pressure from the opposition parties (*IBN Live*, 22 February 2011). A JPC, unlike a Standing Committee, may have a broader scope and is not limited to just the scrutiny of government finances. For instance, the JPC on the stock market scam (2001) was asked to look into financial irregularities, fix responsibility on the persons and institutions involved, check the action taken by investigation agencies like the CBI, identify regulatory loopholes and make suitable recommendations (*Financial Express*, 30 November 2010; *The Times of India*, 28 November 2010).

The Parliamentary Committee's role, however, is advisory and limited to preparing reports that are tabled for discussion and debate in Parliament, in order to initiate the necessary action. The MPs can sometimes choose to ignore the reports of these Committees, if they are in conflict with their political agenda. Sometimes, the creation of these Committees is delayed; for instance, no Standing Committee examination of the Budget occurred in 2009, as Committees were not formed in time (Debroy 2009). The lack of cooperation from the Executive could also impact the functioning of the Committees, since the Executive can decline to produce a document required by the Committee. Ministers are also not obliged to appear before these Committees. Clearly, Parliamentary Committees are often constrained in their objective of holding the Executive accountable.

Delivery Monitoring Unit (DMU)   The government set up a Delivery Monitoring Unit (DMU) under the Prime Minister's Office in 2009 to ensure effective and time-bound implementation of select flagship programmes like the Mahatma Gandhi National Rural Employment Guarantee Act, Bharat Nirman, Sarva Shiksha Abhiyan, National Rural Health Mission, and others (Kumar 2009). The Delivery Monitoring Unit (DMU) monitors the progress of these schemes, fast-tracks implementation and suggests corrective actions, based on periodic reports submitted by the Ministries. Quarterly reports are submitted to the DMU by the Ministries of select programmes, to update the Prime Minister's Office on the implementation status, operational constraints and output achieved. These reports are also available in the public domain to encourage independent assessment of the scheme by citizens, CSOs and the media. The effectiveness of the DMU will be visible only a few years from now, since this initiative is fairly new.

Planning Commission (Programme Evaluation Organization, Independent Evaluation Organization)   The Planning Commission is entrusted with the responsibility of ensuring effective allocation and utilization of the country's resources among the different Ministries and departments within the Executive.

The Planning Commission has independent divisions that look at the implementation of public schemes to ensure effective deployment of the allocated resources.

One division under the Planning Commission is the *Programme Evaluation Organization* (PEO), established in 1952 with the objective of evaluating centrally sponsored schemes in areas like rural development, family welfare and public distribution, among others. The PEO assesses the implementation, effectiveness of delivery, and the outcome of these schemes. The reports based on the PEO's evaluation are different from the progress reports of the DMU, as the former are focused on assessing the impact of the schemes and identifying the areas of success and failure. The PEO has conducted more than 200 studies on various key schemes and brought to light some harsh realities (Planning Commission 2010). An evaluation study to assess the impact of Sarva Shiksha Abhiyan by the PEO reveals that 94 per cent of primary students in India cannot recognize the English language (*DNA*, 27 June 2010). Another study to evaluate the effectiveness and impact of the Khadi and Village Industries Commission revealed that only 37 per cent of the projects sanctioned by them were operationalized in the first year. The major reasons for delay in implementing the other projects were non-availability of funds and procedural issues (Planning Evaluation Organization 2001).

The findings emerging from the evaluation studies are communicated to the implementing departments for follow-up action. For example, the Employment Assurance Scheme was restructured based on detailed guidelines issued by the PEO in 2002 (Programme Evaluation Organization 2009). Similarly, the evaluation reports on the Accelerated Rural Water Supply Programme, the Member of Parliament Local Area Development Scheme, and the functioning of community and primary health centres, have been acted on by implementing agencies. However, not all implementation agencies follow up on the reviews conducted by the PEO. The decision to implement the suggestions of the PEO rests with the Ministries or Departments. In many cases, PEO reports fail to see any action on their recommendations.

Another monitoring agency recently set up by the Planning Commission is the *Independent Evaluation Organization* (IEO), to assess the progress of the government's flagship schemes. The *Programme Implementation Wing* of the Ministry of Statistics and Programme Implementation already exists with a similar objective. It is therefore not entirely clear what objective the IEO aims to achieve, which is not currently met by either the PEO or the Programme Implementation Wing.

Comptroller and Auditor General   The Comptroller and Auditor General (CAG) was established by the Constitution of India to audit all receipts and expenses of the Executive at the central, state and local government levels.

The CAG also audits the accounts of companies owned and financed by the government. The reports of the CAG are submitted to the relevant Parliamentary Committee, which in turn seeks explanations from the Ministry in case of any discrepancy.

CAG reports have highlighted instances of wastage of funds, frauds of appalling proportions and lapses in various PSU transactions. The most recent findings of the CAG are that of the 2G telecom spectrum allocation scam and the Commonwealth Games (CWG) scam. The CAG's scrutiny of the 2G scam suggested that the government had probably suffered a large notional loss due to the flouting of protocols of issuing telecom licenses (*The Times of India*, 10 November 2010). In another report, the CAG indicted the CWG Organizing Committee for financial irregularities and revealed discrepancies in the broadcasting rights and sponsorship deals (PRS Legislative Research 2010; NDTV 2010).

The CAG, however, has inadequate authority as it cannot take any action based on these reports. The CAG has to depend on the Parliamentary Committee to highlight its reports in Parliament, which probes and debates them further. In many cases, the facts brought out in these CAG reports do not lead to effective and timely action. There is a vast backlog of CAG reports and Parliamentary Committees have discussed only a fraction of them so far.

The CAG usually conducts a post-mortem of discrepancies, instead of highlighting them through an ongoing audit process. This delay in reporting can often be traced to delayed or incomplete responses from government departments to the queries raised by the CAG. For example, in 2003, more than 15,000 audit queries raised by the CAG were pending, and some of those pending enquiries were more than 30 years old (Kumar 2003). Once again, we see a horizontal accountability mechanism designed to check the Executive, being handicapped.

Central Bureau of Investigation (CBI)   The CBI is the government's premier investigating agency for anti-corruption cases. The CBI has an anti-corruption division that handles cases of misconduct and fraud committed by politicians, public officials of all central government departments and PSUs. The CBI largely conducts probes into big ticket misgovernance cases, like the CWG and the 2G scam. Besides this, the CBI also apprehends those demanding bribes. For instance, in 2009, an Income Tax Officer was caught accepting Rs 0.45 million as a bribe from an assessee. The CBI also books officials for amassing assets disproportionate to their income. In 2009, the CBI booked an officer for possessing assets of Rs 21.5 million, disproportionate to his sources of income (CBI Annual Report 2009).

The primary obstacle facing the CBI in investigating cases within the government is that it is not truly independent of the government. The CBI is directly under the Centre's control, and this could potentially influence the proceedings of a case. Further, to conduct investigations into public officials at the Joint Secretary rank or above, the CBI requires the prior sanction of that department. For example, one Ministry refused to grant a sanction to the CBI to initiate an enquiry against a senior official with regard to transgression (*Hindustan Times*, 18 November 2010).

Central Vigilance Commission (CVC)   The Central Vigilance Commission is an autonomous body that addresses cases of corruption in the central government and public-sector enterprises. The CVC receives complaints of misconduct or disciplinary matters, investigates the matter and provides impartial advice for necessary   action. Additionally, every government department appoints Chief Vigilance Officers (CVOs) who assist the investigation and ensure speedy processing of vigilance cases within their department. The CVC acts on these complaints within a reasonable time period. In 2009, the CVC received 5,783 complaints, and cleared about 91 per cent of the cases within a year, with around 31 per cent of the cases cleared within three weeks (CVC Annual Report 2009). The CVC also undertakes initiatives, like leveraging technology to prevent corruption, formulating a National Anti-Corruption Strategy, and introducing an 'integrity pact' in large value contracts.

The CVC has no jurisdiction over politicians and is limited only to bureaucrats, who are employed by the Central Government. More than 90 per cent of complaints lodged by citizens are about officials in the local and state governments, which do not fall within the scope of the CVC (*Mint*, 6 September 2010). These restrictions make it difficult for the CVC to take comprehensive action against all public officials who may have misused their power and authority.

The CVC investigates complaints either through the CBI, or through the departmental Chief Vigilance Officers (CVOs). These CVOs are officials from within the department and are therefore less likely to take any action, especially against senior officials (Mitta 2011).

The CVC, being largely advisory in nature, has to depend on a disciplinary authority to take action against guilty public officials, and has no direct powers to ensure that some action is taken. The CVC can only prescribe the penalties to be imposed and send reminders to the disciplinary authority to take action. The final action taken by the department can deviate from this prescribed penalty. The annual report of the CVC, in fact, publishes a list of significant cases in which a department has not complied with or accepted the CVC's advice (CVC Annual Report 2008).

Lokayukta   The steadily increasing misgovernance in India has accentuated the need for an independent redressal organization to examine this critical problem. The idea of constituting an Ombudsman to look into the grievances of citizens was first mooted in 1963. In 1966, the first Administrative Reforms Commission (ARC) suggested a two-tier structure, with the *Lokpal* at the Centre and the *Lokayukta* at the States, to evaluate and address citizens' grievances against public authorities. Acting on the ARC's advice, the Lokpal Bill was introduced in the Parliament for the first time in 1968, but it lapsed with the dissolution of the Lok Sabha. Till early 2011, the Bill has been introduced eight times in the Parliament, but has been thwarted again and again (*The Times of India*, 29 April 2011).

One of the major reasons for the delay in implementing the Bill is the divided opinion over the scope of the Bill; for instance, whether the Prime Minister should be brought under the purview of Lokpal, whether it should investigate only corruption cases or even disciplinary cases, whether it should be an advisory body or have powers to prosecute, and so on. Disappointed by the government's past efforts on this Bill, a massive, nation-wide movement gathered steam in mid-2011, with the creation of an independent Lokpal Bill at the centre of the storm. A group of eminent citizens drafted this independent Lokpal Bill, which proposed that the Lokpal institution should have complete independence, significant powers to conduct investigations, and should adhere to a fixed time frame to complete investigations (*The Times of India*, 31 January 2011). While this independent Bill has received considerable support from CSOs and the media, it remains to be seen whether a Lokpal Bill will be passed in the near future.

Meanwhile, some states have introduced Lokayuktas to investigate cases against state officials. Citizens can file complaints against government officials for abuse of power with the Lokayukta, which assists citizens in prosecuting these officials if the complaint is found to be reasonable. After the allegation is established to the satisfaction of the Lokayukta, it sends its findings and recommended actions to the concerned authority in the State Government. If the Lokayukta is not satisfied with the action taken by the authorities, a special report can be sent to the Governor. The Lokayukta in Karnataka, for example, has played an important role in rooting out poor governance in urban municipalities and hospitals, and has emerged as a key channel for resolving complaints related to service delivery. A study conducted by the University of Leeds, the Karuna Trust and the Indian Institute of Management (Ahmedabad) on the healthcare delivery systems in Karnataka found that independent bodies like the Lokayukta, under strong leadership, played a prominent role in controlling systemic inefficiencies (*Governance Now*, 30 December 2010).

The key hurdle in the functioning of the Lokayukta, however, is lack of independence. Even after investigating complaints, it has no power to take remedial action. Further, since there is no time limit on taking action based on the reports submitted by the Lokayukta, their recommendations seldom materialize. Most state Lokayuktas do not have the power to initiate an investigation themselves, despite having enough incriminating information against a public official. They need a formal complaint to be filed by a citizen to conduct an investigation, and citizens hesitate to do so for fear of retribution from public officials. Even after obtaining a formal complaint from citizens, the Lokayukta needs the prior sanction of the State government to investigate cases involving officials above a certain rank. Another problem is that the powers, resources and functioning of Lokayuktas vary across states. Some states like Tamil Nadu and Sikkim do not even have a Lokayukta. A strong and independent Lokpal at the Centre and Lokayuktas in all the States would aid the combat against corruption.

External Accountability Mechanisms

In the preceding pages, we have encountered the constraints faced by government-appointed agencies in monitoring the performance of the Executive. This makes the role of citizens, CSOs and the media even more important and critical. These three forces of external accountability should, for example, monitor the allocation of funds by the Executive to ensure that they have been distributed appropriately. They should also assess the effectiveness of these funds by comparing the expenditure of the government with its outcomes. There are several mechanisms, initiated by either the government or by the CSOs, that help to externally monitor the allocation and utilization of funds, as well as the performance of the Executive. Some of these mechanisms are explained here.

Right to Information Act Transparency is a necessary precondition for accountability, since it is impossible to judge performance without access to accurate information. The Right to Information (RTI) Act, a significant milestone in the history of accountability, was introduced by the government in 2005 to allow citizens access to government files, records and documents, and to scrutinize government functioning. A citizen has to file a request with the Public Information Officer (PIO) of a public department, specifying the information needed. To ensure that the information request is not delayed, there is a time limit of 30 days in which the information needs to be provided, failing which the PIOs are penalized. The goal of the act is to make information accessible to any citizen in an affordable and convenient manner, within a reasonable time period. The scope of the act extends to all authorities and bodies under the Constitution, and includes all authorities under the central government, state governments and local bodies.

The enactment of the Right to Information Act (RTI) has ushered in a new era in participatory democracy by granting citizens a constitutional right to information. There are several success stories of how common citizens have managed to get their ration cards, water connections, electricity connections, or other public services without paying any bribes. In rural areas, too, citizens have used the RTI successfully to question government officials on issues like delays or non-payment of wages under the MGNREGA scheme, or to access government documents to monitor its performance. It is heartening to see that the number of applications received by the top 10 public authorities has increased from 996 in 2006 to 14,620 in 2010, while the average disposal rate for these applications has gone up from 45 per cent in 2006 to 73 per cent in 2010 (Department of Personnel and Training 2011). The RTI Act thus constrains inefficiency in public office, resulting in more effective functioning of government departments.

There are various constraints that continue to impair the successful implementation of the RTI Act. Lack of awareness of the RTI Act is a key obstacle that limits citizens from accessing information and questioning public officials. According to a study commissioned by the Department of Personnel and Training (DoPT) in June 2009, only 33 per cent of the urban population was aware of the RTI Act. The awareness rate reported in rural areas was a dismal 13 per cent. The study also established that only 12 per cent of women, compared to 26 per cent of the men, were aware of this act (Krishnadas 2009). Additionally, there have been few campaigns by the government to spread awareness about the RTI Act. The existing awareness is primarily due to the efforts of CSOs and the media.

The inadequate functional and behavioural training imparted to the PIOs implementing the RTI Act also acts as a hurdle for citizens. The study conducted by the DoPT also found that around 45 per cent of PIOs had not been provided training in RTI (http://www.rti.gov.in). The training that is provided deals with only the basic provisions of the RTI Act, and key aspects regarding public conduct, usage of technology and service levels have not been addressed. This results in sub-optimal assistance from the information officers, frustrating those citizens who seek information. There are several instances of citizens being discouraged from filing information requests; their RTI applications are rejected, or they are threatened into withdrawing their applications. A panchayat teacher residing in one district received a verbal intimation from the Block (tehsil) office that she had been discharged from her duty, due to the discontinuation of the programme under which she worked. When she was denied a written copy of this order, she decided to file an RTI application. Her husband submitted the application at the Block office, but was beaten up by the Block Development Officer (BDO) when he asked for a receipt. The BDO also filed a case of 'obstructing the work of a government officer' against the husband in the local police station, and had him put in jail (PRIA 2008). While there are still a number of obstacles, the power of the RTI Act to drive accountability is undisputable.

Citizens Charter   The Citizens Charter is an accountability mechanism introduced by the government to encourage citizens to demand better public services. The Charter is an explicit statement of the standard of service that a public department has to offer, the rights and entitlements of citizens using these services, and the redressal path available to citizens should disputes arise in these transactions. For example, the Citizens Charter of the Hyderabad Water Supply and Sewerage Board (HWSSB) guarantees that applications for water or sewage connections will be processed within 30 days of submission, and that acknowledgement of the same will be forwarded to the applicant 15 days thereafter. The charter goes on to state that in the event of the HWSSB taking more than 30 days to process an application, citizens can file a formal complaint. After the complaint has been filed, the HWSSB will process the application within 15 days. If the HWSSB has still not processed the application after the 15-day grace period, the Managing Director of the department must personally handle the file (Public Affairs Centre 2007). Empowered with this charter, citizens are in a position to demand timely action on their applications.

Lack of awareness among citizens is the key constraint that limits the use of Citizens Charters as a tool for demanding accountability. While a large number of public service providers have implemented the Citizens Charter, only a very small percentage of citizens are aware of this mechanism and its effectiveness as a tool of accountability. A study conducted by the Public Affairs Centre in 2007 on the effectiveness of the Citizens Charter as an accountability mechanism indicated that 74 per cent of the users of public services were unaware of the Citizens Charter programme. Of those who were aware, only around 7 per cent had read a charter. What was even more surprising was that even government officials in public departments were unaware of the Citizens Charter initiative. Government officials were found to be familiar with certain charter components, but unfamiliar with the overarching concept of a Citizens Charter. A majority of them had not been trained to implement the departmental Citizens Charters (http://www.darpg.nic.in; Public Affairs Centre 2007). Some public service providers do not even display the Citizens Charter in their offices. Others do not include crucial components like service quality standards or grievance redressal mechanisms in the displayed Charter. According to the study, only 54 per cent of the Charters outlined a grievance redressal mechanism with clarity, and only 4 per cent of the charters outlined a compensation policy when the service was inadequate (Public Affairs Centre 2007).

Budget Advocacy   Budget Advocacy is a tool used by CSOs to improve budget transparency and influence the allocation of funds to reflect citizens' priorities. CSOs demystify and interpret budget information to help citizens analyse the impact of the budget. Based on their analysis, they advocate for changes in fund allocations in the interest of the citizens.

While budget analysis and advocacy initiatives have increased over the years, CSOs face difficulties in these efforts. Access to detailed budget information, especially State budgets, is one of the major constraints faced. DISHA, a CSO based in Gujarat, faced difficulties in analysing the state budget as the government released only a summary of the budget on its website. DISHA had to rely on alternative sources like the Opposition Party to access the documents (www.internationalbudget.org 2007). CSO efforts are also restricted to the local area and lack the scale needed to work across the state. The systemic low awareness about CSOs and the role they play limits their ability to garner mass support and gain traction.

Social Audits   A Social Audit is a participatory mechanism that involves all stakeholders in measuring, reporting and improving the utilization of funds and other resources. The objective of these audits is to compare input resources with outcomes, to measure the extent to which the resources used by a scheme actually benefit citizens. Social Audits are conducted jointly by public officials and citizens, where citizens examine government records, match public expenditures with the entitlements received by them, and ask questions to public officials about leakages of funds, if any. The discrepancies are then exposed in public hearings and the erring officials are publicly denounced. Social Audits empower ordinary citizens to turn into auditors, scrutinize documents, assess gaps and create awareness among beneficiaries about the misappropriation of funds.

With the ever-increasing outlays on social sector programmes and the decentralized implementation, the need for Social Audits is being felt more than ever before. Realizing the criticality of participatory monitoring, the government has taken the first step in this direction by making Social Audits an integral part of the Mahatma Gandhi National Rural Employment Guarantee Act (MGN-REGA). It is now mandatory for local governments in all the states to conduct regular Social Audits under this scheme. Some states like Andhra Pradesh have gone a long way in ensuring the successful use of Social Audits as a monitoring mechanism under the MGNREGA scheme. Around 500 experts have identified and trained about 44,000 village youths, who cross-check official records through a door-to-door verification of muster rolls and physical works. By 2009, these auditors had covered more than 27,000 gram panchayats and 12 million people, recovering embezzled funds amounting to Rs 19 million from government officials (Centre for Good Governance 2009). In most other states, however, the implementation of Social Audits is not underway. A performance audit of the MGNREGA scheme by CAG identified that in many places, the mandatory biannual Social Audits were not taking place (Comptroller and Auditor General of India 2008). In many cases, the villagers were not informed about the date of the Social Audit. A successful social audit is largely dependent on the CSOs' involvement. First, CSOs have to get hold of documents like muster rolls, bills and vouchers from the local authorities. They then have to simplify and collate the information to make it understandable to villagers. CSOs also have to encourage beneficiaries to question government authorities at public hearings, since villagers usually lack the courage to stand up and speak against these officials. Moreover, in a number of cases village authorities have resorted to threatening villagers in order to avoid answering questions about the misuse of funds (Subrahmaniam 2009). During one Social Audit, a ward member was brutally attacked by the representatives of the Gram Panchayat (www.indiatogether.org, January 2010). The government seems to have made only a half-hearted attempt to implement Social Audits. Successful implementation requires equal effort and participation from both the government and the citizens.

Public Expenditure Tracking Surveys The Public Expenditure Tracking Survey (PETS) is a mechanism used by CSOs to monitor the utilization of funds. PETS is based on a 'follow the money' principle, as the flow of resources is traced at each step—from the central government to the state and local government, to the front-line service providers. This information is used to determine how much of the originally allocated resources, financial and non-financial, actually cross each level and ultimately reach the beneficiaries. These surveys are a useful method for locating and quantifying the leakage of funds, identifying bureaucratic capture, and pin-pointing problems in the deployment of non-financial resources like staff, textbooks, or medicines.

The success of PETS is highly dependent on gaining access to information at each level, and analysing this information to detect the misappropriation of funds. Due to lack of proper data management in public institutions, accurate records at each level are not available, which makes it much more difficult to track expenditures. Besides, some public officials have a personal interest in not providing this information to citizens, so as to escape accountability. They often refuse to provide records, or present incomplete data. CSOs have to play an important role here in collaborating with local public officials to obtain the requisite information for the successful implementation of these surveys.

Citizen Report Cards and Community Scorecards Citizen Report Cards
(CRC) and Community Score Cards (CSC) are tools to assess the quality of public
services by measuring the satisfaction level of citizens using these services. They
consist of a sample survey, where the users are asked to rate the public agencies
in terms of their satisfaction, based on factors like cost, accessibility, timeliness,
reliability and responsiveness. The findings are then widely publicized through
the media. Workshops and meetings are then organized with public officials, to
discuss and address the issues exposed through these findings. When CRCs
are prepared over regular intervals, they also help to track changes in quality
over time.

The Citizen Report Card was pioneered in the early 1990s by the Bangalore-based CSO, Public Affairs Centre (PAC). Since then, PAC has repeatedly
used the CRC at regular intervals to evaluate the major service providers of
the city. When PAC first conducted this exercise in 1994, most of the service
providers received very low ratings. Satisfaction levels of the respondents did
not exceed 25 per cent for any of the seven service providers covered by the
survey. The exercise was repeated again in 1999, when it saw partial improvement. The third report card that followed in 2003 revealed substantial improvement in the satisfaction levels of respondents. For the nine service providers
covered in this survey, the satisfaction levels reported were above 70 per cent
(International Budget Partnership 2008). The process also involves a discussion of the findings with the service providers, inter-agency comparisons, and
pressure from citizens and CSOs to bring about improvements. This contributes significantly to improvement in the service quality levels of these public
agencies. For example, based on a user's feedback in the CRC, the Bangalore
Metropolitan Transport Service introduced a monthly pass scheme for frequent commuters, which was well received. The Delhi CRC resulted in the Food
and Civil Supply department distributing kerosene in a sachet, which resulted
in reduced wastage at the point of distribution. In the union territory of Dadra
and Nagar Haveli, the collector pulled up his own department in response to the
findings of the CRC. The whole exercise, however, is not rewarding if the public
institutions do not respond to the findings appropriately. Political commitment
and a willingness to change is important for the successful implementation of this
mechanism.

In summary, while there exist various external accountability mechanisms to
ensure legitimate conduct in the Executive, these mechanisms have not always
been successful, for a variety of reasons. The people of India are not playing as
powerful a role as they should, in ensuring that public officials display conduct
worthy of their positions.

::: Foundation 4—Liability Enforcement

Misgovernance is perceived to be rampant in the Executive, since dishonest officials are seldom penalized. Liability for misdemeanours needs to be strongly enforced by punishing officials for their misconduct, thereby discouraging others from indulging in acts of fraudulence. Let us examine how liability is currently enforced in the Executive.

Internal Accountability Mechanisms

Dismissal, Removal or Reduction in Rank   The Constitution provides that public officials can be penalized if they have been convicted of a transgression. Dismissal, removal or reduction in rank are the mechanisms to penalize public officials for their misconduct. To prevent any abuse of this mechanism, the Constitution does not allow dismissal, removal or rank reduction by any authority subordinate to the authority that appointed the public official. For example, the Centre's sanction is required to investigate and prosecute corrupt officers at the State level. Further, the officials cannot be removed without being offered an adequate opportunity to present their case. For example, three cases were registered against a public official in September 1993, yet permission to initiate prosecution proceedings was granted only after 11 years (Yadav 2008). A 2008 study by *India Today* indicated that the CBI had registered 163 cases against certain public officials since April 1992. Most of these allegedly corrupt officials, however, continued in service and got promoted (ibid.). The findings of an internal civil services survey also reiterated that there is hardly any action taken against corrupt officials. Of the 4,808 officers who participated in this government commissioned internal survey, 79 per cent of the Indian Police Services (IPS) officers and 60 per cent of IAS officials agreed that corrupt officers get away unpunished (*The Times of India*, 13 January 2011).

A constitutional amendment to fast-track trials against corrupt officials was proposed by a Group of Ministers in January 2011. This committee is weighing the option of introducing summary proceedings in cases of grave misdemeanour or blatant misconduct, where proceedings are conducted in a prompt manner, thereby preventing the government from going through a long drawn-out procedure to dismiss corrupt officials (Mitta 2011).

Horizontal Accountability Mechanisms

Police and Judiciary   While many independent agencies exist to monitor and investigate matters of graft and misappropriation in the Executive, they do not have the right to legally prosecute the corrupt. Law enforcement agencies like the Police and the Judiciary have the power to intervene and prosecute public officials for abuse of power. They exercise this power by acting based on complaints filed by citizens, or based on reports submitted by investigating agencies like the CVC and the CBI.

Inadequate infrastructure with the Police and a slow-moving Judicial system, as explained in an earlier section, have directly resulted in weak liability enforcement against corrupt officials.

External Accountability Mechanisms

Public Interest Litigation   Citizens can challenge public officials by filing a Public Interest Litigation (PIL). PILs can be used to challenge the woefully inadequate public services, mal-functioning of public departments, and corrupt practices of public officials.

For example, the Supreme Court, in response to a PIL filed by a lawyer, issued a show-cause notice to the Chief Minister of a State for misusing public money to build statues of the party leader and the party's poll symbol. The citizen alleged that the minister had spent about Rs 20 billion from the public exchequer for this purpose (Bhatnagar 2009). A PIL filed by a CSO, Common Cause, highlighted the misuse of the discretionary quota for the allotment of petrol pumps and gas dealerships. The court found that between 1993–96, a Minister of State for Petroleum and Gas had allotted petrol pumps and gas agencies to his relatives under the 'discretionary quota'. On examining the records with the government, the court confirmed the allegation in the case of 15 allotments. The court nullified all 15 allotments and directed the Minister to pay a sum of Rs 5 million as exemplary damages to the exchequer. The police was also asked to initiate prosecution against him (Desai and Muralidhar 2000). The lack of awareness and understanding about the scope and application of PILs among citizens has resulted in ineffective utilization of this mechanism.

This chapter evaluated the strength of the mechanisms that support the four foundations of accountability in the Executive. The evaluation of these mechanisms reveals that there are many weaknesses in their implementation. These constraints result in low accountability in the Executive, thereby impacting the overall quality of governance (Figure 6.3).

We now turn our attention to the Judiciary and examine the mechanisms that exist to strengthen accountability in the Judiciary.

Weaknesses in Mechanisms of Accountability–Executive			
	Internal Accountability	**Horizontal Accountability**	**External Accountability**
Appropriate Representation	**Objective and Transparent Process** • *Lack of objective process of selection of Council of Ministers* • *Lack of transparency in transfer of public officials*	**Objective and Transparent Process** • *No independent check on selection of Council of Ministers* • *No independent monitoring of the transfers of civil officials*	**Public Disclosure of Appointments** • *No justification for transfers available in public domain*
Participative Conduct	**Participative Policy Implementation** • *No internal check on implementation of citizen's participation mechanisms*	**Participative Policy Implementation** • *No independent agency to check implementation of citizen's participation mechanisms*	**Advocacy and Government Citizen Initiatives** • *Lack of decentralized governance structure to encourage local participation*
Legitimate Conduct	**Annual Performance Assessment Reports, Results Framework Document** • *Performance not linked with salaries* • *Frequent transfers makes assessment difficult* **Whistleblowers Protection** • *Inadequate protection to whistleblowers*	**Legislature, Parliamentary Committees, Delivery Monitoring Unit, Planning Commission, CAG, CBI, CVC, Lokayukta** • *Limited authority to take action* • *Lack of independence in functioning* • *Political interference*	**RTI Act, Citizens Charter, Budget Advocacy, Social Audits, PETS, Report Cards and Community Scorecards** • *Low awareness about mechanisms* • *Low participation by citizens* • *Limited reach of CSOs*
Liability Enforcement	**Dismissal, Removal or Reduction in Rank** • *Lengthy process to prosecute corrupt officials* • *Lack of action due to political interference*	**Police, Judiciary** • *Political interference in appointments and transfers* • *Lack of accountability* • *Inadequate infrastructure*	**Public Interest Litigation** • *Difficulty in using PILs due to lack of understanding of its scope and application*

(Left spanning label: **Foundations of Accountability**)

☐ Mechanism does not exist

Figure 6.3 Assessment of Mechanisms in the Executive

References

'80 transfers within a week of poll results'. 2009. *The Indian Express*, 9 June.

'94% primary students in India cannot recognise English'. 2010. *DNA*, 27 June.

'Accessing Information under RTI: Citizens Experiences in Ten States'. 2008. PRIA. Available at www.pria.org (accessed on 21 January 2010).

'Analysis of 2009 Lok Sabha Winners based on criminal and financial background'. 16 May 2009. *National Election Watch*. Available at www.adrindia.org (accessed on 22 May 2009).

Anand, Eshwar. 2009. 'Civil services: The blunted edge'. *The Tribune*, 25 January.

'Annual Report—Central Bureau of Investigation'. 2009. Available at http://cbi.nic.in/ (accessed on 22 February 2011).

'Annual Report–Central Vigilance Commission'. 2009. Available at www.cvc.nic.in (accessed on 2 March 2011).

'Annual Report—Central Vigilance Commission'. 2008. Available at www.cvc.nic.in (accessed on 2 March 2011).

'Bhagidari: The Concept'. Available at http://delhigovt.nic.in/bhagi.asp (accessed on 12 March 2009).

Bhatnagar, Rakesh. 2009. 'SC raps Mayawati for statue spree'. *DNA*, 29 June.

Bhattacharya, Santwana. 2009. 'In India the comedy of power-sharing'. Available at www.atimes.com/ (accessed on 6 January 2010).

'Budget monitoring and policy influence'. 2007. Overseas Development Institute, March. Available at www.internationalbudget.org (accessed on 15 December 2010).

'Citizens Charters: Indian Experience'. 2009. Available at http://darpg.nic.in (accessed on 28 April 2010).

'Citizens rip govt's Lokpal Bill apart'. 2011. *The Times of India*, 31 January.

'Corrupt forces trying to derail our campaign'. 2011. *The Times of India*, 29 April.

'Corruption has social acceptance'. 2010. *Mint*, 6 September.

'CWG corruption: Endgame Kalmadi and Co?' 2010. *NDTV.* Available at http://cwg.ndtv.com/ (accessed on 7 December 2010).

'CWG Investigations: What is being done?' 2010. PRS Legislative Research. Available at http://prsindia.org (accessed on 7 December 2010).

Debroy, Bibek. 2009. 'Effective legislature'. *The Indian Express*, 9 December.

Desai, Ashok and S. Muralidhar. 2000. 'Public Interest Litigation: Potential and Problems', *International Environmental Law Research Centre.* Available at www.ielrc.org (accessed on 21 December 2009).

'DMK impact: Small Cabinet for a start'. 2009. *NDTV*, 22 May.

'Engineer, who told govt about illegal call racket, harassed'. 2009. *The Times of India*, 1 September.

'Evaluation Report on Sampoorna Gram Rozgar Yojana-SGRY, Jammu & Kashmir'. (2009). Programme Evaluation Organisation. Available at http://planningcommission.nic.in (accessed on 5 November 2009).

'Evaluation Study on Khadi and Village Industries Programme'. 2001. Programme Evaluation Organisation. Available at http://planningcommission.nic.in (accessed on 22 September 2010).

'FE Editorial: Zero hours'. 2008. *Financial Express*, 11 December.

'Goa chief minister sought police transfers: RTI activist'. Available on www.rtiindia.org (accessed on 24 February 2011).

'India's Citizen's Charters: A Decade of Experience'. (2007). Public Affairs Centre. Available at www.partnershipfortransparency.info (accessed on 29 April 2010).

Iyer, Lakshmi and Mani Anandi. 2009. 'Travelling Agents: Political Change and Bureaucratic Turnover in India'. Working Paper, Harvard Business School, November. Available at www.people.hbs.edu (accessed on 3 March 2009).

'JPC vs PAC'. 2010. *The Financial Express*, 30 November.

Kumar, Gaurav and Mayank Singhal. 2003. 'Bhagidari: Good Intention. Bad Implementation?' Available at www.ccsindia.org (accessed on 13 March 2009).

Kumar, Navika. 2003. '15,000 objections by CAG met with silence'. *The Indian Express*, 12 May.

Kumar, Vinay. 2009. 'Delivery Monitoring Unit set up in PMO'. *The Hindu*, 6 September.

'Lokayukta can check systematic corruption: Study'. 2010. *Governance Now*, 30 December.

Mahapatra, Dhananjay. 2011. 'Top babus approach SC to stem civil services rot'. *The Times of India*, 5 March.

'Ministry refuses permission to CBI to probe NHAI official'. 2010. *Hindustan Times*, 18 November.

Mishra, Abhishek and Swati Mishra. 'Formulating the concept, principles and parameters for performance-related incentives in Government'. Report submitted to the Sixth Central Pay Commission. Available at http://india.gov.in (accessed on 18 August 2009).

Mitta, Manoj. 2011. 'Denied teeth, they can't bite'. *The Times of India*, 21 January.

'National Campaign for People's Right to Information RTI Convention 2011'. Available at http://righttoinformation.info (accessed on 22 March 2011).

'Netas defraud India, thanks to spineless babus'. 2011. *The Times of India*, 13 January.

'A new twist to social audits'. 2010. Available at www.indiatogether.org (accessed on 6 February 2010).

'Notification—Govt. of India Resolution on Public Interest Disclosures & Protection of Informer'. 2004. Central Vigilance Commission. Available at www.cvc.nic.in (accessed on 22 March 2011).

'Pending for 3 yrs, Civil Service law gets a push'. 2010. *Hindustan Times*, 7 June.

'Performance Audit of Implementation of National Rural Employment Guarantee Act (NREGA)'. Comptroller and Auditor General of India. Available at http://www.icisa.cag.gov.in/ (accessed on 2 November 2010).

Phadnis, Aditi. 2009. 'Government to introduce bill to protect bureaucracy from political interference'. *Business Standard*, 8 June.

'PM announces JPC probe into 2G spectrum scam'. 22 February 2011. *IBN Live*. Available at www.ibnlive.in.com (accessed on 1 March 2011).

'Policemen transferred on Goa CM's instructions: Social activist'. 2009. *DNA*, 8 October.

'Programme Evaluation Organisation'. 2010. Planning Commission. Available at www.planningcommission.nic.in (accessed on 5 November 2009).

'Public Affairs Centre Develops Citizen Report Cards in India'. 2008. International Budget Partnership. Available at www.internationalbudget.org (Accessed on 15 February 2011).

'Raja cost nation Rs 1.7L cr: CAG'. 2010. *The Times of India*, 10 November.

Rajagopal, Krishnadas. 2009. '26 pc men. 12 pc women aware of RTI, reveals DoPT'. *The Indian Express*, 2 November.

Rajgadia, Vishnu. 2007. 'RTI exposes vendetta by union minister'. Available at http://www.thehoot.org (accessed on 25 January 2010).

'Rajya Sabha passes Women's Reservation Bill'. 2010. *The Times of India*, 9 March.

'RTI-MIS Usage Status'. 2011. Department of Personnel and Training. Available at www.persmin.nic.in (accessed on 4 March 2011).

Paul, Samuel. 2004. 'Public-Private Partnerships for Better Governance'. A Presentation at the Learning Retreat, Antananarivo, 15 January.

'Sittings Held per Lok Sabha'. 2009. Data received from PRS Legislative Research.

'Social Audit of NREGS in Andhra Pradesh. 2009. Centre for Good Governance. Available at www.sasanet.org (accessed on 3 March 2011).

Subrahmaniam, Vidya. 2009. 'NREGA audit: Bhilwara shows the way'. *The Hindu*, 17 October.

'Understanding the key issues and constraints in implementing the RTI Act'. 2009. June. Available at http://rti.gov.in (accessed on 11 January 2010).

'Whistle-blowing, a casualty'. 2003. *The Hindu*, 14 December.

'Who's afraid of a JPC and why'. 2010. *The Times of India*, 28 November.

Yadav, Shyamlal. 2008. 'A lot to hide'. *India Today*, 27 March.

7 Judicial Accountability

*Nobody has a more sacred obligation to obey the law
than those who make the law.*

Sophocles, 497–406 BC

The Judiciary holds an exalted position in the minds of most Indians, despite the lengthy corridors of justice. The presence of a strong and well-developed judicial system differentiates India from many of the emerging economies. This chapter examines the functioning and weaknesses of the key mechanisms enforcing accountability in the Judiciary. The matrix in Figure 7.1 lists the key internal, horizontal and external accountability mechanisms in the Judiciary. We assess these existing mechanisms to determine their ability to reinforce the four foundations of accountability.

Let us take each foundation and closely examine the mechanisms of accountability in the Judiciary that positively or negatively impact it.

::: Foundation 1—Appropriate Representation

The Judiciary is a single integrated hierarchy of courts with the *Supreme Court* as the apex court, the *High Courts* and the *District Courts. Appropriate Representation* in the Judiciary is only possible if an objective and transparent process exists for the appointment of judges in all these courts.

Mechanisms of Accountability–Judiciary		
Internal Accountability	**Horizontal Accountability**	**External Accountability**
Judicial Collegium *Internal check to appoint judges in a neutral and objective manner*	**President and Governor** *Independent check to monitor appointment of judges*	**Public Monitoring of Appointments** *Citizens to monitor the appointment of judges*
Not Applicable *Judiciary cannot seek citizen's participation in the actual process of administration of justice*	**Not Applicable** *Judiciary cannot seek citizen's participation in the actual process of administration of justice*	**Not Applicable** *Judiciary cannot seek citizens participation in the actual process of administration of justice*
Internal Evaluation of Conduct *Internal provision to order an investigation into the conduct of judges*	**Independent Evaluation of Conduct** *An independent agency to investigate the conduct of judges*	**Public Evaluation of Conduct** *Citizens to monitor the conduct and performance of judges*
Impeachment *Internal provision to prosecute judges for misconduct*	**Parliament and President** *Independent authority to impeach judges for misconduct*	**Public Interest Litigation** *Citizens to challenge judges for their misconduct in the court of law*

(Left vertical axis: **Foundations of Accountability** — *Appropriate Representation*, *Participative Conduct*, *Legitimate Conduct*, *Liability Enforcement*)

■ Mechanism not applicable   □ Mechanism does not exist

Figure 7.1   Mechanisms in the Judiciary

Internal Accountability Mechanisms

Judicial Collegium   The Judicial Collegium, comprising the Chief Justice and four senior Supreme Court judges, is an internal body responsible for the appointment of the Supreme Court and High Court judges. The Judicial Collegium evaluates the candidates who can be promoted to the High Court or the Supreme Court, based on their experience and merit. The Collegium conveys their final choice of candidate to the President, who then approves their decision.

Many concerns have been voiced about this process for several years now, due to the apparent lack of transparency and objectivity in the selection and appointment of judges. The appointment process for judges appears to be subjective, since there are no defined criteria or standards for the evaluation of these judges. The process is opaque, with the details of the appointment not being shared with any member external to the Collegium. For example, an Additional Judge of a High Court was being considered for confirmation as a permanent judge of the court in 2005. The Collegium of three senior judges apparently decided not to confirm him, as they had received negative reports with regard to his integrity. Despite this, he was given an extension as an additional judge in 2005, and was confirmed as a permanent judge in February 2007, allegedly based on a higher-level recommendation (Bhushan 2009).

The current method of 'judges appointing judges' has also been criticized by jurists, government and citizens, since it compromises the neutrality of the process. The Judicial Collegium does not have any external individuals or retired Judiciary officials empanelled. Internationally, commissions that appoint judges comprise members external to the existing Judiciary. In South Africa and Germany, elected members of Parliament are also a part of the selection committee. In France, the Minister of Justice and prominent public figures are a part of the selection council (The Scottish Parliament 1999). In the United Kingdom, Supreme Court judges are appointed by the Queen, on the recommendation of the Prime Minister. Realizing the criticality of having a neutral body for the selection of judges, the Government of India is now proposing to lay down Constitutional guidelines for an independent selection body, which will replace the subjective system of appointment by the Collegium (*The Times of India*, 2 November 2010).

Horizontal Accountability Mechanisms

President and Governor   The President and the Governor are neutral and independent checks on the judicial appointment process, to ensure that there are no internal biases. The President has the power to approve or reject the judges recommended by the Judicial Collegium for appointment to the Supreme Court. Similarly, the Governor has the right to sanction the appointment of a judge to the High Court. They have to ensure that the appointment of judges is conducted in a fair manner, and that complaints of misconduct against the judges are considered.

In the past, the President has refused to sanction the recommendation of the Judicial Collegium, when not convinced about the suggested candidate. For example, the President refused to sanction the Collegium's recommendation to promote a Chief Justice of a High Court to the Supreme Court, due to complaints received from jurists and citizens that the judge was allegedly involved in transgression. In another instance, the Collegium recommended the Chief Justices of three High Courts for promotion to the Supreme Court. The President returned the file to the Supreme Court for reconsideration, on the grounds that three other Chief Justices of different High Courts were more senior than the judges recommended by the Collegium, and could not be overlooked for appointment (*Hindustan Times*, 16 November 2008).

In reality, however, the President and the Governor have limited authority over the judicial appointment process. The Collegium has the right to reiterate its recommendation, even if the President does not approve a nominee for appointment to the Supreme Court or the High Court. In such cases, where the Collegium overrides the President's or Governor's suggestion and reiterates its recommendation, the decision of the Collegium is considered final. In February 2007, the President had asked the Collegium to reconsider its decision to confirm an additional judge as a permanent judge of a High Court in the wake of an erroneous judgement by this individual, which attracted a lot of criticism from citizens and the media. A month later, the Collegium reiterated its recommendation, stating that no disqualification should be applied to judges based on past judgements (*The Indian Express*, 15 March 2007). In another instance, the Collegium recommended the elevation of a Chief Justice of a High Court to the Supreme Court, over another senior judge who had a better record. The President, raised concerns about the objectivity of the appointment process. The Collegium reiterated its recommendation to the President, without satisfactory explanation (Venkatesan 2010).

The role of the President and the Governor is thus more signatory in nature. A Parliamentary Committee report has observed that the President and Governor's discretion in the appointment of judges has been negated (Rahman 2009). The Law Commission, in its 214th report, has also highlighted that the President's authority over judicial appointments and transfers is weak (*The Hindu*, 10 August 2009). The process of conducting an independent, horizontal check on the appointment of judges is therefore not as robust as needed.

External Accountability Mechanisms

Public Monitoring of Appointments   The power of civil society and the media in challenging the appointment of tainted judges cannot be underestimated. They have often raised their voices against the appointment of certain judges, especially in the higher Judiciary. In some cases, the protests have been so strong that the Judiciary was forced to act. A corrupt judge of a High Court was recommended for promotion to the Supreme Court in 2009 by the Collegium. There were several damaging allegations against him. A group of lawyers sent a series of representations to the Collegium and the government, detailing allegations against the judge. These allegations were also confirmed by the Law Ministry. The growing objections from the media, civil society, members of the Bar, judicial activists and the Law Minister forced the Chief Justice of India to write to the government, requesting disapproval of the recommendation made by the Collegium (*The Hindu*, 18 December 2009; Campaign for Judicial Accountability and Judicial Reforms).

Citizens find it difficult to evaluate the appointment of judges, since the information regarding their appointment is not available publicly. Activists have filed several petitions and RTI appeals for written justifications of judicial appointments to be disclosed to the public. In response to an RTI appeal, the Chief Information Commissioner released a landmark judgement in early 2009, directing the Supreme Court to provide details regarding the appointment of judges in the apex court. The Supreme Court has challenged this order, on the grounds that the disclosure of the decision-making process would impinge on the independence of the Judiciary (*Rediff News*, 18 November 2010).

To conclude, *Appropriate Representation*, the first foundation of accountability, is weak in the Judiciary due to lack of transparency. It is important to strengthen the accountability mechanisms that can render this foundation stable.

::: Foundation 2—Participative Conduct

The Judiciary's role is to hold corrupt public officials and citizens accountable by prosecuting them in a court of law. Law enforcement is the exclusive prerogative of the Judiciary; citizens cannot be directly involved in the actual process of administration of justice. The second foundation of Participative Conduct is therefore 'Not Applicable' to the Judiciary. We thus move on to study the third foundation of accountability, Legitimate Conduct.

::: Foundation 3—Legitimate Conduct

The Judiciary interprets the law, determines the facts, and declares punitive judgement against government officials and citizens, if guilty. There have been some reports, however, of judges allegedly favouring a litigant in return for a personal favour, or due to coercion. The India Corruption Study (2005) undertaken by Transparency International and the Centre for Media Studies showed that nearly 60 per cent of survey respondents had paid bribes to lawyers, 30 per cent to court officials and 5 per cent to judges. The increasing misgovernance in our society makes it even more critical to oversee the functioning of the Judiciary and ensure that its conduct is of the highest order.

Internal Accountability Mechanisms

Internal Evaluation of Conduct   The members of the Collegium, or the judges of the Supreme Court and the High Court, can seek an investigation against a judge if they believe that the person is involved in some form of misconduct. They can appeal to the Chief Justice of India (CJI) to sanction a detailed enquiry against the judge by providing documents supporting their complaint. The CJI can then constitute an in-house inquiry committee of judges, or appoint the Central Bureau of Investigation (CBI) to conduct a detailed enquiry into the matter. Prior approval by the CJI is needed before filing a formal complaint and conducting an investigation into a judge, to protect them from frivolous complaints (*India Today*, 27 August 2009).

In practice, though, hardly any investigation is approved against judges, in spite of suspicions or indications of power abuse. The case of a senior judge of a High Court demonstrates the lack of action by the judicial system against corrupt judges. There was documentary evidence that a judge had obtained a plot of land at a nominal price through the land mafia. Aware of these facts, a group of senior advocates of the Supreme Court wrote to the CJI, along with evidence like sales deeds. No action, however, was taken on this complaint. A few months later, the group approached the CJI again, seeking permission to register an FIR on the matter, so that at least a police investigation could be conducted. No FIR was registered against the judge. Instead, the allegedly corrupt judge was recommended for promotion as a Chief Justice of a state a month later (*Outlook*, 9 April 2007). In another example, a sum of Rs 65.8 million was fraudulently withdrawn from the Provident Fund accounts of employees posted at a district court between 2001 and 2007. The key accused, an administrative officer in the district court treasury, had provided the names of a Supreme Court judge, 10 High Court judges and 23 lower court judges who were allegedly involved with him in this scam. The apex court, however, permitted the CBI to prosecute only six of them, allegedly due to lack of evidence to prosecute others (*India Today*, 29 July 2010).

Horizontal Accountability Mechanisms

Independent Evaluation of Conduct   The Indian Judicial system has no official independent agency that can be approached to file a complaint against the Judiciary. The Constitution established the High Courts and the Supreme Court as independent institutions, to dispense justice and hold the Executive and the Legislature accountable for any act of civil or criminal misconduct. The independence granted to the Judiciary has resulted in its becoming so powerful that it cannot be questioned or challenged by any mechanism. Internationally, the judicial systems of the UK, USA, Germany and Canada have a Judicial Council, which acts as an independent body to investigate complaints against the Judiciary and suggests relevant punitive action (Sharma 2009). The Canadian Judicial Council, for example, has the power to recommend the removal of judges after holding an enquiry (*Business Standard*, 11 August 2003). In India, however, the Judiciary does not have an independent agency to monitor complaints against them.

The Judicial Standards and Accountability Bill 2010 has suggested the formulation of Committees—a Scrutiny Committee and a National Judicial Oversight Committee—to probe allegations against Supreme Court or High Court judges. The Scrutiny Committee, headed by a retired CJI, will first evaluate all the complaints against judges. If the Scrutiny Committee finds merit in a complaint and feels detailed investigation is warranted, it will place the case before the Oversight Committee. The Oversight Committee, chaired by a retired CJI, will investigate further. Based on the severity of the charges, the Oversight Committee can impose penalties, such as a warning or an advisory to the judge, or can even ask the judge to resign. If the judge does not resign voluntarily, the committee will advise the President to introduce the impeachment motion in Parliament. The Bill has been approved by the Cabinet and was tabled in Parliament in December 2010 (*The Tribune*, 8 December 2010). If this Bill is enacted into a law, there is likely to be an improvement in accountability within the Judiciary, which will strengthen its credibility.

External Accountability Mechanisms

Public Evaluation of Conduct   Citizens should have the ability to monitor the functioning of the Judiciary. In India, citizens are afraid to seek justification from, challenge, or criticize the Judiciary. Although the Constitution guarantees freedom of speech and expression to all citizens, the Judiciary is protected from public criticism due to the threat of '*Contempt of Court*'. The Contempt of Court provision empowers the Judiciary to punish citizens who scandalize the Judiciary, prejudice judicial proceedings, or interfere with judicial functioning. It is still unclear, however, of what constitutes 'scandalizing the court' or 'interfering with the court'. In September 2007, for example, four journalists of a newspaper were sentenced to four months in jail on Contempt of Court charges. The team of journalists had published a report alleging that a former Chief Justice of India had passed orders to seal and demolish several illegal commercial establishments in a city, which would allegedly help his son's business. The High Court sentenced these journalists without completely considering the authenticity of the report (*The Indian Express*, 22 September 2007; *DNA*, 29 September 2007). In many such cases, the contempt law in India does not rely on the truth as the primary test for judging contempt. The Contempt of Court provision limits the right of the citizens to challenge the Judiciary, even if it is in the interest of the citizens at large.

In democracies like the UK and the United States, a contempt judgement is very sparingly exercised, providing greater scope for fair and constructive criticism of the Judiciary (*The Hindu*, 22 January 2007).

Moreover, 'Open Courts', where citizens and the media are allowed to attend court proceedings, are not encouraged in India. This constrains citizens from understanding the justifications for judgements passed in court. It is also difficult for the general public to monitor the Judiciary, since it requires legal expertise to understand the laws, court proceedings and their implications. There are only a handful of CSOs, like the Campaign for Judicial Accountability and Reforms and the Janhit Manch, who advocate judicial accountability and reforms.

::: Foundation 4—Liability Enforcement

The Judiciary is the organization that enforces liability against the corrupt. Accountability mechanisms, however, are also needed to hold the members of the Judiciary responsible for their actions.

Internal Accountability Mechanisms

Impeachment   The only mechanism through which the Chief Justice of India, Supreme Court judges, or High Court judges can be held liable for acts of misconduct is through the process of impeachment. If the members of the Judiciary are of the opinion that a Supreme Court or High Court judge has been involved in misconduct, they can propose impeachment to the Parliament. In 2008, the CJI recommended initiating impeachment proceedings against a High Court judge who was charged with misappropriating funds and giving false explanations thereafter (*The Hindu*, 12 November 2010). In another case, a group of lawyers campaigned for an impeachment motion against a judge who was allegedly involved in amassing disproportionate wealth and acquiring land unlawfully. Eventually, 75 MPs of the Rajya Sabha signed and initiated the impeachment motion in the House, forcing the accused judge to stop discharging judicial functions (Campaign for Judicial Accountability and Reforms).

The impeachment mechanism, however, has been unsuccessful in punishing errant judges. The procedure of impeachment of the judges is slow and lengthy and susceptible to political influence, as we will discuss later. The failure of this mechanism is evident from the fact that not a single judge has been impeached in our country so far (*The Indian Express*, 17 December 2009). Apart from impeachment, there is no other mechanism to penalize judges for misconduct. No penalties are imposed, no salaries are cut and no public explanation is sought.

Horizontal Accountability Mechanisms

Parliament and President   The Parliament and the President are the independent authorities that implement the impeachment of a judge. To start the impeachment process, an impeachment proposal is initiated and signed by the Members of Parliament. The motion should be signed by at least 100 members of the Lok Sabha, or 50 members of the Rajya Sabha, for it to be accepted in the Parliament. The Speaker of the House then forms a three-member committee that investigates the matter in detail and presents its findings before the House. If the judge is found guilty, a parliamentary vote is initiated in one or both Houses to pass the impeachment resolution. If two-thirds of the House votes in favour of the impeachment, the resolution is passed and then presented to the President for approval. If the President signs this resolution, the implicated judge is impeached. This entire process is so slow and lengthy that it often extends over a few years. Of the few attempts made to initiate an impeachment motion in Parliament, only one case has managed to reach the final stage of voting by the MPs so far. One High Court judge was close to being impeached after the investigating committee found him guilty of financial irregularities. An impeachment motion signed by 108 MPs was admitted in the Lok Sabha. The inquiry committee, after examining the documents and a large number of witnesses, found the judge guilty of 'willful and gross misuse of office'. When the motion was finally put to vote in the House, only 196 MPs belonging to the opposition parties voted for his removal. Since the Constitution requires the support of at least two-thirds of the MPs present in the House to impeach a judge, the impeachment did not take place (Campaign for Judicial Accountability and Judicial Reforms).

External Accountability Mechanisms

Public Interest Litigation   Citizens can challenge the Judiciary with issues affecting the public at large using the Public Interest Litigation (PIL). PILs have been filed challenging the functioning of the Judiciary (for example, mass leave by judges, early closure of local courts) and its inadequate infrastructure (number of judges). There is no independent agency, however, to act on the PILs filed against the Judiciary. The Judiciary can itself entertain or dismiss the PILs filed against it. A PIL was filed in April 2004 by a citizen challenging the decision of the judges of a High Court to go on a mass strike. In December 2004, however, the apex court dismissed the PIL as infructuous and unfruitful, on the grounds that the judges had resumed work within 24 hours (Mitta 2004).

In closing, this chapter evaluated the strength of the mechanisms that support the foundations of accountability in the Judiciary. Many constraints exist in the implementation of these existing mechanisms, which result in low accountability of the judiciary (Figure 7.2).

At the end of Part II of this book, we are more *aware* about accountability mechanisms in the three branches of the government. As citizens, we are hopefully better equipped to understand the *actions* we need to take to improve accountability in India. This is the subject of Part III of this book.

		Weaknesses in Mechanisms of Accountability–Judiciary		
		Internal Accountability	**Horizontal Accountability**	**External Accountability**
Foundations of Accountability	Appropriate Representation	**Judicial Collegium** • *Lack of neutral and external members in the Collegium* • *Lack of an objective and defined process for appointment* • *Non-transparent and secretive process to appoint judges*	**President and Governor** • *Limited authority with President and Governor to challenge the appointment of judges*	**Public Monitoring of Appointments** • *No voluntary disclosure of information regarding appointments by Judiciary* • *Citizens cannot file RTI for appointment information*
	Participative Conduct	Not Applicable	Not Applicable	Not Applicable
	Legitimate Conduct	**Internal Evaluation of Conduct** • *Investigation against judges has been rarely initiated by Collegium*	**Independent Evaluation of Conduct** • *No independent agency exists to investigate complaints against the Judiciary*	**Public Evaluation of Conduct** • *Difficult to challenge judges due to threat of 'contempt of court'* • *Difficult to access information about court proceedings*
	Liability Enforcement	**Impeachment** • *Impeachment is seldom initiated by the Collegium* • *No other mechanism of imposing minor penalties or punishing judges*	**Parliament and President** • *Slow and lengthy process of impeachment* • *Political patronage hampers impeachment process*	**Public Interest Litigation** • *No independent authority exists to review PILs against Judiciary* • *Difficulty in using PILs due to lack of understanding of scope and application*

Mechanism not applicable   Mechanism does not exist

Figure 7.2   Assessment of Mechanisms in the Judiciary

References

'Bench shame'. 2009. *India Today*, 27 August.

Bhushan, Prashant. 2009. 'Judging the Judges'. *Outlook*, 21 January.

'Can't make public info on judge transfers: SC'. 2010. *Rediff News*, 18 November.

'CBI for action against 24 judges in PF scam'. 2010. *India Today*, 29 July.

Chibbar, Manish. 2009. 'The law on impeachment of judges'. *Indian Express*, 17 December.

'CJI on Bhayana file: Verdict reversal does not disqualify judge'. 2007. *The Indian Express*, 15 March.

'Collegium decides to drop Dinakaran'. 2009. *The Hindu*, 18 December.

'Contempt of court: need for a second look'. 2007. *The Hindu*, 22 January.

'Ensuring judicial accountability: Provision needed for judges' premature retirement'. 2010. *The Tribune*, 8 December.

'Govt stalls judges' promotions'. 2008. *Hindustan Times*, 16 November.

'Impeaching Justice Sen'. 2010. *The Hindu*, 12 November.

'Judicial Accountability: Impeachment: Justice V. Ramaswamy'. 2011. Campaign for Judicial Accountability and Judicial Reforms. Available at http://www.judicialreforms.org/ (accessed on 10 March 2011).

'Judge Watch on Justice P. D. Dinakaran'. Campaign for Judicial Accountability and Judicial Reforms. Available at http://www.judicialreforms.org/justice_dinakaran.htm (accessed on 8 March 2011).

'Judges and Citizens'. 2007. *The Indian Express*, 22 September.

'Judges appointing judges' likely to be history soon'. 2010. *The Times of India*, 2 November.

'Judicial Appointments'. 1999. *The Scottish Parliament—The Information Centre*. Available at www.scottish.parliament.uk (accessed on 6 January 2010).

'Law Commission moots sweeping reforms'. 2009. *The Hindu*, 10 August.

Mitta, Manoj. 2004. 'PIL on judges' strike: in Sept, SC says great public interest, in December, infructuous'. *The Indian Express*, 11 December.

'PF scam case hearing adjourned'. 2011. *The Hindu*, 19 February.

Rahman, Shafi. 2009. 'Lords on Trial'. *India Today*, 7 September.

'SC collegium clears elevation of Justice Bhalla as CJ'. 2007. *Outlook*, 9 April.

'SC admits journos' plea in contempt case'. 2007. *DNA*, 29 September.

Sharma, Nagendar. 2009. 'Make it possible to judge the judges'. *Hindustan Times*, 3 August.

Venkatesan, V. 2010. 'Trying Times'. *Frontline*, February.

'Who needs the National Judicial Commission'. 2003. *Business Standard*, 11 August.

PART III

Action

8 The Six Initiatives

I hope that I may always desire more than I can accomplish.

Michelangelo, 1475–1564

The last few chapters have helped us to understand the limitations in the internal, horizontal and external mechanisms of accountability within the Legislature, the Executive and the Judiciary. These debilitating weaknesses stress the four foundations of accountability, rendering them unstable (Figure 8.1).

Are there common underlying ailments afflicting these mechanisms? If we could identify the common weaknesses, then perhaps a concentrated effort to overcome them may provide a synergistic improvement across all four foundations of accountability. Fortunately, we can identify these common threads. The lack of transparency in the appointment of judges, the lack of justification for transfers and promotions of public officials, or the insufficient information to evaluate the performance of public schemes, all point to *poor information availability*. The absence of any defined criteria and process for the selection of judges, the absence of objective processes for the transfer of public officials, and the absence of performance-linked incentives indicate a *lack of impartiality in the process of selection, transfer and evaluation*. Similarly, the inability of the Election Commission to prosecute candidates breaching the election code of conduct, the inability of the CBI to investigate judges without prior approval, the inability of the CAG to act based on their audit reports, the absence of authority with the CVC to impose a penalty based on investigations, all indicate the *lack of independence of these agencies to take action*.

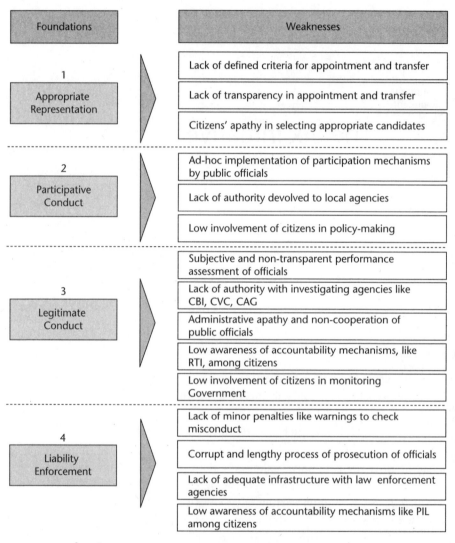

Foundations	Weaknesses
1 Appropriate Representation	Lack of defined criteria for appointment and transfer
	Lack of transparency in appointment and transfer
	Citizens' apathy in selecting appropriate candidates
2 Participative Conduct	Ad-hoc implementation of participation mechanisms by public officials
	Lack of authority devolved to local agencies
	Low involvement of citizens in policy-making
3 Legitimate Conduct	Subjective and non-transparent performance assessment of officials
	Lack of authority with investigating agencies like CBI, CVC, CAG
	Administrative apathy and non-cooperation of public officials
	Low awareness of accountability mechanisms, like RTI, among citizens
	Low involvement of citizens in monitoring Government
4 Liability Enforcement	Lack of minor penalties like warnings to check misconduct
	Corrupt and lengthy process of prosecution of officials
	Lack of adequate infrastructure with law enforcement agencies
	Low awareness of accountability mechanisms like PIL among citizens

Figure 8.1 Key Weaknesses of Accountability Mechanisms

From our search for commonality emerged six underlying threads, which collectively destabilize and stress the four foundations of accountability. We call these common strings the *Six Inadequacies* (Figure 8.2).

These Six Inadequacies, which severely cripple the functioning of the existing accountability mechanisms, can be briefly defined as follows:

- **Inadequate Information**—Lack of available and accessible information
- **Inadequate Impartiality**—Lack of objective and transparent processes of appointment, transfer and evaluation of public officials

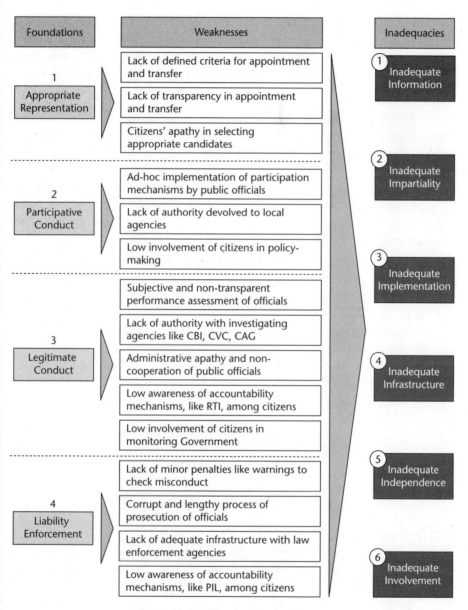

Figure 8.2 The Six Inadequacies

- **Inadequate Implementation**—Ineffective implementation of policies
- **Inadequate Infrastructure**—Inadequate personnel, systems and infrastructure support for accountability agencies

- **Inadequate Independence**—Inadequate authority of accountability agencies and inadequate empowerment given to them
- **Inadequate Involvement**—Low involvement of citizens in the political process due to their indifferent attitude, compounded by lack of awareness

These six inadequacies are the infernal threads that play havoc with accountability as they carelessly tug at the heartstrings of our democracy. These six inadequacies must be overcome to ensure that the internal, horizontal and external accountability mechanisms work as designed, to bring about a systemic improvement in accountability. There are correspondingly *Six Initiatives* needed to strengthen accountability in India. While many of these are common knowledge, what we would like to emphasize here is the synergistic impact that improvement on these six initiatives can have on the mechanisms of accountability, and on the foundations on which accountability rests (Figure 8.3).

Let us study each of these six initiatives in greater detail.

1. **Information:** The availability and accessibility of information in the public domain needs to improve substantially. It is essential to disclose information for public monitoring, since quality and timely information is a critical prerequisite for accountability. It is equally important to provide easy access to information by leveraging technology and the mass media.
2. **Impartiality:** Impartiality implies an objective and defined process for the appointment, transfer and evaluation of public officials. An independent agency overseeing all selections and transfers, as well as objective criteria,

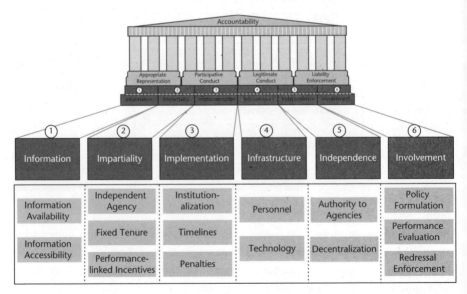

Figure 8.3 The Six Initiatives

are needed to reduce the favouritism that hampers our public administration. A fixed tenure for public officials is essential to protect them from unreasonable transfers. The performance evaluation process for public officials needs to be quantitative and linked to compensation, to hold them accountable.

3. **Implementation:** The issue we face is not the absence of accountability mechanisms, but the ad-hoc implementation of those that already exist. Institutionalizing accountability mechanisms as a part of public schemes will ensure the consistent execution of these mechanisms. Timelines should be prescribed for each mechanism to avoid unnecessary delays. Incentivizing or penalizing public officials involved in implementing these mechanisms is also important to ensure that they cooperate with citizens and deliver results.

4. **Infrastructure:** Infrastructure is the provision of adequate personnel and system support to the agencies responsible for ensuring accountability. Trained personnel need to be provided to improve the productivity of accountability institutions. Technology initiatives also need to be expanded to improve the delivery of accountability mechanisms.

5. **Independence:** Independence refers to the empowerment of accountability agencies so that they can take action against public officials for any abuse of power. It is imperative to provide them with greater power and authority than they currently possess, so that they can function effectively.

6. **Involvement:** Citizens should proactively use accountability mechanisms to monitor policy formulation and budget allocation and provide their feedback. Citizens should also monitor the performance of public services and demand redressal against the poor quality of delivery.

The six initiatives and their corresponding action points would improve the overall performance and effectiveness of our accountability mechanisms. We have tried to capture, within these six improvement areas, a majority of the action points that in some way strengthen the mechanisms of accountability, which in turn stabilize the four foundations of accountability.

To its credit, the Government of India has already taken some initiatives in the areas we mention above. Some initiatives have been widely introduced across the country, while others have been restricted to a particular department, or geography. Some initiatives have been strong, while others have been half-hearted attempts, resulting in no significant improvement in accountability. Similarly, civil society organizations have also initiated campaigns in the areas of governance and accountability, though with limited geographic reach. We decided to subjectively rate the progress made on these initiatives to improve accountability. The initiatives were rated on a 5-point scale, based on their qualitative success in improving accountability and governance in India (Figure 8.4).

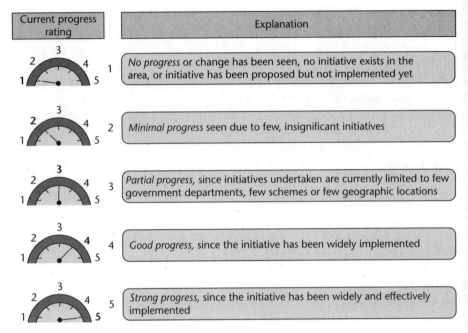

Current progress rating	Explanation
	No progress or change has been seen, no initiative exists in the area, or initiative has been proposed but not implemented yet
	Minimal progress seen due to few, insignificant initiatives
	Partial progress, since initiatives undertaken are currently limited to few government departments, few schemes or few geographic locations
	Good progress, since the initiative has been widely implemented
	Strong progress, since the initiative has been widely and effectively implemented

Figure 8.4 Progress Rating Scale

The following section details the improvement areas required for each of the six initiatives, and evaluates the current progress made in these areas.

::: Initiative 1—Information

Information Availability

Provide information about the amount allocated to public schemes, the amount utilized and the outcome   The government needs to provide information comparing the amount allocated to the amount actually utilized, to aid transparency and optimum utilization of funds. Second, the government should link the actual output of a scheme to the funds spent towards it. For example, it is not only important to know the amount spent towards building new hospitals or recruiting doctors, but also the outcome of this investment on the incidence of diseases, mortality and life expectancy rates.

Current Progress   In India, the usage of public funds is not adequately monitored. Less than 0.5 per cent of the Union budget is utilized to monitor the other 99.5 per cent spent (Misra 2009). The Union budget gives us an indication of the amount allocated for public schemes. There is, however, a

---

Global Example

- **USA:**
  - The US government provides annual performance reports on the effectiveness of various programs, on the website *expectmore.gov* (www.gpoaccess.gov 2009)
  - Recently launched website, www.recovery.gov, publishes details of the sources, recipients and utilization of federal funds appropriated to stimulate the economy (Meskell 2009)
- **Argentina:**
  - The Cristal website provides information on all national policies to evaluate how public funds are assigned and managed (Lic. Gustavo Axel Radics 2001)

---

lack of clarity on how these funds translate into actual outcomes. Major flagship schemes like the Sarva Shiksha Abhiyan (SSA) publicize the outcome of the scheme on their websites. The SSA scheme's website (www.ssa.nic.in) publishes progress reports that provide details of the scheme's performance. The report enables citizens to monitor the outcome under heads like the number of primary and upper primary schools started, the number of teachers recruited, student enrolment and retention ratios, the pupil-teacher ratio, and so on. These reports, however, do not establish a link between outcome indicators and the funds utilized. It is therefore difficult to comment on the effectiveness of the utilization of funds.

Currently, there is no centralized source of information that provides details for all flagship schemes on a single platform. The government has proposed a *Central Plan Scheme Monitoring System (CPSMS)*, a web-enabled application that will be a common platform for monitoring the disbursements and outcomes of flagship schemes under the Central Plan Schemes of the Government of India (www.icisa.cag.gov.in). This portal, when operational, would empower citizens to monitor all schemes and question entitlements that have not reached them.

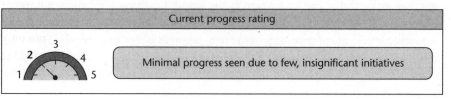

Current progress rating

Minimal progress seen due to few, insignificant initiatives

Provide information on the funds allocated and the amount utilized by the Ministries The Ministries should provide a comparative analysis of the funds allocated to them and their performance based on these funds. Information linking the budget sanctioned with the outcome indicators will aid in the optimum utilization of funds and curb misappropriation.

Current Progress   There has been partial progress in providing citizens with access to expense and performance related information from each of the Ministries. The introduction of *outcome budgeting* in the year 2006–07 was a step in this direction. All Ministries are expected to prepare *outcome budgets* annually, which provide details about the amount allocated, amount utilized and the outcome of these funds. They are also expected to compare this information with the projected utilization and projected output. While the Ministries do prepare outcome budgets, the depth of information provided varies across Ministries. For instance, the outcome budget of one Ministry compares the actual output achieved, the actual expenditure incurred and actual timelines with their projected targets. Another Ministry, on the other hand, provides details of the actual output, expenditure and timelines for various projects, but does not provide a comparison with the projected costs and timelines. To complicate matters further, there is no standard reporting format that the Ministries adhere to, making it difficult to understand and compare performances across Ministries. A standardized reporting format needs to be adopted across all Ministries.

Current progress rating
Partial progress, since initiatives undertaken are currently limited to few government departments, few schemes or few geographic locations

Provide information on the operational expenses incurred by Ministries
Citizens should be aware of how taxpayers' money is spent by the government. Access to information on government expenses is fundamental to holding the government accountable for its actions. Open access to expense-related information prevents public funds from being misused. All Ministries should provide details about their operational expenses, like travel, communication and salaries. A centralized platform providing details of these expenses for all Ministries would help to increase transparency and curb any misappropriation of funds.

Current Progress   The Controller General of Accounts (CGA), the principal Accounts Adviser to the government, provides information on government expenditure through the *annual union finance accounts*. The CGA provides information on the expenses incurred by the government under various heads, like

Global Example

- **USA:**
  - Many state governments in the US (Texas, Georgia, etc.) have published all government expenses online (Meskell 2009)
  - A single searchable website, www.usaspending.gov, allows the public to search and browse information on all federal grants and contracts over the amount of US $25,000 (Fabry 2008)
- **UK:**
  - MPs' allowances-related information is available to the public on the Parliament's website (UK Parliament 2007–08)

salary, allowances and tour expenses, but only for major functionaries of the government, like the President, the Governor and the Council of Ministers. The CGA does not provide this information for each Ministry.

Annual reports published by the various Ministries should ideally provide expenditure-related information. Most Ministries, however, refrain from doing so. For instance, some Ministries do not provide information about the overall operational expenses of the Ministry, like salaries, allowances and tour expenses incurred. Similarly, the only expenditure-related detail provided by the annual report of some Ministries is the amount sanctioned for the various initiatives that come under its purview. They do not provide details of their administrative and general expenses. Citizens have to access the websites of individual Ministries and multiple sources to obtain this expenditure-related information. A single portal providing access to information about Ministries' usage of funds does not exist. The CGA has proposed a central repository for this information, called *E-lekha*. This is a centralized financial management application that consolidates the expenditure incurred by various Ministries and Departments of the central government on a regular basis. A citizens' interface to *E-lekha* is expected to be launched soon (eIndia 2009).

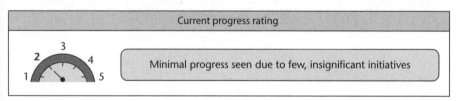

Current progress rating

Minimal progress seen due to few, insignificant initiatives

Allow citizens to track their public service applications (license, ration card, etc.) online An online system that allows citizens to track the progress of their applications, like driving licenses, passports and ration cards, reduces the likelihood of having to bribe officials to expedite these

Global Example

- **South Korea:** The web service OPEN (Online Procedures Enhancement for Civil Applications) allows citizens to track their applications for licenses/ permits online, and thereby curbs exaction (The World Bank 2000).

applications. The reasons for any delay or rejection of the applications should also be provided. This leads to greater transparency and reduces administrative graft.

Current Progress   The application status of a few government documents like passports and Pan Cards can be tracked online. This online system of tracking applications, however, has not been implemented for all government departments. It needs to be scaled up substantially in order to have a major impact on the incidence and prevalence of bribery, which exists at the frictional interface between the life of an ordinary citizen and the role the government plays in it. Besides the online tracking system, the only other way to check status is by filing a Right to Information (RTI) application. RTI has been used by citizens, especially in rural areas, to assess the status of applications for public services such as water connections, electricity connections and the ration card. Government departments, however, should provide this information upfront, so that citizens do not have to depend on the RTI Act to get basic information.

Current progress rating

Partial progress, since initiatives undertaken are currently limited to few government departments, few schemes or few geographic locations

Increase transparency in selections and transfers   The opaque process of selection of judges by the Judicial Collegium needs to be made transparent, by disclosing the criteria for selection and the names and profiles of the judges evaluated for the post. Similarly, rampant transfers of civil service officials should be curtailed by bringing this process before the eyes of citizens and the media. Public disclosure of the reasons and criteria for transfers of public officials should be mandated. These details should be available online, and not just by filing RTI applications.

Current Progress   Civil Society Organizations, citizens and the media have been demanding public disclosure of the process of selection and transfers of judges and public officials for more than a decade. The government has continued to ignore these demands, resulting in negligible progress in this area. The Judiciary too has refrained from public disclosure of the appointments of judges, arguing that their independence would be compromised by doing so.

Similarly, no justifications or details of the transfers of civil service officials are provided in the public domain. Citizens have tried to obtain this information by filing RTI applications, with differing outcomes. In some cases, citizens have managed to expose the politics behind the unreasonable transfer of officials. In other cases, they have been denied this information under the RTI, stating that every public authority is free to deploy its manpower in any manner to optimize efficiency, and that the use of the RTI was uncalled for (Rajagopal 2009). Political willingness and commitment to accountability are lacking, resulting in minimal transparency in the selection and transfers of public officials.

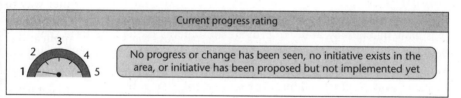

Current progress rating

No progress or change has been seen, no initiative exists in the area, or initiative has been proposed but not implemented yet

Information Accessibility

Leverage Information and Communication Technology (Internet, mobile phones) to foster transparency   Citizens have to interact with the government regularly for the delivery of public services, the issue of documents like birth/death certificates, renewal of licenses and filing of income taxes. Information and communication technology, when used for this purpose, can eliminate geographic and socio-economic divides, foster transparency, reduce misgovernance and strengthen accountability.

Current Progress   A number of successful attempts have been made by the government to leverage technology and make information accessible to citizens. There are several examples: *Bhoomi* refers to the computerization of land records in Karnataka, where the State's Department of Revenue computerized 20 million records of landownership and made these records easily accessible through kiosks—Bhoomi centres in 140 taluk

Global Example
• **Colombia:** The government undertook a two-year 'Connectivity Agenda' that mandated all federal agencies to develop an online presence, make public procedures online and gradually conduct online purchases (Porrua and Rinne 2001)

offices (Chawla and Bhatnagar 2001). The Gyandoot project, which established community-owned Internet kiosks in Dhar, Madhya Pradesh, is another example. These kiosks provided access to services like the auction rates of agricultural produce, copies of land records, online registration of applications, filing of complaints, and updated information about government grants and programmes at a nominal fee (Bhatnagar and Vyas 2001). The *e-seva centres* in Andhra Pradesh are one-stop shops for the payment of utility bills, reservations of train tickets, and obtaining birth and death certificates and vehicle permits. These initiatives have largely been at the state level and need to be scaled up to a national level to benefit all citizens.

With exactly this objective in mind, the National e-Governance Plan (NeGP) was launched in May 2006, to provide an impetus to the long-term growth of e-governance at a national level. The NeGP also covers local bodies like the Panchayats and aims to connect all panchayats in India through the Internet (e-Panchayati Raj Institutions). The implementation of the NeGP is expected to make all government services accessible through an integrated service delivery mechanism, and bring uniformity in e-governance standards. The NeGP has 27 projects covering a basket of services like income tax, customs, excise, passports, land records, agriculture, police and e-procurement, to name a few. Currently, five of these projects are fully operational all over India. Of the remaining 22 projects, 19 are in the implementation stage, where rollout is in progress, and the rest are in the design and development stage. All these projects are expected to be completed and online by 2014 (Ministry of Information and Technology, November 2010). The landmark *Aadhaar* programme undertaken by the Indian government is also one of the 27 projects of the NeGP. This initiative aims to provide every citizen with a 12-digit 'Unique Identification Number', which can be used to access public services and government benefits. This major initiative aims at leveraging technology to reduce leakages in public services by targeting benefits directly to individual citizens. As of October 2011, close to 60 million citizens were issued UIDs (UIDAI).

In addition to the NeGP, a new national-level information network called the Public Information Infrastructure (PII) is being set up. Expected to be operational by 2013, the initiative aims to create a single point information access system for citizens throughout the country, by integrating all central and state government departments and schemes. The existing information framework is scattered, with each state establishing its own data centre for automating land records, municipal applications, and so on. The PII aims to consolidate all the information spread across various schemes, departments and states on a single information platform. The resulting access would encourage citizens to use the information available to demand their rights (*The Economic Times*, 22 July 2010).

The Department of Information Technology has drafted an *Electronic Service Delivery Bill*, which proposes that all Ministries and Departments should compulsorily deliver services to citizens electronically, to reduce the dependence on the manual distribution of services. The first draft of this bill has been made available online for public comments (*Mint*, 11 March 2011).

These short-term and long-term projects will likely develop into powerful tools to facilitate citizen-government interaction.

Current progress rating
Partial progress, since initiatives undertaken are currently limited to few government departments, few schemes or few geographic locations

Build awareness about accountability mechanisms   Citizens should be educated about the mechanisms that exist to demand accountability from the government. A nation-wide awareness campaign about accountability mechanisms is required to build an informed and empowered citizenry. Workshops need to be conducted to train ordinary citizens to use these tools effectively.

Current Progress   The government has introduced many accountability mechanisms, but adequate efforts have not been made to make people aware

Global Example
• **UK:** The UK's Cabinet Office uses search engine placements to promote public awareness of the Freedom of Information Act (eGov Monitor Weekly 2006).

of them. Take for example the iconic accountability mechanism, the Right to Information (RTI) Act, which empowers citizens to access the information available in government records. Lack of awareness of the RTI Act is a major constraint to its success. In the early years of the introduction of the RTI, the government barely made any effort to promote its usage. In 2007, only two television advertisements and a radio spot were released to promote the act. No print media campaign took place on the RTI during 2007 (*Mint*, 23 April 2008). In the last few years, the government has finally begun to step up promotional activities for the RTI with television campaigns, posters in post offices, SMS campaigns and an online portal for information on the RTI. A lot more needs to be done to create rural awareness (*Mint*, 27 September 2010; DMU Report—RTI, March 2010). A good example of how to promote the RTI act has been set by the Maharashtra and Andhra Pradesh governments. These state governments have decided to include the RTI in the school curriculum to introduce this legislation to the younger generation. Students will be introduced to the uses and benefits of the RTI through textbooks, and to the practical aspects of preparing RTI applications as a part of their annual project work (Chandavarkar 2006; *The Hindu*, 27 June 2010). The government also introduced an online RTI course in 2009 (Right to Information 2010).

When the Citizens Charter was introduced more than a decade ago, there was hardly any effort made by the government to spread awareness about it. Recently, the Department of Administrative Reforms and Public Grievances has introduced some measures to improve the awareness levels of the Citizens Charter by listing the charters of various departments on its website, developing a dedicated website (goicharters.nic.in), and conducting regional seminars to build awareness among stakeholders (Public Affairs Centre 2007).

More effort from the government is required to generate awareness about accountability mechanisms, especially when these mechanisms are introduced. An informed society will ultimately lead to a progressive society.

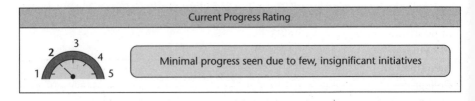

The current progress on the Information Initiative is summarized in Figure 8.5.

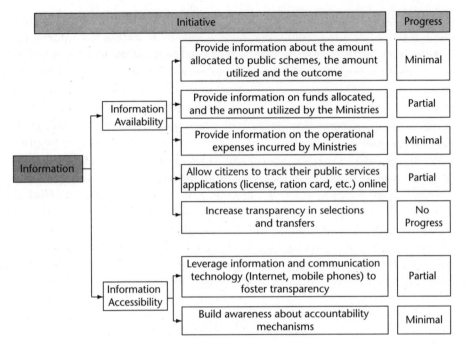

Initiative		Progress
Information	Information Availability	
	Provide information about the amount allocated to public schemes, the amount utilized and the outcome	Minimal
	Provide information on funds allocated, and the amount utilized by the Ministries	Partial
	Provide information on the operational expenses incurred by Ministries	Minimal
	Allow citizens to track their public services applications (license, ration card, etc.) online	Partial
	Increase transparency in selections and transfers	No Progress
	Information Accessibility	
	Leverage information and communication technology (Internet, mobile phones) to foster transparency	Partial
	Build awareness about accountability mechanisms	Minimal

Figure 8.5   Information Initiative—Summary

::: Initiative 2—Impartiality

Independent Agency

Form an independent agency to oversee appointments and transfers   An independent agency should oversee the appointment of public officials, based on a pre-defined process of competitive evaluation to avoid internal biases. The agency should be responsible for filling vacancies based on merit and experience of candidates. It should also be responsible for conducting objective and need-based transfers of public officials.

Current Progress   With the aim of introducing an independent agency for the appointment of judges, the Judicial Collegium was created in 1993, where a team of two Supreme Court judges and the Chief Justice of India jointly took appointment decisions. To make the process more objective and unbiased, the size of the Collegium was increased to five judges in 1998. The Collegium has been in place for over a decade now, but it has increasingly drawn criticism for being a closed system in which the judiciary selects its own judges. The Judiciary needs to take

Global Example

- **Australia:** A Merit Protection Commissioner conducts independent reviews of appointments, transfers and promotion decisions (OECD 2004)

initiative to either rectify this, or propose a new independent agency for merit-based appointments.

On the other hand, the selection of officials in the Administrative Executive is conducted by an independent agency, the Union Public Service Commission. The UPSC, however, does not monitor and conduct the transfers and promotions of these officials. The Civil Services Performance Standards and Accountability Bill does propose the introduction of an independent body to check the transfers of civil service officials. The Department of Personnel and Training is still finalizing the draft bill that will be presented to the Union Cabinet and then tabled in Parliament (*Hindustan Times*, 7 June 2010; *The Telegraph*, 23 June 2010).

Current Progress Rating

No progress or change has been seen, no initiative exists in the area, or initiative has been proposed but not implemented yet

Fixed Tenure

Introduce fixed tenure for civil service officials to avoid rampant transfers A fixed tenure for civil service officials, especially officials at senior posts, will help to reduce unreasonable transfers. This will prevent external forces from transferring these officials for personal or political gain. Barring a few senior-level officials like the Cabinet Secretary, there is no minimum tenure fixed for civil service officials, especially those at the State level.

Current Progress The first initiative by the government in this area was to introduce a fixed tenure of two to five years for police personnel, based on their position and role, through the Model Police Act in 2006 (Corrie 2007). This proposal, however, has not yet been implemented. The other major initiative is the Civil Services Performance Standards and Accountability Bill, which proposes to introduce a fixed tenure of minimum three years for IAS and IPS civil service officials. This act has not yet been implemented (*Business Standard*, 8 June 2009).

Current Progress Rating	
	No progress or change has been seen, no initiative exists in the area, or initiative has been proposed but not implemented yet

Performance-Linked Incentives

Introduce performance-linked incentives for public officials and build an integrated performance management system   Performance-linked incentives should be introduced as a part of the appraisal system, where performance ratings are directly reflected in monetary benefits or penalties. This is important to incentivize officials to perform better, or to penalize them for poor performance. It is also important to link individual incentives with the department's performance by coupling individual performance targets to the overall departmental goals.

Current Progress   The *Annual Performance Appraisal Reports* (APARs) provide a numerical, objective rating of an individual's performance, based on defined performance criteria, functional competency and personal attributes. Similarly, the *Results Framework Document* (RFD) objectively measures a Ministry/Department's performance at the end of the year, based on pre-defined targets.

The key drawback of the current performance appraisal system of civil service officials is that the performance ratings do not translate into tangible benefits for individuals.

Global Example
• **Singapore:** Promotions are based not just on performance assessment, but also on the ranking of officers with respect to each other. Ranking parameters include quality of work, knowledge, reaction under stress and teamwork. Pay, increments and career advancements are performance and competence-linked, not seniority-based (Saxena and Bagai 2010)
• **China:** Rewards and increments are linked to performance. The 'cadre responsibility' system exists at the township level, where local public officials sign performance contracts detailing specific quantifiable targets. Achievement of targets is rewarded with bonuses (Burns and Shen 2002)
• **Finland:** Salary of officials includes pay indexed to individual performance and result-based rewards for the achievement of business objectives (OECD 2005)

Currently, officers are not granted any monetary incentives based on their performance scores. For promotions, the performance score has a minimum threshold, below which the official will not be considered for promotion. Beyond this minimum cut-off, there is no incentive for individual officers to perform better than others. Similarly, there are currently no performance-linked incentives for the top-performing departments. The Performance Management Division has proposed the introduction of performance-linked incentives for the Secretary, who is directly responsible for the performance of the department. The proposal is to provide a bonus of at least 20 per cent of salary to the Secretary, provided the Ministry meets the targets set at the beginning of the year (*The Economic Times*, 27 October 2010). Currently, there is no link between performance scores and the salary received by the officials.

Since the tools to measure the performance of individuals and departments are in place, the next step is to link the individual's targets with departmental goals. An integrated performance management system would ensure that individuals at all levels work towards achieving the broad strategic plan of the department. This would streamline the performance assessment process and bring in greater accountability.

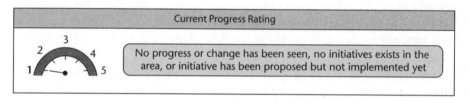

The current progress on the Impartiality Initiative is summarized in Figure 8.6.

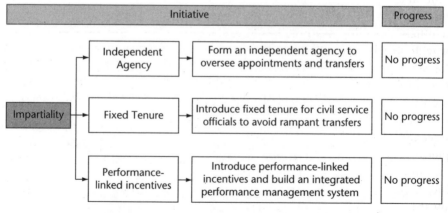

Figure 8.6   Impartiality Initiative—Summary

::: Initiative 3—Implementation

Institutionalization

Institutionalize social accountability mechanisms as part of the governance structure   While formal public institutions have met with limited success in imposing accountability, increased attention is now being paid to 'demand-driven' accountability mechanisms. These socially driven accountability mechanisms, like Social Audits, Public Expenditure Tracking Survey (PETS) and Citizens Reports Cards (CRC), have been used by citizens, civil society organizations and the media to directly demand greater accountability and responsiveness from public officials. The success of these mechanisms has been limited due to the non-cooperative attitude of public officials and the limited geographic spread of these CSOs. While ad-hoc or one-off social accountability initiatives can make a difference, experience shows that the impact is greater when social accountability mechanisms are 'institutionalized' (Malena et al. 2004). By institutionalizing Social Audits and PETS as a part of every flagship scheme, public agencies will be pushed to track and compare the expenditures incurred with the benefits received by citizens. Similarly, by making Citizen Report Cards an integral part of the schemes, public authorities will have to compulsorily conduct citizen satisfaction surveys to improve the quality of their services.

Current Progress   The government has mandated Social Audits for a flagship scheme, the Mahatma Gandhi National Rural Employment Guarantee Scheme (MGNREGS). This is a step forward in citizens' empowerment as local public officials and citizens have to mandatorily conduct a joint audit of muster rolls and cash books. A few states, like Andhra Pradesh and Rajasthan, have taken this initiative seriously. Often, public officials at the grassroots level are not cooperative and are unwilling to provide information. For example, in October 2009 in one district in Rajasthan, thousands of people had set out to conduct audits of the MGNREGS across 375 panchayats. They divided themselves into 125 groups and carried out inspections of attendance rolls, job cards and cash books. They also gathered feedback from villagers and addressed their complaints. This audit was preceded by days of protest by village officials, who were unwilling to answer queries, or were uncomfortable at being held accountable. Although they gave in later, they delayed the process of conducting audits (Subrahmaniam 2009). State governments must demonstrate commitment and seriousness towards such initiatives to successfully implement these mechanisms at the grassroots level.

In the same vein, the Ministry of Housing and Urban Poverty Alleviation is planning to include social auditing in its Basic Services for the Urban Poor, and Integrated Housing and Slum Development Programme schemes. A pilot social audit of both schemes was conducted in Andhra Pradesh and Madhya Pradesh in 2010, to assess and sort out operational issues before full-fledged implementation. Auditing all the other schemes is also important, as millions of rupees exchange hands when these schemes are being implemented.

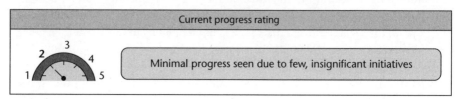

Current progress rating

Minimal progress seen due to few, insignificant initiatives

Timelines

Prescribe timelines for the implementation of accountability mechanisms   Defining timelines to complete a given task, as governed by an act, agency or process, would result in better implementation of accountability mechanisms. A prescribed timeline will not only reduce unnecessary delays in implementation, but will also provide citizens with the power to question delays.

Current Progress   There are no prescribed timelines for most existing accountability mechanisms, resulting in unending delays in holding officials accountable. For example, the process to impeach judges for misconduct continues for years, as there is no prescribed time period for initiating a motion in Parliament, for conducting the inquiry, for discussing the findings in Parliament and reaching a consensus. Corrupt officers freely continue to work and enjoy their regular monetary benefits, while their cases drag on for years with the investigating and law enforcement agencies. In the Judiciary, the lengthy process for the selection of judges, with no deadline for filling vacancies, results in delays in appointments to important positions.

Realizing the criticality of a fixed timeline, some newer mechanisms have introduced this aspect. The RTI Act, for instance, makes it mandatory for Public Information Officers to reply to a query within 30 days. The Delivery Monitoring Unit (DMU) ensures that the Ministries submit their progress reports at the end of each quarter to the Prime Minister's Office. The proposed Judicial Standards and Accountability Bill recommends that the scrutiny panel that will look into complaints against judges submit its reports in three months. One of the key success indicators for all Ministries and Departments in the Results Framework Documents for the year 2010–11 is the timely implementation of Citizen's Charters. The RFDs have mandated that all Departments create a Citizens Charter and grievance redressal mechanism within a year. Introducing similar time-bound indicators as part of the performance assessment of all accountability mechanisms will ensure timely implementation by all Ministries and Departments.

Punitive action in cases of non-adherence to timelines, like monetary fines, lower performance scores, or simply having the delay questioned by higher authorities or by citizens will make this initiative even more effective.

Current Progress Rating

 Partial progress, since initiatives undertaken are currently limited to few government departments, few schemes or few geographic locations

Penalties

Introduce penalties as a part of accountability mechanisms and public schemes   As early as 500 BC, the guide on administration and accountability in the Mauryan Age, the *Arthashastra*, emphasized the importance of penalties for driving accountability. Imposing a penalty for non-compliance or poor performance is necessary to push officials out of their comfort zone, to share information and answer citizens' concerns. Lack of any penalty or liability enforcement limits the success of accountability mechanisms.

Current Progress   Currently, one of the few mechanisms that has an in-built penalty system is the RTI Act. Public Information Officers (PIOs) who fail to provide requested information within a stipulated time period are subjected to a monetary fine of Rs 250 per day of delay, capped at a maximum penalty of Rs 25,000. For example, the PIO of a Municipal Corporation was asked to pay a fine of Rs 25,000 for delaying the requested information for more than 100 days, for the reason that he was too busy to answer the request (*The Economic Times,* 14 January 2011). The PIOs, however, are sometimes casual about implementing RTI requests, since fines are not strictly imposed in all cases. An independent survey conducted by a CSO, Public Cause Research Foundation, in 2009–10 showed that of the 76,813 RTI requests analysed by them, there was a delay in providing information in more than 77 per cent of the cases; only 3.17 per cent of

Global Example

- **USA:** Public officials in Florida are required to pay attorney fees (penalty) to the citizen (plaintiff) if they refuse to provide access to public records requested by the plaintiff, as mandated by the Freedom of Information Act (Central Michigan University)

these violations were actually penalized (*Mint*, 14 January 2011). Studies indicate that even if the Information Commissioner imposes fines on PIOs, the money is recovered from very few. For example, between 2005 and 2009, only 39 per cent of the RTI fines imposed by the Central Information Commissioners have been recovered (Viju 2009). In 2008, only 1 per cent of the RTI fines imposed on the PIOs by a particular State's Information Commissioner were recovered (*Economic and Political Weekly*, 28 November 2009). If the penalty clause was more effective, Public Information Officers would not continue to breach RTI timelines without fear of reprisal.

This system of penalty should be extended to more mechanisms and public schemes. The Delhi government has initiated a penalty system to improve governance delivery. They introduced a scheme in April 2010 to penalize government officers for any delays in providing public services. They also fixed a time frame for the processes involved in major services, like the issue of ration cards and driving licenses. A ration card, for example, has to be issued within 45 days. If the officials do not adhere to the prescribed time period, they will have to bear a penalty. The penalty will range from Rs 10 to Rs 200 for every day of delay, depending on the officer's level of responsibility (Banerjee 2009). The penalty system may result in a more responsive and accountable public service delivery process.

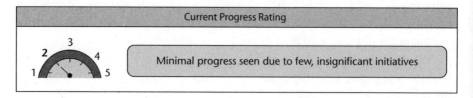

The current progress on the Implementation Initiative is summarized in Figure 8.7.

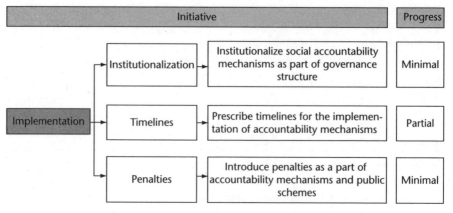

Figure 8.7   Implementation Initiative—Summary

::: Initiative 4—Infrastructure

Personnel

Provide adequate personnel to accountability agencies Agencies responsible for ensuring accountability need to be adequately staffed with competent personnel. The chronic shortage of staff impacts the effective functioning of all these agencies. The Judiciary is a classic example: a large number of vacancies among judges resulted in a backlog of around 30 million cases at the end of 2009 (Rahman 2009). Other institutions like the Police and mechanisms like the RTI also suffer due to poor staff strength. They urgently need to be provided with additional competent staff to ensure effective implementation.

Current Progress The number of judges for every million people in India is only 12–13, compared to 107 judges in the USA and 51 judges in the UK (Transparency International 2007). The Law Commission noted this low ratio of judges way back in 1987 and recommended immediate action to increase the ratio to 50 judges per million people, and to 100 judges per million people by 2000. This recommendation was reiterated by the Parliamentary Standing Committee in 2002 (PRS Legislative Research 2009). The government has also been periodically reminding the Chief Justices of all High Courts to initiate the process of filling up vacancies for judges. In 2009, a 'Roadmap to Judicial Reforms' was prepared by the Law minister, where it was proposed to use the services of retired judges to improve judicial infrastructure and reduce the backlog of cases (*Business Standard*, 20 July 2009). No significant initiative, however, has been undertaken to improve this situation.

Similarly, an Information Commissioner wrote a letter to the Prime Minister drawing attention to the inadequate staff implementing the RTI, resulting in a backlog of pending appeals. The letter stated that if adequate staff were provided, the average annual disposal of cases per Commissioner could be over 4,000, compared to less than 2,000 today (*Outlook*, 24 February 2009). Overall, inadequate staff has compromised the functioning of key government departments, institutions and mechanisms that are responsible for driving accountability.

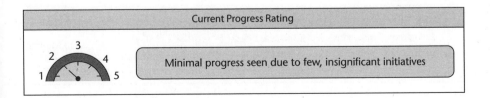

Current Progress Rating
Minimal progress seen due to few, insignificant initiatives

Provide training to improve the effectiveness of personnel Training is a critical component of human resource development, to upgrade knowledge and to build the correct attitude to deal with the many implementation challenges in the government. Functional training should be provided to public officials to help them perform their jobs effectively and meet their targets. They should also be provided behavioural and attitudinal training, to help deal with their internal and external customers.

Providing public officials with intensive training on the usage of information technology is equally important to facilitate the implementation of e-governance initiatives. It is also important to lay strong emphasis on mid-career training for public officials. Successful completion of these training programmes should be made mandatory for promotions of public officials.

Current Progress Training infrastructure has been established to meet the functional training requirements of public officials. For example, the training division of the Department of Personnel and Training administers induction training to recruits of the civil services. States have established Administrative Training Institutes for government employees. Major public services like the Railways and Posts have national training institutes to induct officials. The Ministry of Home Affairs has introduced a scheme of modernization of state police forces to focus on capacity building. Although the training infrastructure is in place, the quality of training needs improvement. The Bureau of Police Research and Development highlights that the police training curriculum is not keeping pace with advancements in technology, instructors are not chosen on merit, and that the course material is rarely revised (Rao 2001).

Public officials involved in managing and administering accountability mechanisms like the Right to Information Act, Social Audit and Citizen's Charter are also provided with short-term training courses to function effectively. The Department of Administrative Reforms and Public Grievances organized two-day workshops to support Ministries with the designing and implementing of their Citizens Charters. Some state governments have also made a concerted effort to train and educate their officials in the usage and application of

Global Example
• **USA:** The Office of Information and Privacy recommended a year's training for the Freedom of Information staff to learn their job (Holsen 2007)
• **India:** An Information Commissioner managed to dispose c. 500 RTI appeals every month by recruiting computer-savvy volunteers (Viju 2009)

these accountability mechanisms. In Andhra Pradesh, for instance, district-level officers and village administrative officers were extensively trained to conduct Social Audits, and this helped in gaining their support and buy-in for the exercise. Similarly, the State Institute of Rural Development in Himachal Pradesh has proposed to conduct 380 training programmes in the year 2010–11, to train the social audit committees involved in conducting the audit exercise.

There is not enough effort to promote the behavioural training that is of key importance in the effective implementation of public schemes. A 2009 study commissioned by the Department of Personnel and Training on the implementation of the RTI Act found that about 55 per cent of Public Information Officers had not been provided training in the RTI. Moreover, the training was restricted to informing the PIOs about the basic provisions of the RTI Act. Key aspects related to behavioural training, such as managing citizens' demands, expectations and service quality levels, were not addressed (http://rti.gov.in/). Overall, a significant amount of effort is still needed to train our public officials to meet the challenge of modern-day governance in an emerging economy.

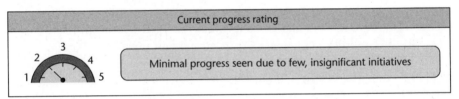

Current progress rating

Minimal progress seen due to few, insignificant initiatives

Technology

Leverage information technology and telecommunications to facilitate the enforcement of accountability   The incredible power of information technology should be leveraged to set up platforms that facilitate the easy usage of accountability mechanisms. Online platforms should be provided to complain against corrupt officials or seek redressal for poor service delivery. Technology should also be used to provide citizens with an accessible platform to provide feedback and opinions. The government should also leverage technology to digitize transactions with citizens—online applications for licenses, permits and e-procurement—to reduce incidences of administrative graft.

Current Progress   The Central Bureau of Investigation (CBI) effectively leveraged telecommunication technology to create awareness about their anti-corruption campaign in 2008. Mobile subscribers of all major telecom service providers were sent text messages, urging them to inform the CBI if they came across any Central, State government, or PSU officer demanding a bribe for any official work (*Outlook,* 11 November 2008). As an outcome

Global Example

- **Philippines:** A National Police initiative allows citizens to complain against corrupt police by sending a text message to a central number (Alampay 2003)
- **USA:**
  - The US Government introduced a website, www.regulations.gov, to seek public comments on upcoming policies and federal rule-making (Sternstein 2009)
  - The White House has launched a blog to discuss the Obama administration's open government initiative (Hoover 2009)
- **San Francisco:** Citizens can register themselves for voting by sending an SMS (www.ega.ee 2005)
- **New Zealand:** Proposal to introduce online voting for disabled voters and voters living abroad (www.edemocracy-forum.com 2008)
- **Estonia:** Citizens could vote online for the 2007 general elections, and 3.5 per cent of the population exercised this option (www.edemocracy-forum.com 2009)

of this campaign, the number of complaints received by the CBI increased. The CBI successfully managed to trap 40 corrupt officials in October 2008, based on these complaints (*The Times of India*, 12 November 2008). The Central Vigilance Commission also sent out SMS to citizens, informing them about their toll free number (1800–11–0180), where citizens could call to lodge complaints against corrupt central government officials. The CVC also introduced a website in December 2010 called Vig-Eye, which allows citizens to file complaints against officials. Citizens can also upload audio and video clips on the website to expose acts of misconduct.

Besides these monitoring agencies, there are other complaint and grievance redressal platforms such as the President's helpline (www.helpline.rb.nic.in) and the portal for public grievances (www.pgportal.gov.in), managed by the Department of Administrative Reforms and Public Grievances. These portals allow citizens to lodge complaints and track status. Citizens can also file a complaint on the RTI website (rti.india.gov.in) if they have not received the information they requested through RTI on time.

Ministries seeking citizens' views on proposed laws publish the draft bills on their websites, inviting citizens' comments. For instance, in March 2011, the Ministry of Environment and Forests published the Draft Animal Welfare Act 2011 on their website and invited public comments. The Department of Information Technology made available the Draft Electronic Service Delivery Bill online for comments.

Overall, the government has initiated several technology-based initiatives to facilitate the process of delivering accountability. These initiatives are restricted to a few departments currently. They should be applied to all institutions, departments and accountability mechanisms gradually, to realize the tremendous potential that information technology and telecommunications can have in improving governance.

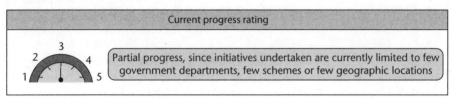

The current progress on the Infrastructure Initiative is summarized in Figure 8.8.

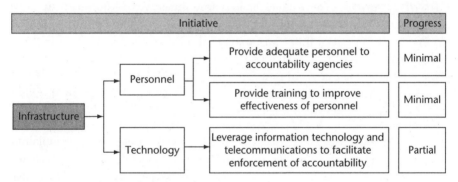

Figure 8.8   Infrastructure Initiative—Summary

⠿ Initiative 5—Independence

Authority to Agencies

Provide adequate authority to monitoring agencies   In India, monitoring agencies like the Election Commission, the CVC and the CBI have not been provided with adequate independence to conduct investigations. Recommendations made by these agencies are only advisory in nature, resulting in a lack of action based on their reports. These monitoring agencies should be provided with adequate authority to operate without any political interference. They should be given the power to conduct investigations on their own, without seeking prior permission. They need to be granted the right to follow up on the disciplinary action recommended by them, to ensure that action is taken based on their reports.

Global Example
• **Hong Kong and Singapore:** Hong Kong's Independent Commission Against Corruption (ICAC) and Singapore's Corruption Practices Investigation Bureau (CPIB) have powers to undertake investigations on their own and freeze the assets of the guilty (Meagher and Voland 2006) • **Thailand:** The Election Commission can seize cash and property of candidates who violate the campaign finance laws (Nelson 2003) • **New Zealand:** The Controller and Auditor General has the power to impose a surcharge on officials involved in fraud, negligence, error or improper use (Misra 2009) • **USA:** The Auditor General can institute action in any federal court for not obeying his authority (Misra 2009)

Current Progress   There have been a few initiatives undertaken by state governments to empower investigating agencies with some punitive authority. The Government of Bihar has enacted the Bihar Special Courts Act 2010, which provides its State Vigilance Department the power to confiscate the property of accused government officials. Under the Act, if vigilance officers are convinced that the government official owns assets in excess of known sources of income, they can file a case in the special courts, which are formed specifically under the Act for speedy trials. While the court is deciding if the official is guilty of misappropriation, the property of the allegedly corrupt official is confiscated. If the official is proven guilty, the confiscated property is used for public services such as building schools or health clinics. If the officer is not guilty, the property is returned with compound interest on its value at the time of its seizure (Singh 2010; Vigilance Department–Government of Bihar).

This initiative received the full support of the Chief Minister, resulting in its successful implementation. The vigilance department has lined up 19 cases to confiscate property valued at Rs 21 crore before the special courts, and is reviewing another 87 cases for possible confiscation of assets (*IBNlive*, 4 February 2011). This is a successful case study in instilling fear of reprisal in the minds of errant officials by equipping the vigilance departments with authority to take action against them. One public official in a district in Bihar was so terrified that he surrendered cash earned through corrupt practices. It is heartening to see states like Madhya Pradesh follow the success of Bihar in planning to implement this initiative. The Karnataka State Government also granted powers to its state Lokayukta to initiate cases against senior officials involved in misgovernance on their own, without any prior citizen's complaint (*Deccan Herald*, 9 July 2010).

Many more such initiatives are required at the national level to bring about a substantial difference in accountability and governance.

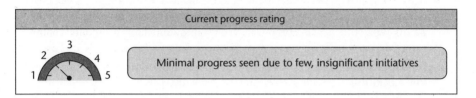

Current progress rating

Minimal progress seen due to few, insignificant initiatives

Decentralization

Strengthen local authorities by delegating power   Authority should be devolved to local governments to take decisions regarding the implementation of public schemes. This will bring citizens closer to the decision-making authorities, enabling greater transparency and trust. This also facilitates greater community participation, as local officials are more accessible to citizens. The closer the local governments are to local problems, the greater impact they have on their constituencies.

Current Progress   Decentralization in India has gone through several stages of evolution since independence. The concept of Panchayati Raj Institutions was carried forward to independent India from the British Raj, although their powers and role in the governance structure was limited and not clearly defined. The Constitution provided decentralization with a new lease of life by formulating the 73rd and 74th Constitutional Amendments in 1993, which devolved significant power to the local governments in rural and urban areas, respectively.

In the rural areas, the 73rd amendment gave constitutional sanctity to Panchayati Raj Institutions (PRIs) and mandated the creation of a three-tier local government structure at the district, block and village levels. The scope, details and pace of implementation were not defined by the regulation, but left to the discretion of state governments. As a result, there is a fair amount of variation in the design, scope and scale of devolution of power across the states. *Political* decentralization has been successful with the setting up of three-tier local government structures across states. *Administrative* decentralization across states has been less successful, as there is no clear demarcation of roles and responsibilities between the three tiers. *Fiscal* decentralization is minimal in all states, and local governments continue to depend on the states for finances, limiting their ability to act on plans developed jointly by the citizens and local authorities.

Global Example

- **Brazil (Porto Alegre):** Municipalities have considerable autonomy over their revenues (local taxes, tariffs and federal transfers) and expenditures. Participatory budgeting is being practised, and budget allocations for public welfare works are made after budgetary debates are held with city residents (www. sasanet.org 2003)
- **India (Kerala):** The Kerala Government launched The People's Campaign for Decentralized Planning in 1996, where around 1,200 local governments were given powers of decision-making and a significant scale of financial devolution (Chaudhuri 2005)

The government is introducing schemes to incentivize states to further decentralize. For instance, the Panchayat Empowerment and Accountability Scheme incentivizes the states to devolve power to the Panchayats. Under the scheme, the Ministry of Panchayati Raj ranks the states based on their performance on decentralization. The top performing states and union territories receive monetary awards as an incentive for higher decentralization (www.planningcommission.nic.in 2006). During the year 2006–07, Rs 80 million was released to the top 10 ranking states, and Rs 20 million was offered to the top six union territories under the scheme (Press Information Bureau, 22 August 2007).

Efforts are also being made to provide a greater role to PRIs in managing schemes that are to be implemented at the local level. The MGNREGA scheme is the first to have legally declared PRIs as 'the principal authorities for planning and implementation' of the scheme and assigned them a wide role, right from the registering of workers up to monitoring and social auditing (National Social Watch 2010). The President, in her address to both Houses of Parliament on 4 June 2009, also provided some directives for assigning a definite and important role to the PRIs to manage programmes like the Nutrition Delivery Programme and the Rural Water Supply Programme (*IBNLive*, 4 June 2009). The Panchayats, however, have to be supported with adequate infrastructure to be able to implement these programmes in an effective manner.

In urban areas, the 74th Constitutional Amendment led to decentralization by forming a two-tier structure of Ward Committees under the Municipal Corporation. Each Ward Committee comprises of an elected councillor of the ward, along with residents of wards as members. To fully realize the intent of the 74th Amendment, a Community Participation Law proposed the creation of a third level of governance, where each Ward is further divided into Area Sabhas. This will result in greater devolution and greater participation of citizens with the local government. The enactment of this Community Participation Law is still pending, as several states still have to pass this law and incorporate the relevant provisions into the existing laws (www.urbanindia.nic.in 2010). Overall, reasonable progress has been made in the decentralization of local governments, but administrative and fiscal devolution of powers still remains a 'work-in-progress'.

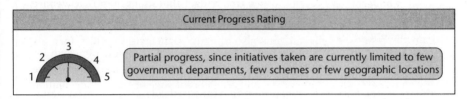

The current progress on the Independence Initiative is summarized in Figure 8.9.

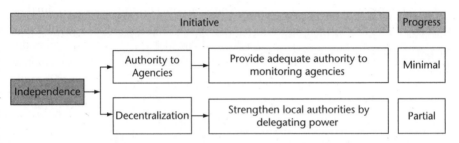

Figure 8.9   Independence Initiative—Summary

⠸ Initiative 6—Involvement

The five initiatives set out earlier revolved around action points for the government. The sixth and final initiative, Involvement, gravitates around the actions that citizens, the media and CSOs must take to increase accountability. This is undoubtedly the most important of all the Initiatives, and probably the most neglected one. Only with this continuous 'Involvement' will the current equilibrium of poor accountability finally reach a tipping point, paving the way for a higher quality of governance to be ultimately established.

Policy Formulation

Participate in policy formulation   Citizens and CSOs should proactively participate in the process of public policy formulation to ensure that pragmatism and on-the-ground realities are factored from inception. Integrating public opinion into the policy crafting process strengthens citizens' trust in the government, allows the government to tap into a wider base of perspectives, and increases the overall transparency and robustness of the political process.

Current Progress   A few CSOs are quite actively engaged in the process of policy formulation. CSOs like PRS Legislative Research, Democracy Connect, and think-tanks like the Centre for Policy Research provide parliamentarians with extensive research and supporting data on bills to be discussed in the Parliament, in order to augment the analytical capacity of the MPs. They also provide MPs with a broader view on bills under discussion by presenting expert opinions and stakeholder feed-back on the proposed bills. Citizens also directly participate in policy formulation by voicing their concerns and sharing their opinions about the bills online, through email or on the websites of the Ministries. For example, in July 2008, the Ministry of Environment and Forests invited public opinion on a draft bill of the Coastal Manage-ment Zone (CMZ), to understand the issues and concerns of stakeholders impacted by the bill. Many objections were raised and modifications suggested by fishermen, coastal communities and environmental activists. The stakeholders felt that the Bill was inadequate to control industrialization on coastlines, or to address issues like the livelihood rights of the fishing community. These objections were then examined in detail by the Ministry, following which the draft CMZ notification was rejected (*The Hindu*, 18 June 2010).

Apart from advocating changes in the bills proposed and debated in the Parliament, citizens and CSOs also put pressure on the government to introduce and endorse bills that would significantly improve governance and accountability in India. The advo-cacy efforts spearheaded by a CSO called Mazdoor Kisan Shakti Sangathan (MKSS) is truly one of the best examples of how persistent external pressure can result in fruitful action. In 1994, MKSS initiated a movement to get a legislation introduced in Rajasthan that would provide easy access to government records on financial expen-diture. In 1995, the Chief Minister announced that they would introduce such a law, but no subsequent action was taken. MKSS then conducted a series of protests to put pressure on the government to enact the law. As these demonstrations gained momentum, the government issued an order providing access to documents on local development expenditure. This, however, proved to be only an eyewash. The CSOs were not allowed to obtain photocopies of the documents they were inspecting, and therefore could not utilize the information to question the concerned authorities. Once again MKSS conducted demonstrations, this time joined by more citizens and activist groups. The opposition party promised to enact the Right to Information Act if they came to power in the state elections of 1998. Following their victory in the election, they formed a committee—which included MKSS members—to prepare a draft of the bill. After consultations with many stakeholders, the draft bill was pre-pared and eventually enacted into law in Rajasthan on 26 January 2001.

The CSOs involved in advocating for policy formulation are few in number, since understanding and analysing public policies is a difficult and tedious task. Substantially more involvement is needed from ordinary citizens to improve the process of participative policy formulation.

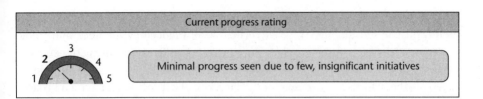

Participate in budget formulation   Citizens and CSOs should participate in the budget formulation process to directionally influence government expenditures, allowing them to reflect the priorities of society. They should evaluate budgetary allocations to assess if they meet the proposed commitments of the government, and the needs of the poor and underprivileged sections of society. They can then advocate for changes in fund allocations in the interest of the general public.

Current Progress   Over the past decade, CSOs have gradually become more involved in advocacy activities aimed at influencing public spending. CSOs have analysed budgetary allocations from the perspective of the poor and the marginalized, and advocated for a higher share of allocations for them. A Gujarat-based CSO, DISHA, analysed state expenditure patterns and found that government spending on the well-being of tribal groups was well below the 15 per cent level mandated by law. Sustained advocacy efforts, including marches and demonstrations, pressed the government to increase their allocations as a percentage of total expenditures. More significantly, implementation of the budget improved dramatically, by pressuring local governments to ensure that resources for local development were used for that purpose (Overseas Development Institute 2007). Similarly Janaagraha, a CSO in Bangalore, encouraged citizens from various wards to provide their suggestions regarding budgetary allocations towards infrastructure planning, like the maintenance of roads, footpaths, sidewalks and drains. The Bangalore government incorporated these suggestions in the budget, committing Rs 100.79 million, or 20 per cent of the total budget to these suggestions (Clay 2007).

Several budget-focused CSOs like the Centre for Budget and Policy Studies, Centre for Budget and Governance Accountability, and the Budget Analysis Rajasthan Centre increase public literacy about budgets and build citizens' capability to engage in Participatory Budget sessions with local governments. Participatory Budgets are platforms where citizens deliberate, prioritize and negotiate budgetary allocations with the local government authorities. Through this platform, citizens and CSOs have managed to advocate and modify funds allocation based on their suggestions. For example, the Participatory Budgeting initiated by the Pune Municipal Corporation (PMC) in 2005 generated a positive response from the citizens. In the 2007–08 PMC budget, about 575 citizens' suggestions, adding up to Rs 176 million of budgetary allocation, were included in the budget (Centre for Environment Education).

The CSOs have been reasonably successful in building the ordinary citizen's capacity to participate in budget development in certain regions and cities. This work needs to broaden and deepen, so that more citizens become aware of this process and increase their involvement in it.

Current progress rating
Partial progress, since initiatives undertaken are currently limited to few government departments, few schemes or few geographic locations

Performance Evaluation

Track public expenditure   Leakages in public expenditure are an indication of both system's inefficiency and systemic corruption. This results in the bottom 20 per cent of the poorest people receiving only 10 per cent of the subsidies meant for them (CUTS International). This makes the participation of citizens and CSOs critical in tracking the flow and utilization of funds. Citizens and CSOs should monitor the flow of funds from the government to the citizens, to determine what proportion of the allocated funds actually reaches the beneficiaries.

Current Progress   Civil society organizations have actively taken up public expenditure tracking as a part of the overall objective of ensuring accountability and transparency. To facilitate public expenditure monitoring, CSOs have been insisting that the government release statements of budgets and records of expenses incurred by them. For instance, a public campaign called Public Record of Operations and Finance (PROOF) began in 2002 in Bangalore, to persuade the city government to release quarterly public statements on its financial performance, comparing revenues and expenditures with the original budgets. With the help of this information, CSOs have successfully deployed various tools such as Social Audits and Public Expenditure Tracking Surveys (PETS) to carefully monitor the flow of public funds under specific programmes. They have managed to identify delays in the transfer of monetary and non-monetary benefits, leakage rates and general inefficiencies in public spending. For example, a social audit of the MGNREGA scheme was conducted in one district of Bihar with the support of Jan Jagaran Abhiyan, a CSO. Two thousand villagers participated in this exercise along with the panel of public officials. The public hearings and inspection of panchayat records exposed the siphoning of funds through fake muster rolls, bills and vouchers. The panchayat records showed that 76 per cent of the 1,710 job holders registered on the muster did not get even one day of work in the year 2008–09 (www.jjabihar. org 2009).

In another example, Consumer Unity and Trust Society, a CSO based in Rajasthan, undertook PETS to evaluate the implementation of the Mid-Day Meal Scheme in 211 schools in a district of Rajasthan. PETS was used to gather information on budget allocations and expenditure. They tracked the release of funds and food grains across the four tiers of the governance structure (state, district, block and village), along with the timeliness and efficiency of such releases. The survey highlighted gross inefficiencies in implementation, such as unutilized food grains, delays, poor quality, and poor cooking and storage infrastructure (www.sasanet.org 2007).

Citizens are also using the RTI to track public expenditure and highlight inefficiencies. The RTI helped a social activist to expose misappropriation of Rs 12.5 million in the Sampoorna Gram Rozgar Yojana (SGRY) scheme, which was launched to provide employment and food security to rural areas. The activist did not receive the monetary benefits he was entitled to under the scheme. He filed an RTI application with the Ministry of Panchayat and Rural Development of the state, seeking information regarding fund allocations for SGRY. A few months later, the social activist had received only partial information. A scrutiny conducted thereafter revealed a number of discrepancies in the purported list of beneficiaries; some names on the list had not received any benefit at all. The probe, using the RTI and social scrutiny, successfully exposed the misappropriation of funds (Public Cause Research Foundation 2009).

While this process of closely examining public expenditure has begun, it needs to gain substantial momentum so that public officials are always under the watchful eyes of citizens.

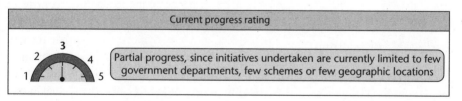

Current progress rating

Partial progress, since initiatives undertaken are currently limited to few government departments, few schemes or few geographic locations

Evaluate the quality of public services   While tracking expenditure improves transparency and legitimacy in the utilization of funds, it is equally important to evaluate the qualitative aspect of public services, such as efficiency and responsiveness. Citizens and CSOs should compare the quality of the service they experience at any public office with the quality of service promised by the government. The level of satisfaction of the citizens should then be communicated to these public agencies so they can take corrective steps to improve quality and efficiency.

Current Progress   A few CSOs have embarked on initiatives to monitor the quality of public services and provide this feedback to public officials. CSOs like Parivartan, MKSS, CUTS and the Public Affairs Centre conduct surveys in different parts of the country to gather citizens' feedback on the performance of public agencies. The findings of these surveys are widely publicized using the media, and through workshops and seminars. The resultant public pressure compels government agencies to take corrective action. A Hyderabad-based CSO called Centre for Good Governance conducted a pilot study to assess the performance of two primary health centers in Visakhapatnam and developed performance scorecards. The users of these primary health centers arrived at a list of indicators to measure the quality of service delivery. The users' community was then asked to rate these indicators on a scale of 0–100, based on their perception. Factors like staff behaviour, infrastructure, support services and low awareness of service entitlements were the key factors that undermined the quality of service delivery the most. These results were then shared with the service providers and action plans were prepared with defined responsibilities and timelines.

It is difficult for CSOs to conduct such audits on an ongoing basis due to the lack of citizens' awareness and the scarce resources at their disposal. CSOs need the active support of citizens to build institutional capacity in this area.

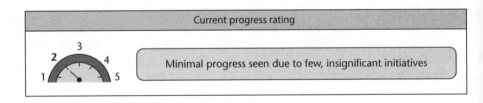

Current progress rating

Minimal progress seen due to few, insignificant initiatives

Redressal Enforcement

Complain against poor delivery of public services   Citizens often resort to bribing government officials to obtain public services, due to the absence of complaint channels against errant officials. Now, with the redressal mechanisms introduced by the government, citizens should raise their voices against the poor delivery of public services.

Current Progress   Many public service agencies have leveraged technology to provide easy access to grievance redressal mechanisms to citizens. Citizens are actively using these portals and mobile-messaging facilities to demand better quality of public services. For example, Mumbai's Central Railway train service started an SMS campaign in 2009, where citizens could provide their feedback, suggestions and complaints about the railways by sending an SMS. Thousands of citizens used this provision and sent messages to the railways demanding better services. To their surprise, a lot of their complaints were answered promptly by the railway authorities. For example, a commuter on the Central Railway used this service to complain that the seats in the first-class compartments of certain trains were uncomfortable. Incredibly, in a couple of weeks, he received a call from railway officials informing him that they had addressed his complaint by replacing the old seats. He was even invited to visit the workshop to check the new seats (Verma 2009).

Citizens are also actively using the President's helpline (http://helpline.rb.nic.in) to file petitions regarding their grievances. The helpline receives an average of 60 petitions daily, and has received 34,376 complaints since its inception in July 2009. Citizens complain about diverse issues like difficulties in obtaining passports, delay in receiving pensions, or errant postal services (*The Hindu*, February 5 2011). Similarly, citizens actively complain about civic issues to the Municipal Corporation of Mumbai by dialling their helpline 1916, or filing complaints online on their website (mcgm.gov.in). The civic body receives close to 150–200 complaints daily from citizens, indicating the active participation of citizens in demanding better civic amenities. Praja, a CSO based in Mumbai, played a key role in providing citizens with this interface to connect with their civic administrators (www.praja.org). Clearly, if the government wants to work towards improving the delivery of public services, there are several avenues they can use.

The active usage of these helplines and complaint mechanisms by citizens indicates the success of these mechanisms. The fact that citizens do not require technical expertise or intense subject knowledge, as in the case of policy formulation or budget advocacy, makes this initiative widely successful. Greater awareness and access to the Internet will further drive the usage of these complaint mechanisms by citizens.

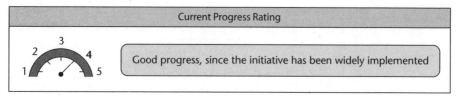

Current Progress Rating

Good progress, since the initiative has been widely implemented

Complain against corrupt officials   Citizens should escalate matters of misgovernance by filing complaints with the CVC, the CBI, or Lokayukta, and seek legal recourse against the guilty. Citizens can also file a Public Interest Litigation in a court of law if an issue affects the public interest at large.

Current Progress   Many citizens have reported corrupt officers by complaining to the CVC and the Lokayuktas. For example, a citizen of Karnataka had filed a complaint against a police officer who had demanded a bribe of Rs 1 lakh to return his passport. The Lokayukta investigated the complaint and caught the police officer while he was accepting the bribe (*The Hindu*, 8 March 2011). During a visit to the Government Community Hospital, the Karnataka State Lokayukta chief found the hospital to be in perfect condition. The citizens informed him that this clean-up had been done just two days prior to his visit, that the doctors hardly visited the hospital, and that medicines were not available when needed. Acting on the people's complaints, the Lokayukta Chief warned the district health officer of stern action if he failed to take corrective measures (*Deccan Herald*, 29 January 2006).

Citizens have started exercising their power to bring the corrupt to justice. An increase in awareness about these complaint mechanisms will bring greater power to the force that can truly keep governance honest.

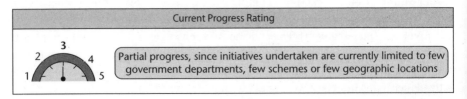

The current progress on the Involvement Initiative is summarized in Figure 8.10.

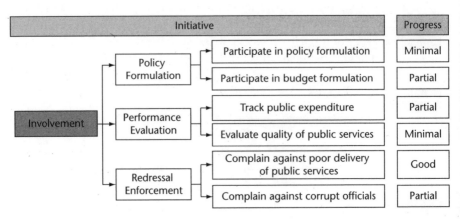

Figure 8.10   Involvement Initiative—Summary

We have now completed an exhaustive and comprehensive review of the Six Initiatives that must be undertaken to improve accountability in India. Figure 8.11 provides a summary of these Initiatives.

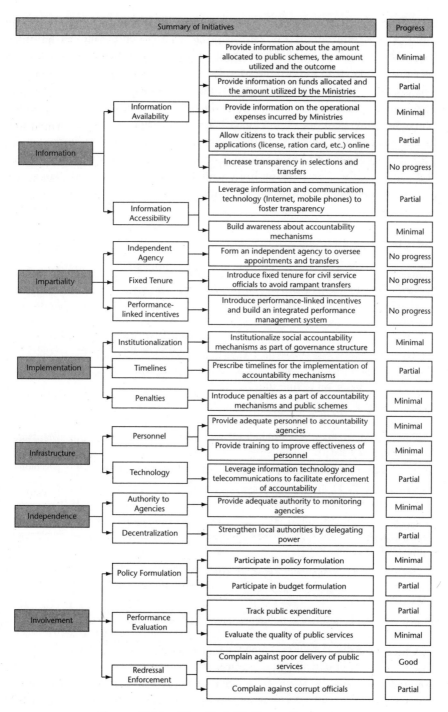

Summary of Initiatives			Progress
Information	Information Availability	Provide information about the amount allocated to public schemes, the amount utilized and the outcome	Minimal
		Provide information on funds allocated and the amount utilized by the Ministries	Partial
		Provide information on the operational expenses incurred by Ministries	Minimal
		Allow citizens to track their public services applications (license, ration card, etc.) online	Partial
		Increase transparency in selections and transfers	No progress
	Information Accessibility	Leverage information and communication technology (Internet, mobile phones) to foster transparency	Partial
		Build awareness about accountability mechanisms	Minimal
Impartiality	Independent Agency	Form an independent agency to oversee appointments and transfers	No progress
	Fixed Tenure	Introduce fixed tenure for civil service officials to avoid rampant transfers	No progress
	Performance-linked incentives	Introduce performance-linked incentives and build an integrated performance management system	No progress
Implementation	Institutionalization	Institutionalize social accountability mechanisms as part of governance structure	Minimal
	Timelines	Prescribe timelines for the implementation of accountability mechanisms	Partial
	Penalties	Introduce penalties as a part of accountability mechanisms and public schemes	Minimal
Infrastructure	Personnel	Provide adequate personnel to accountability agencies	Minimal
		Provide training to improve effectiveness of personnel	Minimal
	Technology	Leverage information technology and telecommunications to facilitate enforcement of accountability	Partial
Independence	Authority to Agencies	Provide adequate authority to monitoring agencies	Minimal
	Decentralization	Strengthen local authorities by delegating power	Partial
Involvement	Policy Formulation	Participate in policy formulation	Minimal
		Participate in budget formulation	Partial
	Performance Evaluation	Track public expenditure	Partial
		Evaluate the quality of public services	Minimal
	Redressal Enforcement	Complain against poor delivery of public services	Good
		Complain against corrupt officials	Partial

Figure 8.11 The Six Initiatives—Summary

As is visible from the subjective progress ratings that we have assigned, in most cases only minimal or partial progress has been achieved. A task of mammoth proportions awaits both the government and the citizens. While the government has set in motion the wheel of reforms in many of the six improvement areas, it needs a more rigorous approach to drive this process faster. Citizens must proactively participate in the process of improving the quality of governance and accountability. The CSOs have already taken an active role over the last two decades, in building their capacity and driving citizens to demand action from the government. The next chapter stresses the growing importance of CSOs in transforming accountability, and highlights the role that citizens and businesses can play in supporting these CSOs.

References

Alampay, Erwin. 2003. 'Reporting Police Wrongdoing via SMS in the Philippines'. Available at www.egov4dev.org (accessed on 2 July 2009).

'Annual Report 2008–09'. 2009. *Ministry of Civil Aviation—Government of India*. Available at www.civilaviation.nic.in/ (accessed on 4 November 2009).

'Annual Report 2008–09'. 2009. Ministry of Home Affairs—Government of India. Available at www.mha.nic.in/ (accessed on 4 November 2009).

'Anti-Corruption Initiative for Asia and the Pacific'. 2004. *ADB/OECD*. Available at www.oecd.org (accessed on 22 June 2009).

'Application shows that RTI law is under-publicized'. 2008. *Mint*, 23 April.

'Background papers: Meeting of The National e-Governance Advisory Group'. 2010. Ministry of Information and Technology. Available at http://www.mit.gov.in/ (accessed on 7 December 2010).

'Bajpe constable caught accepting Rs. 1 lakh'. 2011. *The Hindu*, 8 March.

Banerjee, Rumu. 2009. 'If driving license not issued in a day, babu to pay fine'. *The Times of India*, 16 December.

Bhatnagar, Subhash and Nitesh Vyas. 2001. 'Gyandoot: Community-Owned Rural Internet Kiosks'. *e-Government Case Studies—The World Bank*. Available at www.worldbank.org (accessed on 25 June 2009).

'Bill proposes to phase out manual distribution of govt services'. 2011. *Mint*, 11 March.

'Bribeless in Bihar'. 4 February 2011. Available at www.ibnlive.in.com (accessed on 1 March 2011).

'Budget monitoring and policy influence'. 2007. Overseas Development Institute, March. Available at www.internationalbudget.org (accessed on 15 December 2010).

Burns, John P. and Chau-Ching Shen. 2002. 'Country Reform Summary—China'. Available at http://www1.worldbank.org. (accessed on 8 December 2010).

'Case Study 3—Rajasthan, India: An Assessment of the Mid-Day Meal Scheme in Chittorgarh District'. 2007. *Social Accountability Series*. Available at www.sasanet.org (accessed on 16 April 2010).

'CBI's SMS campaign nets 40 corrupt babus'. 2008. *The Times of India*, 12 November.

'CBI's SMS campaign pays rich dividends'. 2008. *Outlook*, 11 November.

Chandavarkar, Pia. 2006. 'Now, RTI in school textbooks'. *The Indian Express*, 20 October.

Chaudhuri, S. 2005. 'Building democracy: The people's campaign for decentralized planning in Kerala'. The World Bank. Available at www.worldbank.org (accessed on 26 June 2009).

Chawla, Rajeev and Subhash Bhatnagar. 2001. 'Bhoomi: Online Delivery of Land Titles in Karnataka. India'. *e-Government Case Studies—The World Bank*. Available at www.worldbank.org (accessed on 25 June 2009).

'CIC imposes Rs 25,000 fine on MCD PIO for delay in giving info'. 2011. *The Economic Times*, 14 January.

'Citizen Selection Procedure (Nominee: Akhil Gogoi)'. RTI Awards 2009 Section-Public Cause Research Foundation. Available at www.pcrf.in (accessed on 6 January 2010).

Clay, Elizabeth. 2007. 'Community-led Participatory Budgeting in Bangalore'. Available at www.dspace.mit.edu (accessed on 15 December 2010).

Corrie, Priyasha. 2007. 'Providing an enabling environment for effective policing—The new Police Act'. Available at http://papers.ssrn.com/ (accessed on 25 January 2010).

'Country reports on judicial corruption (India and UK)'. 2007. *Global Corruption Report*. Available at www.transparency.org (accessed on 19 May 2009).

'Curb Wastage to Contribute 8.9% to National Income'. Memorandum to the Hon'ble Finance Minister for Budget 2004–05. Available at www.cuts-international.org (accessed on 27 January 2010).

'e-Lekha—A Stride towards a Core Accounting Solution'. Available at www.eindia.net.in (accessed on 4 November 2009).

'European Elections: 15% of Estonians voted by Internet'. 2009. Available at www.edemocracy-forum.com (accessed on 2 July 2009).

Fabry, Sandra. 2008. 'Transparency in Government Spending: An Idea who's Time Has Come for Florida'. Available at www.jamesmadison.org (accessed on 6 June 2009).

'Finance Accounts: 2007–08'. Available at www.cga.nic.in/ (accessed on 4 November 2009).

'Full text of President's address to Parliament'. 4 June 2009. Available at www.ibnlive.in.com (accessed on 23 January 2011).

'Government to introduce bill to protect bureaucracy from political interference'. 2009. *Business Standard*, 8 June.

'Half Yearly Progress Monitoring Report—Sarva Shiksha Abhiyan'. 2008. Available at www.ssa.nic.in (accessed on 23 November 2009).

Holsen, Sarah. 2007. 'Freedom of information in the U.K., U.S., and Canada'. *Information Management Journal*. Available at www.entrepreneur.com (accessed on 23 June 2009).

Hoover, Nicholas. 2009. 'White house launching transparency blog'. *Information Week*. Available at www.informationweek.com (accessed on 6 June 2009).

'Incentive system for govt staffers next year: Secy'. 2010. *The Economic Times*, 27 October.

'India's Citizen's Charters: A Decade of experience'. 2007. *Public Affairs Centre*. Available at www.partnershipfortransparency.info (accessed on 29 April 2010).

'Inputs for Delivery Monitoring Unit, as on 3/03/2010'. Available at http://rti.gov.in/ (accessed on 7 December 2010).

'Inside the govt, a certain degree of misunderstanding still persists'. 2010. *Mint*, 27 September.

'Jawaharlal Nehru National Urban Renewal Mission Monitoring Formats'. 2010. Available at www.urbanindia.nic.in (accessed on 30 January 2011).

'Lack of Staff Key Reason for CIC's Under-Performance'. 2009. *Outlook*, 24 February.

Lic, Gustavo Axel Radics. 2001. 'Cristal: A Tool for Transparent Government in Argentina'. e-Government Case Studies, The World Bank. Available at http://web.worldbank.org (accessed on 25 June 2009).

'Lokayukta may get suo motu power to investigate Government officers'. 2010. *Deccan Herald*, 9 July.

'Lokayukta orders suspension of two officials'. 2006. *Deccan Herald*, 29 January.

Malena, Carmen, Reiner Foster and Janmejay Singh. 2004. 'Social Accountability: An Introduction to the Concept and Emerging Practice'. *Social Development Papers*. Available at www.worldbank.org (accessed on 12 December 2008).

'Managing For Results'. 2009. Budget of the United States Government for fiscal year 2009. www.gpoaccess.gov/ (accessed on 4 November 2009).

Meagher, Patrick and Caryn Voland. 2006. 'Anticorruption Agencies (ACAs): Anticorruption Program Brief'. United States Agency for International Development. Available at www.usaid.gov (accessed on 24 June 2009).

'Members' Allowances'. 2007–08. MPs. Lords and Offices Section, UK Parliament. Available at www.parliament.uk/ (accessed on 19 June 2009).

Meskell, Darlene. 2009. 'Transparency in Government'. *Transparency and Open Government—Intergovernmental Solutions Newsletter.* Available at www.usaservices.gov (accessed on 6 June 2009).

Misra, Neelesh. 2009. 'Dude, where's my money?' Inspired India series, *Hindustan Times*, 16 July.

_____. 2009. 'Give muscle to this paper tiger'. Inspired India series, *Hindustan Times*, 24 July.

'Mobile services in Tartu-Estonia'. 2005. Available at www.ega.ee (accessed on 3 July 2009).

'Monitoring of Plan Scheme Expenditure–CPSMS an e-governance initiative'. Available at www.icisa.cag.gov.in (accessed on 2 November 2009).

National Social Watch. 2010. *Citizens' Report on Governance and Development 2010*. New Delhi: Sage Publications, pp. 114–16, 120–27.

'NCAER's report on devolution index'. 2007. Press Information Bureau. Available at www. pib.nic.in (accessed on 9 August 2011).

Nelson, Sue. 2003. 'Elections law enforcement—International Comparisons'. *Electoral Insight*. Available at www.elections.ca (accessed on 15 June 2009).

'New Zealand: e-Voting pilots for 2014–20'. 2008. Available at www.edemocracy-forum.com (accessed on 3 July 2009).

'Online Complaint Monitoring System (OCMS)'. Praja. Available at 216.197.119.113/artman/uploads/ocms_write-up.doc (accessed on 27 January 2010).

'OPEN: Seoul's Anticorruption Project'. 2000. *e-Government Case Studies—The World Bank.* Available at www.worldbank.org (accessed on 25 June 2009).

'Outcome Budget: 2008–09'. 2009. *Ministry of Steel—Government of India*. Available at http://steel.nic.in/ (accessed on 4 November 2009).

'Participatory Budgeting in Pune'. 2007. Centre for Environment Education. Available at http://government.wikia.com (accessed on 7 July 2009).

'Pending for 3 yrs, Civil Service law gets a push'. 2010. *Hindustan Times*, 7 June.

'Performance-related Pay Policies for Government Employees'. 2005. Available at www. oecd.org (accessed on 25 January 2010).

'Pitroda now sets sights on creating public information infrastructure'. 2010. *The Economic Times*, 22 July.

Porrua, Miguel and Jeffrey Rinne. 2001. 'Colombia's Government Portal'. *e-Government Case Studies—The World Bank*. Available at www.worldbank.org (accessed on 25 June 2009).

'Porto Alegre, Brazil: Participatory Approaches in Budgeting and Public Expenditure Management'. 2003. Available at www.sasanet.org (accessed on 15 June 2009).

'Pre-draft CRZ notification rejected'. 2010. *The Hindu*, 18 June.

'President's Helpline whirrs away'. 2011. *The Hindu*, 5 February.

Rahman, Shafi. 2009. 'Lords on Trial'. *India Today*, 7 September.

Rajagopal, Krishnadas. 2009. 'Want to stall husband's transfer? CIC says RTI Act helpless'. *The Indian Express*, 14 April.

Rao, Vijay Rama. 'Research Studies on Police and Prison Issues (1970–2007) Compendium, Report no. 120: Training Policemen of the Future (2001)'. Available at http://bprd.nic.in/. (accessed on 9 December 2010).

'Report of the Working Group on Democratic Decentralisation & PRIs'. 2006. Available at www.planningcommission.nic.in (accessed on 20 February 2011).

'The Right to Know'. 2009. *Economic and Political Weekly*, 28 November.

'Roadmap for judicial reforms soon: Moily'. 2009. *Business Standard*, 20 July.

'RTI in school curriculum, law courses soon'. 2010. *The Hindu*, 27 June.

'RTI penalties for delay in information are rarely imposed'. 2011. *Mint*, 14 January.

Saxena, Naresh and Dipa Singh Bagai. 2010. 'The Singapore Success Story'. UNDP. Available at http://www.scribd.com/doc/40966835/The-Singapore-Success-Story.

Singh, Santosh. 2010. 'MLAs lose fund; officer loses property as Nitish fights corruption'. *The Indian Express*, 13 December.

'Social Audit Report—Araria district'. 2009. Available at www.jjabihar.org/ (accessed on 9 December 2010).

Sternstein, Aliya. 2009. 'Regulations.gov wins praise for public outreach'. Available at www.nextgov.com (accessed on 27 January 2010).

Subrahmaniam, Vidya. 2009. 'NREGA audit: Bhilwara shows the way'. *The Hindu*, 17 October.

'Sukrity becomes the one millionth resident whose Aadhaar Number is generated'. 2011. UIDAI. Available at http://uidai.gov.in (accessed 10 March 2011).

'Sunshine Laws: How Are States Making Lawbreakers Pay?' AEJMC Archives–Central Michigan University. Available at https://ls2.cmich.edu/ (accessed 1 July 2009).

'Understanding the key issues and constraints in implementing the RTI Act'. 2009. Available at http://rti.gov.in (accessed 11 January 2010).

Verma, Kalpana. 2009. 'SMS feedback a hit, keeps railway officials busy'. *The Indian Express*, 23 June.

'Vital Stats: Pendency of Cases in Indian Courts'. 2009. Available at www.prsindia.org (accessed on 30 June 2009).

Viju, B. 2009. 'Pending cases biggest threat to RTI'. *The Times of India*, 9 March.

_____. 2009. 'RTI's penalised PIOs escape paying fines'. *The Times of India*, 7 September.

'Without Fear or Favour'. 2010. *The Telegraph*, 23 June.

'Yahoo! boosts Freedom of Information awareness'. 2006. eGov Monitor Weekly. Available at www.egovmonitor.com/ (accessed on 22 June 2009).

9 | The Five-Fold Path

What would life be if we had no courage to attempt anything?
Vincent Willem van Gogh, 1853–1890

The overwhelming feeling among many of us is a sense of helplessness with the state of our nation. Our inner voice echoes the words, *'no point complaining, nothing will change'*, and resonates with the *'chalta hai'* attitude, penetrating deep into the Indian soul. The prevalence of this thinking paralyses our hope for the future. We must seek to break free from this 'complacency trap'. Increased importance should be given to the engagement of citizens, with public officials in an organized manner. This 'demand-side' effort to improve governance is generally spearheaded by Civil Society Organizations (CSOs). These CSOs work towards strengthening accountability and governance by raising *awareness* among citizens, *assessing* government performance, and *advocating* new policies or suggesting modifications to the existing ones. The following section elaborates these three areas, so that the reader can develop a greater appreciation of the role that CSOs play in improving accountability.

::: Create Awareness

Civil Society Organizations strive to raise awareness among citizens, especially the marginalized and rural populations, about their rights and responsibilities. They undertake campaigns to inform citizens about the specific tools they can employ to demand accountability. They also inform citizens on the performance of the elected government, and the extent to which it has managed to deliver on the promises made to citizens. CSOs use many platforms to create this awareness among citizens:

Public Awareness Campaigns—CSOs regularly conduct workshops to raise awareness about accountability mechanisms. For instance, CSOs like Society for Participatory Research in Asia (PRIA), Centre for Youth and Social Development, and Satark Nagrik Sangathan conduct workshops to create awareness about the usage and benefits of the RTI Act. CSOs such as PRIA and Janaagraha have set up booths in business premises and colleges, to educate the youth about the importance of voting, and also assist them in the electoral registration process.

Publications—CSOs publish reports highlighting the performance of the government. For example, Social Watch annually publishes a report called the 'Citizens Report on Governance and Development', which analyses the performance of the key institutions of governance like the Parliament, the Police, the Judiciary and local self-governments. PRIA publishes a bi-annual journal called *Participation and Governance*, which provides perspectives on issues of governance, citizenship, accountability and democracy, highlighting different avenues for citizens to be involved in improving accountability.

Websites and Helplines—CSOs are increasingly using technology to make information accessible to citizens. For instance, the Public Interest Foundation designed a web-campaign called 'No Criminals' (www.nocriminals.org) to inform citizens about the criminal backgrounds of candidates prior to elections (Prasad 2009; NASSCOM Foundation). National Election Watch started a campaign to enable voters to obtain information on candidates from their constituencies by dialling a toll free number, or by sending an SMS (Seetha 2008). The Centre for Policy Research has set up a web portal called the 'Accountability Initiative', which regularly publishes research and articles promoting accountability, especially in the area of service delivery. Kabir, a CSO based in New Delhi, runs a dedicated helpline to address RTI-related queries, serving around 2,000 people every month.

⠿ Conduct Assessments

CSOs also monitor the ongoing functioning of the government using a number of methods, some of which we have discussed previously:

Policy and Budget Advocacy—This involves analysing the impact of budget allocations, demystifying the technical content of budgets and policies, and undertaking public education campaigns to improve budget and policy literacy.

Expenditure Tracking—This involves tracking how the government actually spends funds, with the aim of identifying leakages in the usage of financial resources. The tools commonly used to monitor the usage of funds are Public Expenditure Tracking Surveys and Social Audits.

Performance Evaluation—This involves monitoring the performance of public services by surveying the level of satisfaction of citizens using these services. The report cards based on these survey findings are presented to public officials and shared with citizens. Some CSOs also assess the performance of elected representatives in the Parliament by developing report cards, and publicizing them.

::: Constantly Advocate

Advocacy is the organized process through which CSOs engage with decision-makers in the government to influence public policies and legislations, with the objective of achieving better outcomes. Advocacy comprises activities like research, campaigns, consensus-building and mobilizing the community to ensure that the voice of the people is heard. Advocacy can be achieved in a number of ways, which are now explained:

Building Mass Support—CSOs build alliances and networks with like-minded groups to create solidarity, share resources and achieve critical mass. For example, the Centre for Budget and Governance Accountability works with CSOs from across the country in the area of budget advocacy. The CSOs meet annually to discuss issues and expectations from the forthcoming budget, and then reach out to Members of Parliament and Parliamentary Committees with their recommendations (Sirker et al. 2007). *National Election Watch* is a coalition of 1,200 CSOs working on electoral reforms and improving democracy in India (http://nationalelection-watch.org; Rahman 2009). Similarly, the *Wada Na Todo Abhiyan* is a national coalition of citizen groups that monitors the manifestos of political parties and checks the promises made by the government in areas like poverty reduction and social inclusion. Engaging citizens as active participants in advocacy through signature campaigns and petitions increases the bargaining power of these CSOs.

Lobbying—Lobbying is an organized attempt to positively shape the opinions of public officials. Lobbying is used by CSOs to influence policy-makers and build consensus on policy issues. To lobby effectively, CSOs need to be familiar with the legislative process, the interplay of power, and the ecosystem within which policy-makers thrive.

Think Tanks—A number of CSOs function as research and advocacy institutions, commonly called think-tanks. These think-tanks have qualified staff who specialize in key policy areas. They conduct extensive research on areas where new policies or amendments are required, and recommend their policy suggestions to the government.

Organized, constructive and peaceful civic activism always will be at the forefront of efforts to increase citizen participation in the political process and enhance the accountability of the state. The most pragmatic way for an ordinary citizen to participate in the process of improving accountability is perhaps to support a CSO that is aligned to their interest areas. Hundreds of CSOs have emerged across the country, each one doing its bit to improve governance and accountability in India. Below is an indicative, though not exhaustive, list of CSOs working to uplift accountability in some way, many of whom we had an opportunity to briefly interact with in the early stages of our research (Figure 9.1). Readers are advised to thoroughly research the background and working of any CSO they consider supporting.

• AGNI, Mumbai	• DISHA, Ahmedabad
• Anti Corruption Movement, Chennai	• Janaagraha, Bangalore
• Association for Democratic Reforms, New Delhi	• Janhit Manch, Mumbai
• Budget Analysis Rajasthan Center, Jaipur	• Liberty Institute, New Delhi
• Campaign for Judicial Accountability & Judicial Reforms, New Delhi	• Mazdoor Kisan Shakti Sangathan, Rajsamand
• Catalyst Trust, Chennai	• National Centre for Advocacy Studies, Pune
• Centre for Budget and Governance Accountability, New Delhi	• National Foundation for India, New Delhi
• Centre for Budget and Policy Studies, Bangalore	• PRIA, New Delhi
• Centre for Civil Society, New Delhi	• PRS Legislative Research, New Delhi
• Centre for Good Governance, Hyderabad	• People's Union for Civil Liberties, New Delhi
• Centre for Legislative Research and Advocacy, New Delhi	• Praja, Mumbai
• Centre for Policy Research, New Delhi	• Public Affairs Centre, Bangalore
• Centre for the Study of Developing Societies, New Delhi	• Sanket, Bhopal
• Centre for Youth and Social Development, Bhubaneswar	• Satark Nagrik Sangathan, Mumbai
• Charkha, Gurgaon	• Social Watch India, New Delhi
• Commonwealth Human Rights Initiative, New Delhi	• Transparency International India, New Delhi
• CUTS-International, Jaipur	• 5th Pillar, Chennai
• Democracy Connect, New Delhi	• ...

Figure 9.1 Indicative List of Civil Society Organizations

Most CSOs have insufficient resources, which limit their scalability. For the most part, they rely on volunteers to execute their campaigns. With limited financial resources, it is difficult for CSOs to attract high quality talent. The challenge of building institutional capacity in a CSO remains a constant one, and so the task of enforcing accountability on the government becomes even more difficult. The easiest way for a citizen to support a CSO is to provide monetary assistance. There are several other avenues available to interested citizens to help build these keystone organizations that are at the centre of an ecosystem, striving to create the accountable India that we all aspire towards. Volunteering time, sponsoring media campaigns, and providing knowledge and infrastructure support are some of the ways in which we can help build institutional capacity in CSOs. There are five paths that businesses, citizens and the media can traverse to support the CSOs that are helping to improve accountability and governance in India. Below, we look at several examples of how CSOs, and NGOs in general, can benefit from external help.

::: Path 1—Provide Time

In a time-challenged world, one of the most precious gifts that we can provide CSOs is finite slices of time. The few permanent staff members who work for CSOs are often stretched as they juggle planning, execution and administration. The CSOs therefore rely heavily on ordinary citizens, who assist the core team in the execution of their campaigns. With more volunteers contributing their time, CSOs can substantially increase their effectiveness by expanding the scale and scope of their operations. Citizens need to devote just a few hours on a regular basis to support a CSO. As a citizen, you can volunteer in campaigns held by CSOs to support mechanisms like the RTI or Social Audits, or provide support during events like the elections, when CSOs conduct nation-wide campaigns to increase awareness about candidates. The opportunities for ordinary citizens to make a significant difference are many.

Businesses and large corporations can also play a key role in helping to improve accountability. They should encourage their employees to support CSOs in their activities. The trend of employees emerging from their cubicles and boardrooms to help CSOs is gathering force. Many organizations provide platforms for their employees, to facilitate this process. IBM, for example, inculcates the culture of volunteering through its 'On Demand Community Program'. IBM employees have access to a number of technology tools that they use to provide CSOs with technology training, administration support and mentoring (*The Times of India*, 26 July 2006). Infosys launched a 'Community Empathy Policy' in 2008, which encourages employees to opt for a sabbatical for a year to engage in charitable causes, while still being paid half their salary (Mishra and D'Monte

2008; *Financial Express*, 7 November 2010). HSBC and Standard Chartered encourage their staff to officially dedicate some time and energy to social causes (HSBC 2010; Standard Chartered 2010; Wadia 2008). Voltas supports CSOs located in the proximity of their office, to make it practical for employees to volunteer for a few hours. Almost 1,200 Voltas employees take time out for these activities, during and after work hours (Wadia 2008). Organizations like IBM, Infosys and Delhi University have also taken up the challenge to become 100 per cent voter registered, by encouraging their employees to register and vote (*The Times of India*, 13 December 2008). Hindustan Unilever sent out internal mails providing electoral process details and a detailed list addressing voters' concerns, prior to the elections (Zachariah and Singh 2009).

To facilitate volunteering, there are online networking platforms like iVolunteer (www.ivolunteer.in), NGO Marketplace (www.ngomarketplace.com) and Indianngos (www.indianngos.com), where citizens, corporates, researchers and CSOs can interact with each other. CSOs can upload their proposals on these websites, where they describe the nature and length of projects for which volunteers are needed. Citizens and corporates can evaluate the projects proposed by various CSOs, and offer help based on their personal interests and backgrounds. The combined force of citizens and corporates will provide the external energy that CSOs need to supercharge their critical agenda.

::: Path 2—Provide Media Access

A vigilant, vibrant and vigorous media leads to a more accountable and responsive public administration, since it enhances citizens' ability to scrutinize government actions. The unfailing energy and passion of the CSOs, mingled with the voice of the media, creates the chemistry that is needed to shape public policy and debate. Through the media, CSOs can build awareness of the rights of citizens, and the accountability mechanisms that citizens can use to fight for their rights. The media assists CSOs in building critical mass to advocate for policy changes and acts as a channel to disseminate their findings from surveys and audits.

Businesses can provide significant visibility to CSOs through media sponsorship. Tata Tea supported the campaign of a Bangalore-based CSO, Janaagraha, to build citizen's awareness about the importance of voting (*DNA*, 11 November 2005). The campaign, called 'Jaago Re!', released multiple television advertisements asking citizens to register for voting in general elections. Tata Tea provided a link to the 'Jaago Re!' campaign on their website. They also promoted the campaign by printing the 'Jaago Re!' logo on their tea packets.

Media organizations themselves can be a great source of support to CSOs by proactively being more accessible and propagating the CSO' initiatives.

The television channel NDTV, for example, supported and screened the 'RTI Awards' organized by a CSO called Public Cause Research Foundation, which recognizes the outstanding work of citizens and public officials in the arena of the RTI Act (*Business Standard*, 26 November 2009). *Rajasthan Patrika*, a newspaper, published the promises made by candidates prior to the 2005 state elections and tracked their performance against these promises, thereby directly holding them accountable (Bahri 2008). The Doordarshan TV news channel, in association with a CSO, Kabir, created a weekly show called '*Janne Ka Haq*' (Right to Know) to increase public awareness of the RTI. The show featured live discussions and phone-ins to address viewers' queries about the RTI (Changemakers 2007). A number of media houses, including NDTV, Hindustan Times and The Hindu, initiated a 15-day 'Drive Against Bribe Campaign' in July 2006, where they discouraged citizens from paying bribes to government departments to clear pending applications for passports, voter IDs, licenses or certificates. They instead recommended the use of the RTI Act to question delays in the process (*Hindustan Times*, 4 July 2006).

Media organizations should also consider providing CSOs with free or subsidized airtime and print space. As a part of their corporate social responsibility, Zee Entertainment Enterprise leveraged the huge viewership of its channel and launched Zee Touch India, an initiative to enable businesses to air films focusing on social causes across Zee channels without paying for airtime (Karmayog 2008). Public relations firms and advertising agencies can also develop documentaries and promotional literature to support CSOs' marketing campaigns. In the run-up to the 2009 general elections, Lodestar Universal, an advertising and marketing agency, developed a pro-bono voter awareness campaign, '*Sache Ko Chune, Ache Ko Chune*'. The campaign, in support of two CSOs working towards improving governance, Association for Democratic Reforms (ADR) and National Election Watch, was widely publicized on TV and the print media, and asked people to make informed electoral choices. Lodestar won a 2010 Media Abbey award for the campaign's tagline (Exchange4media 2009). Both media and non-media businesses can leverage the richness and reach of the media to help CSOs project their voices.

::: Path 3—Provide Intellectual Capacity

Central to any CSO's work is information gathering, processing, analysing and publishing research. This mammoth task is one of the biggest challenges CSOs face. They conduct a large amount of research to support and advocate for the issue they are working on. Surveys and audits generate a huge amount of data, which makes data analysis and storage a critical function. Citizens and businesses can very effectively support CSOs by providing them with the research and analytical skills they need. Businesses can undertake research assignments specific to their sector, whether in healthcare, education, food, communication or infrastructure, on behalf of these CSOs. Accenture, for example, extends its expertise and skills to local CSOs by conducting research assignments at low charges (Accenture 2006). Business schools like the S. P. Jain Institute of Management and Research have mandated CSO internships for their students, where students help CSOs to improve their marketing campaigns and economic viability (SP Jain Institute of Management and Research 2009).

Civil Society Organizations also require technical expertise to work in areas like budget advocacy, policy analysis and litigation, which require specialized knowledge. Finance or accounting firms can help CSOs to understand the impact of government budgets in socially important sectors like health and education. Legal firms can support CSOs by sharing legal expertise in matters related to the Judiciary. For example, the Public Interest Legal Support and Research Centre is a public interest law firm based in New Delhi, which supports social justice groups, NGOs, human rights institutions and marginalized communities by providing them with legal advice, legal research and litigation support. The portal www. indianngos.com, supported by Mahindra & Mahindra, provides guidance to CSOs in the form of articles on taxation, fund raising, and legal and financial issues they need to be aware of.

::: Path 4—Provide Technology and Infrastructure

The effective usage of information technology enables CSOs to broaden their geographic reach, access a larger population and accelerate the impact of their initiatives. Citizens or businesses with Information Technology (IT) skills can help CSOs develop an effective web presence, regularly update web content, participate in discussion forums, build an online community of volunteers and create a solid presence through social media.

Corporates can support CSOs by providing them with the required IT infrastructure for data management. Microsoft India, for instance, donates software products to CSOs to support their welfare and community development work. It also runs a Microsoft Authorized Refurbisher Programme along with the industry body FICCI, which makes available low-cost refurbished computers for CSOs. The 'ConnectIT' workshops run by the NASSCOM Foundation are also an initiative to build IT capacity in NGOs. The workshops include practical training on the use of applications for evaluating, managing and documenting data, creating project proposals and presentations for donors, as well as streamlining internal organizational processes and systems (www. nasscomfoundation.org).

Providing CSOs with access to physical infrastructure is also useful. Organizations of all shapes and sizes can provide temporary access to office space, which helps CSOs to reduce their operational costs. Voltas has provided office space to a CSO, Akanksha, at its Mumbai premises. This also enables Voltas employees to interact with the CSO regularly (Wadia 2008). The S. P. Jain Institute of Management and Research provides a classroom to a CSO called Satark Nagrik Sangathan to conduct workshops at minimal cost. Businesses can also provide CSOs with platforms at corporate seminars, to conduct workshops about the usage of accountability tools like the RTI, PIL and Citizens Charter. The leaders of CSOs should be invited to speak at corporate forums, where they can share the stories of citizens who have demanded accountability and succeeded in their efforts.

::: Path 5—Provide Monetary Support

Economic viability is a critical aspect for the sustainability of CSOs, since most of these organizations in India suffer from severe fund constraints. Financial support is clearly needed to meet their operational expenses, as well as to embark on their planned initiatives. Less than 1 per cent of the NGOs in India have professionally trained fund-raisers (*Rediff News*, 5 March 2008). Funding is the key to building institutional capacity and maintaining inter-generational sustainability.

Larger businesses and organizations can set up dedicated trusts or foundations that provide grants to CSOs. The Ford Foundation established by Ford Motor Company (www.fordfoundation.org), or the Sir Ratan Tata Trust established by the Tata Group (www.srtt.org), provides grants to CSOs working in India for several causes.

Corporates can also provide monetary support to capacity-building organizations, which in turn provide grants to CSOs active in specific areas. These capacity-building organizations conduct credibility checks on target CSOs and act as an intermediary between potential donors and CSOs. For example, the National Foundation of India (www.nfi.org.in) collects funds from corporates and provides them to CSOs focused on specific issues. CSO Partners is a Chennai-based non-profit organization committed to strengthening CSOs in India. Other institutes like the India Sponsor Foundation (www.indiasponsor. org), Funds for NGOs (www.fundsforngos.org) and Murray Culshaw Consulting Pvt Ltd (www.fundraising-india.org), among others, act as facilitators between donors, corporates, individuals, and those CSOs that need monetary support. Citizens can, in their individual capacity, choose to provide direct monetary support to CSOs that target areas close to their heart, and thus do their bit to build a culture of accountability in India.

For the interested and motivated citizen of India who wants to make a difference, there are clearly many ways to make a significant contribution to improve accountability. The five-fold path prescribed above may provide the navigating lights for this journey.

A completely different, though more difficult, option is also available to citizens. Rather than improving accountability from the outside, citizens could consider joining the government to help improve accountability from within. This route could result in a slow, but lasting improvement in accountability.

In my closing comments in the Epilogue that appears next, you will see how the change in accountability levels will play out over the next few decades, leading to a better India.

References

'Autumn Project: SP Jain Institute of Management and Research'. 2009. Available at www. spjimr.org/ (accessed on 26 March 2010).

Bahri, Bedi Puneet. 2008. 'Language papers in poll mode; gear up to roll out pre-electoral campaigns'. Available at www.exchange4media.com/ (accessed on 15 April 2010).

'Campaign to encourage youngsters to vote'. 2008. *The Times of India*, 13 December.

'ConnectIT Program'. Available at: www.nasscomfoundation.org (accessed on 1 April 2010).

'Corporate Citizenship Review 06: Giving for a better tomorrow'. 2006. Available at www. accenture.com/ (accessed on 25 March 2010).

'CSR Activities: Zee Entertainment Enterprises Ltd'. 2008. Available at www.karmayog. org/ (accessed on 25 March 2010).

'Elections 2009: McCann, Lodestar, ADR join forces to create voter awareness'. 2009. Available at www.exchange4media.com/ (accessed on 17 December 2010).

'Employee Volunteering'. 2010. Available at http://www.hsbc.co.in. (accessed on 14 December 2010).

'Employee Volunteering'. 2010. Available at http://sustainability.standardchartered.com. (accessed on 14 December 2010).

'I Volunteer!' 2006. *The Times of India—Ascent*, 26 July.

'Indians: Charity rich, philanthropy poor'. 2008. Rediff News, 5 March. Available at www. rediff.com (accessed on 2 April 2010).

'Jaago re campaign wakes up voters'. 2008. *DNA*, 11 November.

'Kabir: A communication initiative on Right to Information'. 2007. Available at http://geo-tourism.changemakers.com/ (accessed on 26 March 2010).

Mishra, Bibhu Ranjan and Leslie D`Monte. 2008. 'Infosys exhorts employees to go on 1-yr sabbatical, work for NGOs'. *Business Standard*, 15 November.

'NDTV and PCRF join hands to announce the first ever RTI Awards'. 2009. *Business Standard*, 26 November.

'No Criminals Campaign'. Available at www.nasscomfoundation.org (accessed on 13 April 2010).

'On Day 13, numbers speak of campaign's popularity'. 2006. *Hindustan Times*, 4 July.

Prasad, Swati. 2009. 'India's election campaigns get Net-savvy'. Available at http://m.zdnetasia.com/india-s-election-campaigns-get-net-savvy-62053192.htm.

Rahman, Shafi. 2009. 'Include electoral and political reforms in parties manifestos: National Election Watch'. *India Today*, 18 March.

Seetha. 2008. 'Vote's the matter'. *The Telegraph*, 16 November.

Sirker, Karen, Sladjana Cosic and Public Affairs Foundation. 2007. 'Empowering the Marginalized: Case Studies of Social Accountability Initiatives in Asia'. The World Bank Institute, pp. 12–18. Available at www.sasanet.org (accessed on 13 April 2010).

Wadia, Jai. 2008. 'A shoulder to lean on'. Available at www.tata.com (accessed on 14 April 2010).

'Well worth a break'. 2010. *The Financial Express*, 7 November.

Zachariah, Reeba and Namrata Singh. 2009. 'Go vote, India Inc tells employees'. *The Times of India*, 12 March.

Epilogue

There is a tide in the affairs of men.
Which, taken at the flood, leads on to fortune;
Omitted, all the voyage of their life
Is bound in shallows and in miseries.
On such a full sea are we now afloat,
And we must take the current where it serves,
Or lose all our ventures.

William Shakespeare, 1564–1616
Julius Caesar, Act 4

The literary genius William Shakespeare perhaps did not have India on his mind when he penned those prescient words hundreds of years ago. If there was indeed such a 'tide' in the affairs of India, which could lead either to fortune or to miseries, this decade could well be the one that stands jury on his words.

In early 2011, two important and seemingly unrelated events were being reported in the press. First, foreign direct investment into India fell by a stunning 31 per cent in 2010, down to USD 24 billion, although global investors were still actively investing in emerging markets. In just two months from November 2010, foreign investors vanished with USD 1.4 billion from the Indian stock markets, driving the BSE Index (Sensex) down by 16 per cent. While there were a number of reasons for this mass exodus from India, many analysts felt that the multitude of corruption scandals exposed in 2010 contributed in no small measure to this phenomenon. There is a real *cost of poor governance* and India is most certainly paying the price for it.

Second, in the deserts of the Middle East and North Africa, the shrill war cry of democracy rung in the dawn of 2011, heralding the 'Arab Spring'. Decades of rule by suppressive, autocratic and corrupt regimes, the absence of civil liberties, freedom and justice, coupled with misgovernance, poverty and hunger, resulted in a massive uprising of citizens against the self-proclaimed rulers. Initially Tunisia fell, then Egypt, and later Libya, with Bahrain on the brink. Jordan, Yemen, Algeria, Syria, even Saudi Arabia, all were on edge. In the final analysis, it was a fight for good governance and greater accountability.

By August 2011, the 'Arab Spring' had turned into an 'Indian Summer'. A massive citizen's movement sparked anti-corruption protests nationwide with countless thousands joining the rallies. Good governance and accountability were once again the focus.

The important question that we must now ask, is: Will we see some serious governance and administrative reform in India that can improve accountability?

Over the past six decades since independence, the government has implemented a number of policies that have set the framework of our existing accountability institutions and mechanisms. While the post-independence decades of the 1950s and 1960s saw the establishment of public institutions and policies to facilitate the monitoring of government performance, the introduction of governance policies slowed down in the 1970s and 1980s. The 'Emergency Rule' in the late 1970s curbed the political and civil rights of citizens, censored the media and increased the opaqueness of government actions. Power and authority shifted squarely into the hands of government officials, reinforcing nepotism and graft in the administrative machinery. Never before in the history of independent India was the importance of civil rights and liberty felt more acutely. Fortunately, the 1990s and the first decade of the twenty-first century saw the introduction of some important accountability mechanisms to encourage citizens' participation in governance. These policies are summarized in Figure E1.

It is instructive to look at the key economic policies over the same 60-year period and contrast the velocity and density of their introduction with those of the accountability policies. The first 40 years of independence led to a set of socialist economic policies that delivered little for the country by way of economic and social prosperity. The economic crisis of 1991 led to the 'big bang' of liberalization and a bouquet of economic reforms, which laid the foundation for the sustained growth we have seen over the last two decades (Figure E2).

A simple visual comparison of this 60-year period, within which both economic policies and accountability policies were introduced, shows the relative intensity of economic reforms, in stark contrast to the paucity of governance reforms over the last two decades (Figure E3).

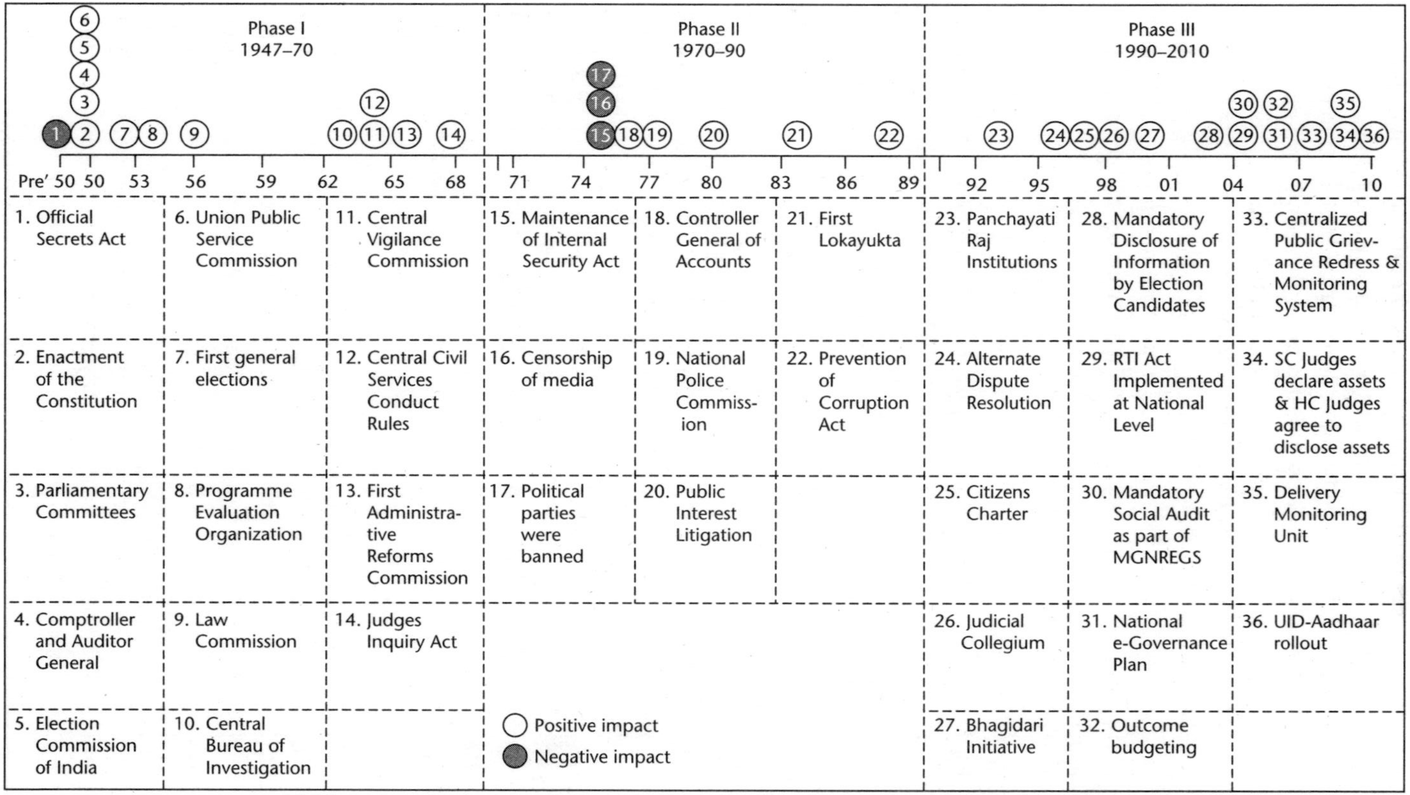

Figure E1 Key Accountability Policies, 1947–2010

Phase I 1947–70 | Phase II 1970–90 | Phase III 1990–2010

Timeline: Pre' 50, 50, 53, 56, 59, 62, 65, 68, 71, 74, 77, 80, 83, 86, 89, 92, 95, 98, 01, 04, 07, 10

Legend: ○ Positive impact ● Negative impact

1. Official Secrets Act
2. Enactment of the Constitution
3. Parliamentary Committees
4. Comptroller and Auditor General
5. Election Commission of India
6. Union Public Service Commission
7. First general elections
8. Programme Evaluation Organization
9. Law Commission
10. Central Bureau of Investigation
11. Central Vigilance Commission
12. Central Civil Services Conduct Rules
13. First Administrative Reforms Commission
14. Judges Inquiry Act
15. Maintenance of Internal Security Act
16. Censorship of media
17. Political parties were banned
18. Controller General of Accounts
19. National Police Commission
20. Public Interest Litigation
21. First Lokayukta
22. Prevention of Corruption Act
23. Panchayati Raj Institutions
24. Alternate Dispute Resolution
25. Citizens Charter
26. Judicial Collegium
27. Bhagidari Initiative
28. Mandatory Disclosure of Information by Election Candidates
29. RTI Act Implemented at National Level
30. Mandatory Social Audit as part of MGNREGS
31. National e-Governance Plan
32. Outcome budgeting
33. Centralized Public Grievance Redress & Monitoring System
34. SC Judges declare assets & HC Judges agree to disclose assets
35. Delivery Monitoring Unit
36. UID-Aadhaar rollout

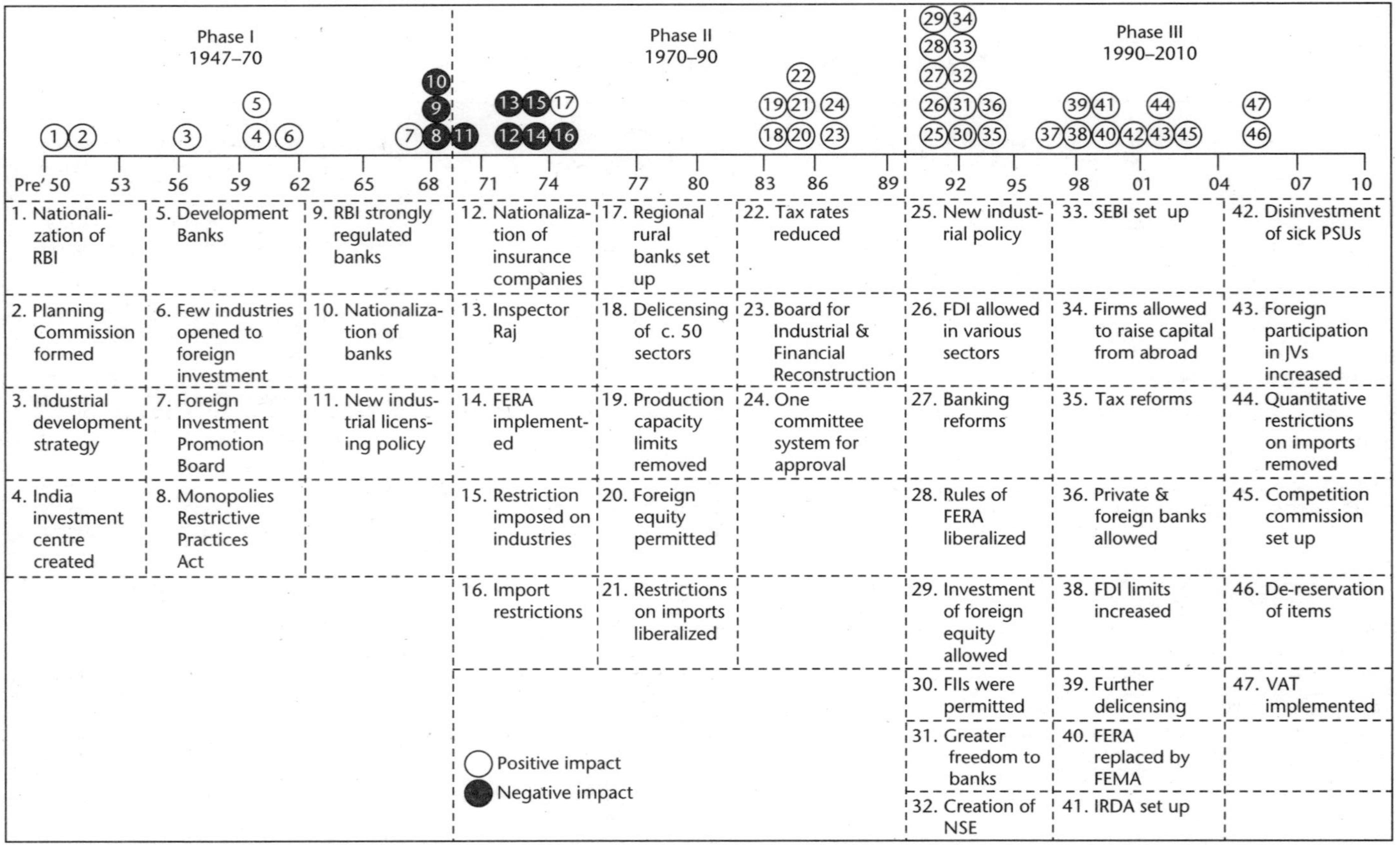

Phase I 1947–70 Phase II 1970–90 Phase III 1990–2010

Timeline: Pre' 50 · 53 · 56 · 59 · 62 · 65 · 68 · 71 · 74 · 77 · 80 · 83 · 86 · 89 · 92 · 95 · 98 · 01 · 04 · 07 · 10

1. Nationalization of RBI
2. Planning Commission formed
3. Industrial development strategy
4. India investment centre created
5. Development Banks
6. Few industries opened to foreign investment
7. Foreign Investment Promotion Board
8. Monopolies Restrictive Practices Act
9. RBI strongly regulated banks
10. Nationalization of banks
11. New industrial licensing policy
12. Nationalization of insurance companies
13. Inspector Raj
14. FERA implemented
15. Restriction imposed on industries
16. Import restrictions
17. Regional rural banks set up
18. Delicensing of c. 50 sectors
19. Production capacity limits removed
20. Foreign equity permitted
21. Restrictions on imports liberalized
22. Tax rates reduced
23. Board for Industrial & Financial Reconstruction
24. One committee system for approval
25. New industrial policy
26. FDI allowed in various sectors
27. Banking reforms
28. Rules of FERA liberalized
29. Investment of foreign equity allowed
30. FIIs were permitted
31. Greater freedom to banks
32. Creation of NSE
33. SEBI set up
34. Firms allowed to raise capital from abroad
35. Tax reforms
36. Private & foreign banks allowed
38. FDI limits increased
39. Further delicensing
40. FERA replaced by FEMA
41. IRDA set up
42. Disinvestment of sick PSUs
43. Foreign participation in JVs increased
44. Quantitative restrictions on imports removed
45. Competition commission set up
46. De-reservation of items
47. VAT implemented

Legend:
○ Positive impact
● Negative impact

Figure E2 Key Economic Policies, 1947–2010

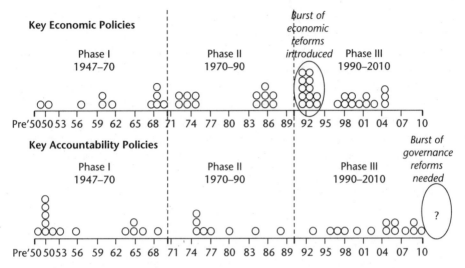

Figure E3 Mapping Key Economic and Accountability Policies

A similar burst of governance and accountability reforms, mirroring the explosion of the economic reforms of 1991, would put India on an accelerated path of growth. These much-needed reforms, while difficult to push through due to political considerations, would have the power to launch a new era of good governance and better accountability, simultaneously increasing global confidence in the 'India story'. A jump in foreign direct investment and foreign institutional investment is more than likely, besides turbo-charging domestic investment.

The recent flood of scams, however, leaves some big questions unanswered. Will accountability among our public officials change with the passage of time? Could it become much worse than we see today, horrifying as it may sound? Will it improve at some point in the not-so-distant future? These are undoubtedly difficult questions to answer, but nevertheless important ones to consider. Grappling with these subjective questions necessarily requires us to take a more qualitative approach to charting the possible trajectory of accountability out into the future.

To paint this new world, let us draw from the palette of business, where organizations constantly have to re-invent themselves to cope with the unrelenting pressure from customers, competitors and collaborators, as well as from the aspirations of their own employees. Whenever a change occurs in an organization, forced by the application of an exogenous force, there tends to be a dip in organizational morale and productivity to a new low point. This transition period is often called the 'valley of despair', as people adjust to the new realities set by a change in strategy, structure or systems. This is ultimately followed by what appears, at a macro-level, to be a slow and gradual improvement in morale, as both endogenous (similar to the internal and horizontal accountability imposed by government departments) and exogenous forces (similar to the external accountability imposed by citizens, civil society and the media) push morale and productivity to a higher level of equilibrium. This would appear as a gradual improvement in the level of accountability and governance, although if one were to drill deeper into the nature of this change, you would see an improvement in fits and starts, followed by periods of relatively little change, as described in an earlier chapter. A model of the undulating path that accountability will likely take is described in the 'Accountability Change Curve' in Figure E4.

A question to ponder on: Where is India positioned on the 'Accountability Change Curve' in 2011? Are we teetering on the edge of the 'Valley of Despair', waiting to slide further off the precipice; are we already half-way down in our descent; or are we almost at the bottom of the pit, just shy of the tipping point that will goad us to clamber up the opposite hill, to an improved state of accountability? No amount of quantitative or qualitative analysis can reveal the true answers to these questions. But we can hazard a somewhat educated guess. It is likely that the next few years will see even more corruption cases and scams brought to the surface, with the tremendous power of the media, civil society, citizens and even the government, all acting in unison to enforce accountability. With the ever-increasing pace of misgovernance, citizens will demand more stringent action against the corrupt. We may even perceive that accountability has worsened (although hidden from view in the background, it may have actually

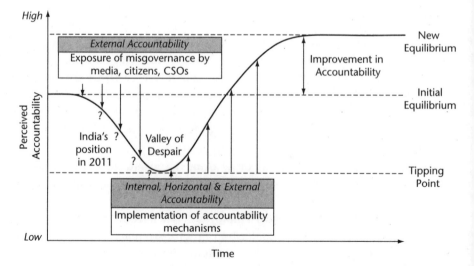

Figure E4   The Accountability Change Curve

begun to improve), even as the government takes stronger action. This would send a strong message against poor governance. Accountability levels would ultimately rise to a higher level, to a new equilibrium, we fervently hope.

How long will this whole process of change take? My best guess, given the current pace at which misgovernance is being unearthed, as well as the recent efforts that have been made to improve accountability, is that it would be a good 10 to 15 years from now, well into the 2020–25 time frame, when we will see a measurable improvement in accountability, and better governance. I have no empirical method with which to test my grand assumption, of course, but I draw comfort in the knowledge that the 'Accountability Change Curve' will inevitably follow the Holy Grail of all processes of change; from the current condition we find our country in, to a more distant but better future, so that our children and grandchildren will live in a more accountable India. Provided, of course, we citizens play a part in this improvement process.

I started this book with a question on accountability, posed to me by a friend. This endeavour brings to completion only one leg of the journey to answer this question. I can only hope that it is the beginning of a new journey for you, as you think through what you can do to improve accountability in our country. In doing our duty, we will help India make its 'tryst with destiny'.

Jay P. Desai

***

'India never will allow me to ferment in the sleep of my own desires; But keeps me ever wakeful to a consciousness that embroiders patterns that decorate my Body and my soul, and anoints me as the bride of its soil. Born wrapped in the placenta of many cultures, I breathe a life of knowingness uniquely Different from those with chaste tongues of scriptures and divides.

From the gullies and shanties, dark shadows pattern the cities like fake lace of a bridal Gown, whilst the wail of sirens block out the screams of the innocent whose spilt blood are The only reminders of their vanquished dreams. Legacies of a past cannot hold the brace of my spine upright, Nor does the stoop of my weariness find me my bed of comfort.

As my body wrinkles and my breasts become heavy with the stories of all those I carry close to my heart, I listen, wakeful ever, just for the smallness of hope.'

Rekha Rodwittiya
Artist

Bibliography
....

'A concise history of India'. Available at www.geographia.com (accessed on 9 February 2010).

'A controversial judicial appointment'. 2006. *The Hindu*, 1 December.

'A handbook for Trainers: The Right to Information Act 2005'. 2006. Capacity. Building for Access to Information Project. Available at www.rti.org.in (accessed on 22 January 2010).

'A Study on Management of Public Expenditure by State Governments in India'. Available at http://planningcommission.nic.in (accessed on 19 February 2009).

'A walk through India's history'. Available at www.indianembassy.ru (accessed on 21 July 2009).

'Achievements—Association of Democratic Reforms'. Available at www.adrindia. org (accessed on 7 July 2009).

'Activities and Programs: Budget Advocacy'. Available at www.cbgaindia.org/ (accessed on 23 May 2009).

Adegite, Elizabeth. 2010. 'Accounting, accountability and national development'. *The Guardian*, 6 January.

'Aggarwal brothers delve deep into the "soul of India" to tap talent'. 2010. *DNA*, 14 September.

Agarwal, O. P. and T. V. Somanathan. 'Public Policy Making In India: Issues and Remedies'. Available at www.cprindia.org (accessed on 5 February 2009).

Agarwal, S. K. 2007. 'Judicial Corruption Fuels Impunity, Corrodes Rule of Law'. Available at www.transparency.org (accessed on 14 March 2009).

Ahmad, R. 2008. 'Governance, Social Accountability and the Civil Society'. *JOAAG*, 3 (1).

Aiyar, Yamini. 'Who Cares About Outcomes?' Available at www.accountabilityindia.in (accessed on 12 January 2011).

Aiyar, Yamini and Bala Posani. 2009. 'State of Accountability: Evolution, Practice and Emerging Questions in Public Accountability in India'. AI Working Paper No. 2, May. Available at www.accountabilityindia.org/ (accessed on 3 August 2009).

Ali, Mubarak. 2009. 'Time check—Ancient India: The Arthashastra of Kautilya'. *Dawn*, 19 December.

'All India Seminar on Judicial Reforms'. 2008. Available at www.supremecour-tofindia.nic.in (accessed on 18 February 2009).

'Ancient India Government'. Available at www.culturalindia.net (accessed on 22 July 2009).

'A new twist to social audits'. 2010. Available at www.indiatogether.org (accessed on 6 February 2010).

'Annual Report—Central Vigilance Commission'. 2009. Available at www.cvc.nic. in (accessed on 2 March 2011).

Ansari, M. M. 2008. 'Impact of Right to Information on Development: A Perspective on India's Recent Experiences'. Available at http://portal.unesco.org (accessed on 3 March 2011).

'Appraisal of babus'. 2010. *The Economic Times*, 9 May.

'Archive of General Elections 2009—Political Party and Symbols'. Available at http://eci.nic.in (accessed on 14 March 2009).

'Are judges over-reaching?' 2007. Available at www.indiatogether.org/ (accessed on 26 February 2009).

Arora, Ramesh and Rajni Goyal. 1996. *Indian Public Administration: Institutions and Issues*. New Delhi: Wishwa Prakashan.

Arroyo, Dennis and Karen Sirker. 2005. 'Stocktaking of Social Accountability Initiatives in the Asia and Pacific Region'. Washington, D. C.: World Bank Institute Community Empowerment and Social Inclusion Learning Program.

'As games begin, India hopes to save its pride'. 2010. *International Herald Tribune—The New York Times*, 2 October.

'Background Note: Improving Public Service Delivery—Management Aspects and Technology Applications'. Available at www.darpg.nic.in (accessed on 9 November 2009).

'Background papers; Meeting of The National e-Governance Advisory Group'. Available at http://www.mit.gov.in/ (accessed on 7 December 2010).

Baisakh, Pradeep. 2007. 'Are judges over-reaching?' Available at www.indiato-gether.org/ (accessed on 2 February 2009).

————. 2005. 'The Lokpal Cycle'. Available at www.indiatogether.org/ (accessed on 25 February 2009).

Bajpai, Nirupam and Sangeeta Goyal. 2004. 'Primary Education—Low coverage, poor quality'. *The Hindu Business Line*, 9 June.

Balakrishnan, K. G. 2008. 'Growth of Public Interest Litigation in India'. Available at www.supremecourtofindia.nic.in (accessed on 23 February 2009).

'Bangalore Agenda Task Force'. Available at www.janaagraha.org (accessed on 12 December 2008).

'Battling the babu raj'. 2008. *The Economist*, 6 March.

Bedekar, V. V. 2002. 'Law and Justice in Ancient India'. Available at www.orien-talthane.com (accessed on 5 February 2010).

Behl, Abhishek. 2008. 'Understaffed, under policed India raise new battalions to check Naxals'. Available at www.merinews.com (accessed on 20 January 2010).

Besley, Timothy and Robin Burgess. 2000. 'Political Agency, Government Responsiveness and the Role of the Media'. Available at http://econ.lse.ac.uk (accessed on 30 March 2010).

'Best Practice Guidelines: Voluntary Organisations'. Available at www.ivolunteer. in (accessed on 26 March 2010).

'Bhagidari: The Concept'. Available at http://delhigovt.nic.in/bhagi.asp (accessed on 12 March 2009).

'Bhagidari monitoring system launched'. 2008. *The Hindu*, 7 February.

Bhanu, Vinod. 2007. 'Making the Indian Budget: How Open and Participatory'. *Economic and Political Weekly*, 31 March.

Bharucha, Nauzer K. 2010. 'Adarsh society members got Rs 8.5cr flats for Rs 85L'. *The Times of India*, 28 October.

Bhat, Vishal. 'Public Interest Litigation'. Available at www.legalserviceindia.com (accessed on 3 February 2009).

Bhati, Manoj. 'Right to Information in India: Need for it & Perspectives'. Available at www.legalserviceindia.com (accessed on 3 February 2009).

Bhatnagar, Rakesh. 2004. 'SC to hear PIL against HC judges mass leave'. *The Times of India*, 20 April.

Bhatnagar, Subhash. 'Administrative Corruption: How Does E-Government Help?'. Available at www.iimahd.ernet.in (accessed on 6 November 2009).

Bhattacharya, A. K. 2010. 'One captain for all flagships'. Available at www.sify. com/finance (accessed on 10 January 2011).

Bhattacharya, Amit. 2010. 'Food fight: When will we get freedom from hunger?' *The Times of India*, 14 August.

Bhattacharya, Santwana. 2009. 'In India the comedy of power-sharing'. Available at www.atimes.com/ (accessed on 6 January 2010).

Bhattarcharjya, Satarupa. 2006. 'House in Turmoil'. *India Today*, 2 January.

Bhushan, Prashant. 2009. 'Accountability, M' Lord'. *Outlook*, 15 September.

————. 2006. 'Illusion of Accountability '. *Outlook*, 23 November.

————. 2005. 'Contempt of court and the triple shield'. *The Hindu*, 7 September.

————. 2005. 'Judicial Impunity'. *Outlook*, 13 September.

'Bill on judicial accountability approved'. 2010. *The Hindu*, 5 October.

Bishnoi, Baldev. 'Akbar and the Era of Multi-Religious Empire'. Available at www. rajputbrotherhood.com (accessed on 5 April 2010).

Blair, Harry. 2007. 'Gaining state support for social accountability mechanisms'. Paper prepared for the World Bank's CommGAP Workshop, 1–2 November, Paris. Available at www.sasanet.org (accessed on 26 March 2010).

Bovens, Mark. 2007. 'New Forms of Accountability and EU-Governance'. *Comparative European Politics*.

Boyd, Michael. 'Hofstede's Cultural Attitudes Research - Cultural Dimensions'. Global Human Resource Management. Available at www.boydassociates.net (accessed on 29 April 2009).

'British India—Government under the East India Company'. Available at http://library.thinkquest.org (accessed on 4 February 2010).

'Brochure On Preparation and Maintenance Of Annual Performance Assessment Report For Central Civil Services'. Available at http://www.ddindia.gov.in (accessed on 31 January 2011).

'Building Public Awareness on Elections and Candidates'. 2004. *The Financial Express*, 5 April.

Burden, Barry. 2009. 'The Dynamic Effects of Education on Voter Turnout'. Available at https://mywebspace.wisc.edu (accessed on 28 April 2010).

Burgess, Heidi and Cate Malek. 2005. 'Public Participation'. Available at www.beyondintractability.org (accessed on 9 February 2009).

Burns, John P. and Chau-Ching Shen. 2002. 'Country Reform Summary—China'. Available at http://www1.worldbank.org. (accessed on 8 December 2010).

'Cabinet divided over Judicial Bill'. 2010. *The Hindu*, 15 March.

Carrington, Wesley, Jim DeBuse and HeeJin Lee. 2008. 'The Theory of Governance and Accountability'. The University of Iowa: Centre for International Finance and Development.

Caruthers, R. W. 2009. 'State Bank of India Wins Developer Award for Central Plan Scheme Monitoring System'. Available at www.windowsfs.com (accessed on 2 November 2009).

'Case Study 1—Andhra Pradesh, India: Improving Health Services through Community Score Cards'. 2007. *Social Accountability Series*. Available at www.sasanet.org (accessed on 16 April 2010).

'Case Study—Bangalore, India: Citizen Report Cards'. 2005. Available at www.sasanet.org (accessed on 15 April 2010).

'Cash and caste playing role in Punjab and UP elections'. 2002. *The Financial Express*, 13 February.

'Caste System in Post Mauryan India'. Available at www.historytution.com/ (accessed on 3 February 2010).

Champakalakshmi, R. 2002. 'Cultural Technologies of Colonial Rule'. *The Hindu*, 3 November.

'Chapter 1: Judiciary under British Rule in India'. Available at http://prr.hec.gov.pk (accessed on 8 February 2010).

'Chapter IV: India—Introduction to Budgeting and Accounting'. Available at www.asosai.org (accessed on 23 February 2009).

'Chapter 5: Annual Report'. 2008. *Central Vigilance Commission*. Available at http://cvc.nic.in/ (accessed on 7 January 2010).

'Chapter 35: Colonialism in India'. Available at http://nos.org (accessed on 2 February 2010).

Chaturvedi, Rakesh Mohan. 2008. 'Rural jobs scheme needs independent social audit, say activists'. Available at www.thaindian.com (accessed on 8 June 2009).

Chaudhuri, Jay, Yamini Aiyar and Jessica Wallack. 2009. 'Outcomes Rule: Getting Development from Development Expenditure'. Available at www.accountabilityindia.org (accessed on 4 November 2009).

Chaudhuri, Sayak. 2006. 'Impeachment of Judges: A Theoretical Stroke on Judicial Accountability'. Available at http://papers.ssrn.com (accessed on 23 February 2009).

Chaudhury, Shoma. 2008. 'Religion's Double Role'. *Tehelka Magazine*, 5 (48).

Chauhan, Radha. 2009. 'National E-Governance Plan in India'. Available at www.iist.unu.edu (accessed on 4 May 2010).

Chawla, Anil. 'Republic in Ancient India—Need for A New Paradigm in Political Science', Available at www.samarthbharat.com (accessed on 5 February 2010).

Chhatre, Ashwini. 2008. 'Political Articulation and Accountability in Decentralisation: Theory and Evidence from India'. India Environment Portal. Available at http://unpan1.un.org (accessed on 8 December 2008).

Chibbar, Manish. 2009. 'The law on impeachment of judges'. *Indian Express*, 17 December.

Chowdhury, Mahfuz. 2008. 'The impact of continued population growth'. Available at www.upiasia.com (accessed on 18 March 2010).

'Citizen Selection Procedure (Nominee: Ajay Dubey)'. RTI Awards, 2009 Section. Available at www.pcrf.in (accessed on 6 January 2010).

'Citizen Selection Procedure (Nominee: Akhil Gogoi)'. RTI Awards, 2009 Section. Available at www.pcrf.in (accessed on 6 January 2010).

'Citizens Charters: Indian Experience'. 2009. Available at http://darpg.nic.in (accessed on 28 April 2010).

'Civil Services Survey—A Report'. 2010. Available at http://darpg.nic.in (accessed on 13 December 2010).

'Colonialism, Caste Order and Tribal Movements'. Available at www.egyankosh.ac.in (accessed on 2 February 2010).

'Complaint Registration'. Available at www.mcgm.gov.in (accessed on 4 June 2010).

'Community Affairs—Microsoft India'. Available at www.microsoft.com/ (accessed on 1 April 2010).

'Conditions of Service (Articles 309, 310, 311 of Constitution)'. Available at http://apvc.ap.nic.in (accessed on 19 February 2009).

'Corporate Citizenship Review 06: Giving for a better tomorrow'. 2006. Available at www.accenture.com/ (accessed on 25 March 2010).

Corrie, Priyasha. 2008. 'Instilling Public Confidence in Administration: The needs for an Ombudsman like Institution in India'. Available at http://papers.ssrn.com (accessed on 22 January 2009).

'Corruption Catalogue—Judiciary'. 2005. India Corruption Study. Available at www.livemint.com (accessed on 18 February 2009).

Costa, Roana Maria and Chinmayi Shalya. 2009. 'Competition targets keep rail TCs on their toes'. *The Times of India*, 24 February.

'Country reports on judicial corruption (India and UK)'. 2007. *Global Corruption Report*. Available at www.transparency.org (accessed on 19 May 2009).

'Criminalization of Politics—Cause or Consequence?' Available at http://fdrindia. org (accessed on 21 January 2009).

'CSO within the Company'. Available at www.mcxindia.com (accessed on 14 April 2010).

'Curb Wastage to Contribute 8.9% to National Income'. Memorandum to the Hon'ble Finance Minister for Budget 2004–05. Available at www.cuts-international.org (accessed on 27 January 2010).

Datar, Arvind. 2003. 'Judicial Appointments—The Indian Perspective'. University of Cambridge: Centre for Public Law.

Datta, Saikat. 2010. 'With An Arm Tied'. *India Today*, 8 March.

Das, Gurcharan. 2010. 'It is criminal to close schools for the poor'. *The Times of India*, 19 September.

Deal, Christopher. 'Application of the Concepts of Individualism and Collectivism to Intercultural Training'. Available at www.dealglobalcommunication.com (accessed on 8 March 2010).

Dean, Cornelia. 2008. 'Public Outreach, Done Right, Aids Policy Making'. *New York Times*, 22 August.

'Decentralization for empowerment of rural poor'. Available at www.fao.org (accessed on 4 May 2010).

'Decentralisation and Political Accountability'. 2002. Available at www.odi.org.uk (accessed on 5 February 2009).

'Declaration of Principles on Tolerance'. 1995. Culture of Peace. Available at www. unesco.org (accessed on 20 April 2010).

'Definition of basic concepts and terminologies in governance and public administration'. 2006. Available at http://unpan1.un.org (accessed on 17 February 2010).

'Delhi snub to CM in judge joust'. 2009. *The Telegraph*, 11 March.

Desai, Jamshed. 2010. 'Bihar election results—a political renaissance in India'. Available on www.rexiter.co.uk (accessed on 9 December 2010).

'Details of CSR of 500 Companies'. Available at www.karmayog.org (accessed on 25 March 2010).

'Details of procedure followed in the allotment of cadre to the officers of the All India Service'. Ministry of Personnel. Available at http://persmin.nic.in (accessed on 3 March 2009).

Devasahayam, M. G. 2002. 'Whither electoral reforms?' *The Hindu*, 3 September.

Dey, Anindita. 2009. 'Performance appraisal: Govt takes a cue from private sector'. *Business Standard*, 6 June.

Dhar, Aarti. 2008. 'Survey: 3 years into RTI Act, information is hard to come by'. *The Hindu*, 9 September.

'Dharma, cardinal theme of the Mahabharata'. *The Hindu*, 16 August.

Dhavan, Rajeev. 2005. 'Separation of Powers'. *The Hindu*, 18 March.

Dhavan, S. S. 'The Indian Judicial System: A Historical Survey' Available at www.allahabadhighcourt.in (accessed on 8 February 2010).

'Dialling Delhi for corruption'. 2010. *The Financial Times*, 25 November.

Dirks, Nicholas B. 2001. 'Castes of Mind'. Princeton, NJ: Princeton University Press.

'Dissent isn't defection'. 2005. Available at www.indiatogether.org (accessed on 6 February 2009).

'DMK sulks over cabinet berths for Karuna's kin; Mamata mollified'. 2009. *Hindustan Times*, 22 May.

'DMU-Report Monitoring formats for Quarterly Report—July 2010 to September 2010'. 2010. Available at http://urbanindia.nic.in/ (accessed on 30 December 2010).

Drabu, Haseeb A. 2010. 'Structure of corruption'. *Mint*, 12 December.

Dwivedi, Anju and John Gaventa. 'Working on both sides of the equation: The role of NGOs in strengthening champions of participation in India'. Available at www.drc-citizenship.org (accessed on 5 February 2009).

'EC's response sought on incomplete affidavits'. 2008. *The Hindu*, 16 April.

Edwardes, Stephen and Herbert Leonard Offley Garrett. *Mughal Rule in India*. New Delhi: Atlantic Publishers and Distributors.

'Efficacy of Public Audit System in India: C & AG—Reforming the Institution'. 2001. Consultation paper, National Commission to Review the Working of the Constitution. Available at http://lawmin.nic.in (accessed on 21 January 2009).

'E-governance'. Available at http://india.gov.in (accessed on 9 November 2009).

'Election Expenses: Sky is not the limit'. 2008. *Deccan Herald*, 15 August.

'e-Lekha'. Available at www.cga.nic.in (accessed on 4 November 2009).

'Empowering Rural India'. 2010. Available at http://www.egovonline.net/. (accessed on 10 December 2010).

'Empowering the Civil Services'. 2006. Presentation at the Regional Conference on Fostering Excellence in Governance, Department of Personnel and Training, 6 October.

'Engagement in Scotland's Policy-Making System'. 2007. Available at www.scotland.gov.uk (accessed on 5 February 2009).

'Engaging Citizens in Policy making: Information, Consultation and Public Participation'. 2001. OECD. Available at www.oecd.org (accessed on 5 February 2009).

'EOC Bill, women's quota on House agenda'. 2009. *The Indian Express*, 17 November.

Eraly, Abrahim. 'Ten Indian flaws bequeathed by history'. Available at www.rediff.com (accessed on 13 August 2009).

'Evaluation Report on Sampoorna Gram Rozgar Yojana-SGRY, Jammu & Kashmir'. 2009. Programme Evaluation Organisation. Available at http://planningcommission.nic.in (accessed on 5 November 2009).

'Events: Workshop for Journalists on Tracking Legislators'. Available at www.prs-india.org (accessed on 17 December 2009).

'Executive—Its Accountability to Parliament'. Available at http://rajyasabha.gov.in (accessed on 16 February 2009).

'FAQs—Election Machinery'. Available at http://eci.nic.in (accessed on 25 February 2009).

'Finance Accounts: 2007–08'. Available at www.cga.nic.in/ (accessed on 4 November 2009).

Fish, Steven M. and Brooks, Robin. 2004. 'Does Diversity Hurt Democracy?' *Journal of Democracy*, 15 (1).

'Firms in Corrupt Countries Pay a Price in Market Value'. 2010. Available on http://www.gsb.stanford.edu/ (accessed on 10 January 2011).

'FOI Act and Fighting Corruption'. 2004. Available at www.humanrightsinitiative.org/ (accessed on 7 July 2009).

Fox, Leslie and Priya Helweg. 1997. 'Advocacy Strategies for Civil Society: A Conceptual Framework and Practitioner's Guide'. Available at http://pdf.dec.org (accessed on 30 March 2010).

Francis, Bijo. 'Judge transfers may not stop corruption'. Available at www.upiasia.com (accessed on 20 February 2009).

'Gallup World Poll'. 2002–08. Available at www.gallup.com (accessed on 30 April 2009).

Gangadhar, V. 2004. 'Roots of corruption'. *The Hindu*, 6 June.

'Gazette Notification dated March 14 2007'. 2007. Available at http://persmin.nic.in/ (accessed on 8 January 2011).

Gedam, Pranali and Ajay Agashe. 'Information Literacy Competencies and Programmes in India'. Available at http://crl.du.ac.in (accessed on 11 May 2010).

Geetika and Neeraj Pandey. 'National E-Governance Plan Revisited: Achievements and Road Ahead'. Available at www.iceg.net (accessed on 9 November 2009).

Ghose, Bhaskar. 2004. 'Colonial baggage'. *Frontline*, February.

Ghosh, Sanmitra. 2006. 'The Phenomenon of Voter Turnout in the Parliamentary Elections of India'. *Contemporary Issues in Social Sciences*, June.

Gier, Nicholas 'Dharma Morality as Virtue Ethics'. Available at www.class.uidaho.edu (accessed on 3 February 2010).

'Global E-democracy Best Practices—Case Study Summaries'. Available at http://dowire.org (accessed on 9 February 2009).

'Global Integrity Report—India'. 2007. Available at www.globalintegrity.org/ (accessed on 6 April 2009).

'Global Integrity Report—India'. 2004. Available at www.globalintegrity.org/ (accessed on 6 April 2009).

'Goa chief minister sought police transfers: RTI activist'. Available on www.rtiindia.org (accessed on 24 February 2011).

Godbole, Madhav. 1997. 'Bureaucracy Bashing'. *The Times of India*, 14 May.

Gordillo, Manuel Vega and Jose L. Alvarez-Arce. 2003. 'Economic Growth and Freedom: A Causality Study'. Available at www.freetheworld.com (accessed on 19 May 2010).

Goetz, Anne Marie and Rob Jenkins. 2002. 'Voice, Accountability and Human Development: The Emergence of a New Agenda'. Background Paper for HDR 2002. Available at http://hdr.undp.org (accessed on 21 April 2009).

Gopalakrishnan, V. N. 'Kautilya's Arthashastra'. Available at www.karmayog.org (accessed on 4 February 2010).

'Govt for filling up vacancies of judges in SC, HC'. 2009. *Business Standard*, 27 August.

'Govt reshuffles cabinet, seeks to improve image'. 2011. *Mint*, 19 January.

'Govt suspends 19 CMC officials'. 2003. *The Times of India*, 11 December.

'Guidelines for Results-Framework Document (RFD) 2010–11'. Available at http://performance.gov.in (accessed on 8 January 2011).

Gupta, Anand. 2005. 'It's all in the outcomes'. *The Sunday Express*, 24 September.

Gupta, Anand P. 2007. 'Outcome budgets and budget outcomes'. *The Indian Express*, 8 January.

Gupta, V. P. 2002. 'The President's role'. *The Times of India*, 26 August.

'Half Yearly Progress Monitoring Report—Sarva Shiksha Abhiyan'. Available at http://ssa.nic.in/ (accessed on 23 November 2009).

Haque, Shamsul. 2002. 'E-governance in India: its impact on relations among citizens, politicians and public servants'. Available at http://profile.nus.edu.sg (accessed on 11 December 2008).

Hazra, Arnab. 2009. 'Bureaucrats on the loose'. *Hindustan Times*, 22 January.

'HC judges to declare assets on May 21'. 2010. *The Tribune*, 19 May.

Hebbar, Neria Harish. 2002. 'History of Islam in India'. Available at http://www.boloji.com/ (accessed on 8 February 2010).

'History of Social Relations in India'. Available at http://india_resource.tripod.com/social.htm (accessed on April 5, 2010).

'How much does an election cost'. (2004). *Rediff News*. March 26. Available at www.rediff.com (accessed on April 28, 2010).

'How should elections be made clean?'. (2005). *The Tribune*. January 24.

'How to root out corruption'. (2010). *The Times of India*. November 2.

'IAS officers to be put on PAR'. (2005). *The Indian Express*. May 8.

'Identity Politics In India (Caste, Religion, Language And Ethnicity)'. Available at www.egyankosh.ac.in (accessed on February 2, 2009).

'In Pursuit of Democratic Reforms – Lok Satta's Experiences'. (2003). Presentation by Loksatta at ADR. 10–11 May. Ahmedabad.

'India: A Historical View. 2008. Available at www.asiasociety.org (accessed on 28 August 2010).

'India: Asia's Next Tiger?' Essays in Public Policy. Available at www.hoover.org (accessed on 19 February 2009).

'India: Lack of accountability has corrupted Judiciary'. 2008. Asian Human Rights Commission, 10 September. Available at www.ahrchk.net (accessed on 9 December 2008).

'India Corruption Study 2005'. 2005. Transparency International India. Available at http://www.prajanet.org (accessed on 28 May 2009).

'India Statistics—Literacy Rate'. Available at www.indiastat.com (accessed on 9 December 2008).

'Indian electoral exercise becoming big biz for many'. 2004. Available at www.siliconindia.com (accessed on 9 February 2009).

'Indian National Movement'. Indian History Section. Available at www.currentgk.com (accessed on 5 February 2010).

'Individualism versus Collectivism'. Available at www.via-web.de (accessed on 6 May 2010).

Inglehart, R. and Christian Welzel. 2009. 'How Development Leads to Democracy'. *Foreign Affairs*, March/April.

'International Day of Democracy 2009: Democracy and political tolerance'. Available at www.ipu.org (accessed on 17 March 2010).

'International Experience of PRIS'. Available at http://india.gov.in/ (accessed on 6 January 2010).

'Is EC helpless about model code violations?' 2004. *The Hindu*, 22 April.

'Is The Anti-Defection Law Suppressing MPs?' 2009. Available at www.india-server.com (accessed on 6 January 2010).

Iyer, Krishna V. R. 2007. 'Judicial reform in the Indian context'. *The Hindu*, 12 May.

————. 2002. 'Judicial review in a democracy'. *The Hindu*, 11 June.

Iyer, Lakshmi, 2004. 'The Long-term Impact of Colonial Rule: Evidence from India'. Available at www.people.hbs.edu (accessed on 2 February 2010).

'Jaago Re! One Billion Votes Campaign Awakens young India!'. 2008. Available at www.janaagraha.org (accessed on 13 April 2010).

Jain, Ashok. 2008. *Public Administration*. Mumbai: Sheth Publishers.

Jain, R. B. 'Parliament and Policy in India'. Available at www.lib.hku.hk/ (accessed on 23 February 2009).

Jain, Vaishali. 2006. *Crisis in Indian Democracy and Gandhian Alternative*. Chandigarh: Panjab University.

Jamatia, Hamari. 2008. 'Poll process discouraging'. *The Indian Express*, 12 November.

'Jawaharlal Nehru Urban Renewal Mission-Overview'. Available at http://jnnurm.nic.in/ (accessed on 23 November 2009).

'Jawaharlal Nehru National Urban Renewal Mission Monitoring Formats'. 2010. Available at www.urbanindia.nic.in (accessed on 30 January 2011).

Jayal, Niraja Gopal. 2008. 'New Directions in Theorising Accountability', *IDS Bulletin*, 38 (6).

Iyengar, Jayanthi. 2004. 'Elections and the funding conundrum'. *The Hindu Business Line*, 10 April.

Jha, Sanjay. 2010. 'Performance scare sinks in—Ministers fret after signing up'. *The Telegraph*, 2 February.

'Jharkand: Addressing the challenges of inclusive development'. World Bank. Available at http://web.worldbank.org (accessed on 2 March 2011).

Jing, Su. 2007. 'Corruption by design? A comparative study of Singapore, Hong Kong and mainland China'. ANU College of Asia and the Pacific: Crawford School of Economics and Government.

Johnson, Craig. 2003 'Decentralization in India: Poverty. Politics and Panchayati Raj'. Available at www.odi.org.uk (accessed on 29 April 2010).

Johnson, Isabelle. 1997. 'Redefining the Concept of Governance'. Canadian International Development Agency. Available at www.acdi-cida.gc.ca (accessed on 17 February 2010).

Joshi, Anuradha. 2008. 'Uncivil servants'. *India Today*, 25 September.

Joshi, Preeta. 2003. 'Accountability, Indian Administrative Culture and Trust'. Available at http://unpan1.un.org (accessed on 19 February 2009).

'Judges get hike with a footnote on corruption'. 2009. *The Times of India*, 20 February.

'Judicial Accountability'. Available at www.judicialreforms.org (accessed on 4 January 2010).

'Judicial excesses'. 2002. *The Hindu*, 9 December.

'Judicial System and Reforms in Asian Countries: The Case of India'. IDE Asian Law Series No. 3, Institute of Developing Economies. Available at www.ide.go.jp (accessed on 19 February 2009).

'Judiciary comes under RTI ambit, says House panel'. 2008. *The Financial Express*, 30 April.

'Justice and Judicial Delay'. 2007. *The Hindu*, 6 September.

'Justice Ashok Kumar's Appointment Challenged'. 2007. *The Hindu*, 31 July.

K., Muthukumar. 2000. 'CVC—quo vadis?' *The Hindu*, 28 November.

Kapur, Devesh. 2005. 'India's Promise'. *Harvard Magazine*, July–August. Available at http://harvardmagazine.com (accessed on 8 December 2008).

Kapur, Devesh and Pratap Bhanu Mehta. 2006. 'The Indian Parliament as an Institution of Accountability'. Available at www.unrisd.org (accessed on 16 February 2009).

————— (eds). 2005. *Public Institutions in India*. New Delhi: Oxford University Press.

Karisiddappa, C. R. and Iqbalahmad U. Rajgoli. 2007. 'Blooming knowledge society and information literacy in India'. *Sri Lankan Journal of Librarianship and Information Management*, 3 (1). pp. 1–13.

Kashyap, Subhash. 2000. 'Working of Parliament And Need For Reforms'. Available at http://lawmin.nic.in (accessed on 6 February 2009).

Katju, Markandey. 2007. 'Contempt of court: a need for second look'. Available at http://districtcourtallahabad.up.nic.in (accessed on 4 January 2010).

Katyal, Anita. 2009. 'Now, Congmen battle it out for berths'. *The Tribune*, 26 May.

Kaufmann, Daniel, Art Kraay and Pablo Zoido-Lobaton. 1999. 'Governance Matters'. Washington, D.C.: The World Bank.

Kaur, Sumandeep. 2008. 'Electoral Reforms in India: Proactive Role of Election Commission'. *Mainstream Weekly*, XLVI (49).

Kaushik, K. Ram. 2009. 'What ails e-governance in India'. Available at www.merinews.com (accessed on 3 May 2010).

'Kejriwal Arvind. 'One year of unfreedom'. 2007. Available at www.indiatogether. org (accessed on 19 December 2008).

Kesharwani, Madhusudan. 'Judges and Judicial Accountability in India with reference to the Judge's bill of 2005'. Available at www.indialaws.info (accessed on 4 February 2009).

Khan, Salar. 'Judicial Accountability: No Adjournment, Please!'. Available at www. hrsolidarity.net (accessed on 18 February 2009).

Khandavalli Bharadwaj, Shankara and Krishna Maheshwari. 'Dharma'. www. hindupedia.com/ (accessed on 3 February 2010).

'Kingship'. Available at www.indiaheritage.org (accessed on 2 February 2010).

Klasing, Mariko. 2008. 'The Cultural Roots of Institutions'. University of St. Gallen: Department of Economics.

Knack, Stephen and Omar Azfar. 2003. 'Trade intensity, country size and corruption'. *Economics of Governance*, 4, pp. 1–18.

_____. 2000. 'Are Larger Countries Really More Corrupt?'. IRIS—University of Maryland. Available at www.worldbank.org (accessed on 18 March 2010).

'Know your MLA: Did he serve you, or his cronies?' 2008. *The Times of India*, 31 October.

'Know Your Parliament'. Available at www.prsindia.org (accessed on 6 February 2009).

Kondo, Norio. 2007. 'Election Studies in India'. Discussion Paper, Institute of Developing Economies, March. Available at http://ir.ide.go.jp (accessed on 10 December 2008).

Kripalani, Manjeet. 2008. 'Hiking Indian bureaucrats' salaries: Smart or silly?' *Business Week*, 25 March.

Krishna Murthy, T. S. and Vijay Patidar. 'Case Study: India—Getting to the CORE'. ACE—The Electoral Knowledge Network. Available at http://aceproject.org (accessed on 6 February 2009).

Krugman, Paul. 1998. 'The Role of Geography in Development'. Available at http://www.signallake.com (accessed on 14 May 2010).

Kumar, Abeer. 'Whistle-blowers and the law'. Available at www.legalserviceindia. com (accessed on 20 April 2009).

Kumar, Kamal. 'Police-Executive Relationship in India'. Available at www.human-rightsinitiative.org/ (accessed on 19 May 2009).

Kumar, Rajesh. 'Doing Business in India: Beware the Similarities'. Centre for Intercultural Learning. Available at www.international.gc.ca (accessed on 3 February 2010).

Kumar, Sanjay and Suhas Palshikar. 2004. 'Participatory Norm: How Broad-based Is It?' *Economic and Political Weekly*, 18 December.

Kumara Swamy, V. 2010. 'Portals with punch'. *The Telegraph*, 4 January.

Lahiri, R. K. 2005. 'Caste System in Hinduism: A Historical and Analytical Approach'. Available at www.boloji.com (accessed on 8 February 2010).

Lakshmi, Rama. 2008. 'Indian Cities Eye New Delhi's Quiet Citizen Revolution'. *The Washington Post*, 2 March.

'Landmark SC orders on right to food'. Available at www.empowerpoor.org (accessed on 31 December 2009).

'Later Vedic civilization'. History of India Section. Available at www.indianetzone. com (accessed on 2 February 2010).

'Legal System and Judiciary'. Available at www.egyankosh.ac.in (accessed on 5 February 2010).

Lian, A. S. 2008. 'Singapore Experience—Dealing With Governance and Corruption'. Available at www.apsacc.com.au (accessed on 15 June 2009).

Lic, Gustavo Axel Radics. 2001. 'Cristal: A Tool for Transparent Government in Argentina'. *e-Government Case Studies—The World Bank*. Available at http://web.worldbank.org (accessed on 25 June 2009).

'Life and Works of Thomas Robert Malthus'. Available at www.blupete.com (accessed on 23 April 2010).

'Loksabha 2009'. Available at http://myneta.info/ (accessed on 13 April 2010).

'Loopholes in Right to Information Act'. 2004. *The Times of India*, 19 January.

Maddison, Angus. 1971. 'The Economic and Social Impact of Colonial Rule in India' In *Class Structure and Economic Growth: India and Pakistan*. London: George Allen and Unwin.

Madhawan, M. R. and Namita Wahi. 2008. 'Measuring the Effectiveness of the Indian Parliament'. Available at www.prsindia.org (accessed on 20 February 2009).

Mahapatra, Dhananjay. 2010. 'Judges accountability bill watered down'. *The Times of India*, 24 August.

Mahapatra, Dhananjay and Akshaya Mukul. 2010. 'Late or dozing in court? Judges could be in the dock'. *The Times of India*, 1 January.

Mahapatra, Dhananjay. 2009. 'SC collegium scraps Dinakaran's chances of promotion'. *The Times of India*, 18 December.

Maheshwari, S. R. 2001. *Indian Administration*. New Delhi: Orient Longman.

'Make appointment of judges transparent'. 2007. *Express India*, 30 November.

'Make it possible to judge the judges'. 2009. *Hindustan Times*, 3 August.

'Making Population Stabilization a Peoples' Programme'. National Commission on Population. Available at http://populationcommission.nic.in (accessed on 12 May 2010).

Malajovich, Laura and Mark Robinson. 2006. 'Budget Analysis and Social Activism: The Case of DISHA in Gujarat, India—Executive Summary'. Available at www.internationalbudget.org (accessed on 13 April 2010).

Malhotra, M. L. 2007. 'Instrumentality of the CAG and the Executive's Accountability'. *Mainstream Weekly*, XLV (49).

'Managing For Results'. Budget of the United States Government for fiscal year 2009. www.gpoaccess.gov/ (accessed on 4 November 2009).

Mandal, Debaki. 2004. 'Beg Your Pardon. My Lord'. *The Telegraph*, 17 November.

Mathaiyan, R. 2004. *Social Science*. Chennai: Tamilnadu Textbook Corporation.

'Manusmriti: the Laws of Manu'. Available at www.hinduwebsite.com (accessed on 5 April 2010).

Marker, Sandra. 2003. 'Effects of Colonization'. Available at www.beyondintractability.org/ (accessed on 8 February 2010).

McCandless, Henry. 2008. 'The Issue of Public Accountability: A Summary for Citizens'. Available at www.accountabilitycircle.org/ (accessed on 8 December 2008).

McDermott, Jim. 2001. 'Ensuring Accountability: The Role of Parliament'. National Endowment for Democracy. Available at www.ned.org/ (accessed on 3 February 2009).

Mehdudia, Sujay. 2004. 'Government faces accountability crisis'. *The Hindu*, 3 September.

————. 2004. 'Bhagidari runs into rough weather with MLAs'. *The Hindu*, 2 January.

Mehta, J. L. 2009. 'Aurangzeb'. In *Advanced Study in the History of Medieval India*. New Delhi: Sterling Publishers.

Mehta, Mandavi. 2003. 'The Role of Hindutva in Indian Politics'. *South Asia Monitor*, 1 February.

'Members' Allowances'. 2007–08. MPs. Lords and Offices Section. Available at www.parliament.uk/ (accessed on 19 June 2009).

Milner, Henry. 2001. 'Civic Literacy: How Informed Citizens Make Democracy Work'. Available at www.sase.org (accessed on 28 April 2010).

————. 2001. 'Civic Literacy in Comparative Context'. Available at www.irpp.org (accessed on 28 April 2010).

Misra, Sanjay. 2010. 'Fixing the leaking pipe'. *Mint*, 30 March.

Mishra, Abhishek and Swati Mishra. 'Formulating the concept, principles and parameters for performance-related incentives in Government'. Report submitted to the Sixth Central Pay Commission. Available at http://india.gov. in (accessed on 18 August 2009).

Mishra, R. K. 2001. 'National Civil Service System in India: A Critical View'. Available at http://citeseerx.ist.psu.edu (accessed on 28 July 2009).

Mitta, Manoj. 'Standing in for Parliament'. 2008. *The Times of India*, 28 December.

'Mobile services in Tartu-Estonia'. 2005. Available at www.ega.ee (accessed on 3 July 2009).

Mohanty, Biswaranjan. 2007. 'Indian Polity and Constitution'. *Pratiyogita Darpan*, March.

Monga, Anil. 2008. 'E-government in India: Opportunities and challenges'. *JOAAG*, 3 (2).

'Monitoring of Plan Scheme Expenditure—CPSMS an e-governance initiative'. Available at http://www.icisa.cag.gov.in/ (accessed on 2 November 2009).

'Mughal Administration'. Available at www.columbia.edu (accessed on 8 February 2010).

'Mughal era in India'. Available at www.indianchild.com (accessed on 22 July 2009).

'Mughal Administration: Mansab and Jagir'. Available at www.egyankosh.ac.in (accessed on 29 July 2009).

Mukul, Akshaya and Sanjay Dutta. 2009. 'Rs 6000 cr poll stimulus'. *The Times of India*, 18 February.

Murphy, John. 2009. 'Recovery.gov reveals details of the stimulus spending'. *Transparency and Open Government—Intergovernmental Solutions Newsletter.* Available at www.usaservices.gov (accessed on 6 June 2009).

Naik, J. V. 1997. 'Early intellectual resistance to British colonial rule'. *The Indian Express,* 9 May.

Narayan, Jayaprakash. 2003. 'Liberalization, literacy and governance'. Available at www.indiatogether.org (accessed on 16 March 2010).

———. 2003. 'Decentralisation. Voting and the Public Good'. Available at www. indiatogether.org (accessed on 4 May 2010).

'NCPRI RTI Convention 2011'. Available at http://righttoinformation.info (accessed on 22 March 2011).

Nelson, Sue. 2003. 'Election Law Enforcement—International Comparisons'. *Electoral Insight.* Available at www.elections.ca (accessed on 15 June 2009).

Ngowi, Daniel. 'Best Practices In Civil Society Involvement in Budget Monitoring and Policy Accountability'. Available at www.tanzaniagateway.org/ (accessed on 6 July 2009).

'Notification—Setting up of a Delivery Monitoring Unit in the Prime Minister's Office'. 2009. Available at http://pmindia.nic.in (accessed on 5 November 2009).

O'Donnell, G. 1999. 'Horizontal Accountability in New Democracies', in Andreas Schedler, Larry Jay Diamond and Marc F. Plattner (eds), *The Self-Restraining State: Power and Accountability in New Democracies*. London: Lynne Reinner.

Okediji, T. 2008. 'Social Diversity Index—The Color of Brazil: Law, Ethnic Fragmentation, and Economic Growth' *Chicago Kent Law Review*, 82 (3).

'Ongoing key activities undertaken by Kabir'. Available at www.kabir.org.in (accessed on 12 April 2010).

'OnlineComplaintMonitoringSystem(OCMS)'.*Praja*.Availableat216.197.119.113/ artman/uploads/ocms_write-up.doc (accessed on 27 January 2010).

'Only two of every 100 RTI Act violations get penalised: Study'. 2009. *Business Standard*, 22 October.

'Open up, Let the sunshine in'. 2009. *Best Practices*, 6 (1).

Ouedraogo, Dawn. 2009. 'British India, Creator of Indian Caste System?' Available at http://indian-history.suite101.com (accessed on 3 February 2010).

'Overview—Civil Society Organisations'. Available at www.icicifoundation.org (accessed on 25 March 2010).

'Overview—CSO Partners Website'. Available at www.csopartners.org.in (accessed on 25 March 2010).

'Overview of Rural Decentralization in India'. 2000. Available at www.worldbank. org (accessed on 16 January 2009).

'Panchayat Raj Act'. Available at http://panchayat.nic.in (accessed on 23 November 2009).

'Panchayat Empowerment & Accountability Incentive Scheme'. 2010. Available at www.pib.nic.in (accessed on 20 February 2011).

Pande, Suchi Nikhil Dey and Aruna Roy. 'The Law Above All?' www.judicialreforms.org (accessed on 14 January 2009).

Pandey, Sandeep. 2008. 'Social audit of jobs programme in UP'. Available at www. indiatogether.org/ (accessed on 2 July 2009).

Pandit, Vivek. 'Advocacy concepts and techniques'. Available at www.internationalbudget.org (accessed on 26 March 2010).

'Parliament Library'. Available at http://loksabha.nic.in/ (accessed on 20 February 2009).

'Parliamentary Committees'. Available at http://parliamentofindia.nic.in (accessed on 4 March 2011).

'Participatory Budgeting in Pune'. 2007. Centre for Environment Education. Available at http://government.wikia.com (accessed on 7 July 2009).

Paul, Samuel. 1994. 'Does voice Matter: For Public Accountability, Yes'. Policy Research Working Paper. Washington, D. C.: The World Bank.

'Perform or perish a signal for bureaucrats'. 2010. *Bureaucracy Today*, 1 September.

'Performance appraisal of Civil Servants'. Background paper prepared by Sardar Patel Institute of Public Administration. Available at www.darpg.nic.in (accessed on 20 February 2009).

'Performance Management in Government': Civil Services Day 2009—Proceedings. Available at www.cgg.gov.in (accessed on 12 January 2011).

'Period of Religious Upheaval'. Available at www.webindia123.com (accessed on 5 February 2010).

'Petitioning President a click away'. 2009. *The Times of India*, 27 July.

Pillai, Ramachandran S. 2007. 'Judiciary and the Ongoing Debates'. Available at http://pd.cpim.org (accessed on 19 March 2009).

'PIL on DGP appointment sparks debate on judicial activism'. 2008. *The Indian Express*, 5 January.

Pokriyal, Geetika. 'Just seen, never heard: 15 MPs who didn't speak'. 2009. Available at http://ibnlive.in.com (accessed on 19 January 2010).

'Police Organisation in India'. 2008. *Commonwealth Human Rights Initiative.* Available at www.humanrightsinitiative.org. (accessed on 9 December 2010).

'Police Services'. 2007. *TII-CMS India Corruption Study 2007—With Focus on BPL Households.* Available at http://cmsindia.org (accessed on 19 May 2009).

'Political forms of Ancient India'. Available at www.onlineessays.com (accessed on 22 July 2009).

'Poll panel gets notice over loophole in electoral law'. 2008. Available at www.thaindian.com (accessed on 26 March 2009).

'Powers of Samiti or Parliament'. Available at www.indiaheritage.org (accessed on 2 February 2010).

'President Kalam's file noting on Vijender Jain appointment'. 2006. *The Hindu*, 1 December.

'Pressures of Loyalism during British Rule'. Available at http://india_resource. tripod.com (accessed on 4 February 2010).

'PRIA Journals and Newsletters'. Available at www.pria.org (accessed on 13 April 2010).

'Prior sanction not needed in corruption cases, says SC'. 2006. *The Financial Express*, 7 December.

'Process of Public Accountability—Public Accountability Chain'. www.cag.gov.in (accessed on 8 December 2008).

'Programme Evaluation Organisation'. Divisions. Available at www.planningcommission.nic.in (accessed on 5 November 2009).

'Proposed Electoral Reforms'. 2004. Available at http://eci.nic.in (accessed on 6 January 2009).

'Proposed Govt Lokpal Bill is an eyewash'. Available at http://indiaagainstcorruption.org/ (accessed on 2 March 2011).

'Public Affairs Centre Develops Citizen Report Cards in India'. 2008. Available at www.internationalbudget.org (accessed on 15 February 2011).

'Public Participation in Budgeting in India'. 2007. Available at http://content. msn.co.in (accessed on 3 February 2009).

'Public Interest Legal Support and Research Centre'. Available at www.wiserearth. org (accessed on 31 March 2010).

'Public Interest Litigations (PILs)'. Available at www.janhitmanch.org (accessed on 2 March 2009).

'Public participation in reforms is low'. 2003. *Financial Express*, 14 February.

Pye, Lucian W. 2002. 'Book Review: Castes of Mind: Colonialism and the Making of Modern India'. *Foreign Affairs*, May/June.

Raghavan, B. S. 2008. 'Appointment of Judges'. *The Hindu Business Line*, 24 November.

Rajagopal, Krishnadas. 2009. '26 pc men. 12 pc women aware of RTI, reveals DoPT'. *The Indian Express*, 2 November.

Rahman, Shafi. 2003. 'Commission's omissions'. *India Today*, 12 February.

Rajadhyaksha, Niranjan. 2009. '"Aam aadmi" and oligarchies'. *Mint*, 30 June.

Raja, N. K., G. Sundararaman, G. Vasumathi and K. Palanisamy. 2005. *Political Science*. Chennai: Tamilnadu Textbook Corporation.

Rajan, Sudanshu. 2008. 'Judicial appointments and transfers: need for transparency' *Deccan Herald*, 31 October.

Rajan, Raghuram. 2010. 'Afterword: What lies ahead for India'. In *Fault Lines: How Hidden Fractures Still Threaten the World Economy*. Noida: Harper Collins.

Ramshaw, Graeme. 'Independent Monitoring Organizations: A Qualitative Look at Performance'. Available at www.internationalbudget.org (accessed on 4 May 2010).

Ramanujam, T. and T. Sangeetha. 2002. 'Cleansing the electoral process'. *The Hindu Business Line*, 2 August.

Ramkumar, Vivek. 2004. 'Case Study, Part 2: The Right to Know Movement in India. Making Change Happen'. Available at www.sasanet.org (accessed on 13 April 2010).

Rana, Ajit. 2007. 'CBI's impartiality has taken a beating'. Available at http://indiainteracts.in (accessed on 29 April 2010).

'Ranking Our Netas'. 2010. Available at http://business.in.com (accessed on 8 January 2011).

Rao, Arati. 2006. 'Janaagraha: Harnessing the force of the people. Available at http://infochangeindia.org (accessed on 7 July 2009).

Rao, S. R. 2009. 'e-Governance in India: Premises & Promises'. Available at www.csi-sigegov.org (accessed on 10 November 2009).

Rao, Vijay Rama. 'Research Studies on Police and Prison Issues (1970–2007) Compendium, Report no. 120: Training Policemen of the Future (2001)'. Available at http://bprd.nic.in/. (accessed on 9 December 2010).

'Recruitment & Promotion': Public Sector Governance. Washington D. C.: The World Bank.

Reichenbach, Bruce. 1988. 'The Law of Karma and the Principle of Causation'. *Philosophy East and West*, 38 (4), pp. 399–410.

Reinke, Saundra. 2005. 'Exploring the Unknown: What We Know, and Don't Know, About Civic Engagement in College Students'. Available at www.teachingpa.org (accessed on 26 April 2010).

'Refurbishing of Personnel Administration'. Tenth Report of Second Administrative Reforms Commission. Available at http://arc.gov.in (accessed on 20 February 2009).

'Registration of Political Parties'. Available at www.indian-elections.com (accessed on 2 March 2009).

'Report cards on the performance of Delhi MLAs'. 2008. Available at www.snsindia.org (accessed on 19 January 2010).

'Report for Delivery Monitoring Unit (DMU) of PMO'. Sarva Shiksha Abhiyan. Available at www.ssa.nic.in (accessed on 5 November 2009).

'Report on the Public Interest Disclosure and Protection of Informers'. 2001. Available at http://lawcommissionofindia.nic.in (accessed on 20 April 2009).

'Results-Framework Document of Ministries / Departments for the year 2010–11'. Available at http://performance.gov.in (accessed on 8 January 2011).

'Results Framework Document for Department of School Education and Literacy for 2010–11'. Available at www.education.nic.in (accessed on 22 March 2011).

Reuben, William. 2003. 'The Role of Civic Engagement and Social Accountability in the Governance Equation'. *Social Development Note Series*. Available at www.sasanet.org/ (accessed on 26 March 2010).

'Right of Children to free and compulsory education act'. Available at www.indg.in (accessed on 23 November 2009).

Rinne, Jeffrey and A. Lage. 2001. 'Citizen Service Centers in Bahia, Brazil'. e-Government Case Studies. Washington, D. C.: The World Bank. Available at www.worldbank.org (accessed on 25 June 2009).

Robinson, Mark. 'Resources, Citizen Engagement And Democratic Local Governance'. Available at www2.ids.ac.uk (accessed on 5 February 2009).

Roy, Bhaskar. 2006. 'Immunity cover for top babus may go'. *The Times of India*, 14 October.

Roy, R. R. 2008. 'Key pro-poor schemes miss targets'. Available at http://igovernment.in/ (accessed on 30 June 2009).

'RTI exposes 481 transfer requests by mumbai police officials written by MLAs and ministers in just 19 months'. 2006. Available at www.rtiindia.org (accessed on 22 March 2011).

'RTI-MIS Usage Status'. 2011. Department of Personnel and Training. Available at www.persmin.nic.in (accessed on 4 March 2011)

Rukambe, Joram. 2009. 'Promoting Political Tolerance: Experiences From Selected Countries'. A presentation at the Namibia 2009 Electoral Symposium, 17–18 March, Windhoek.

Sabharwal, Y. K. 2006. 'Valedictory Address'. National Colloquium on Ethics in Governance—Moving from Rhetoric to Results, 2 September, Bhopal.

Sachdeva, Samir. 2010. 'Accountability will help us develop faster'. *Governance Now*, 2 December.

Sachs, Jeffrey, Andrew Mellinger and John Gallup. 2000. 'The Geography of Poverty and Wealth'. *Scientific American*, 284 (March), pp. 70–75.

'Sack unfit bureaucrats: Moily panel'. 2008. *The Indian Express*, 12 December.

Saeed, Shahbaz M. 2007. 'Caste System in India and its Impact on Politics'. *Strategic Studies*, XXVII (1).

Sainath, P. 2008. 'They lock on to the NREGA'. Available at www.indiatogether.org (accessed on 28 December 2009).

Sangar, Pramod. 2001. 'There was widespread corruption in Mughal India'. *The Tribune*, 8 December.

Sarma, Mahesh. 'Contending paradigms for contested public spaces: role of CSOs in shaping Delhi's transport policy'. Available at www.odi.org.uk (accessed on 17 December 2009).

Satish, M. 2004. 'Civil Service Reforms'. Available at www.cgg.gov.in (accessed on 20 February 2009).

'SC allows contempt plea in Kapadia case'. 2009. *The Times of India*, 10 October.

'SC judges ready to declare assets, but with riders'. 2009. *The Economic Times*, 17 March.

'Scheme for Modernization of State Police Forces'. Available at http://mha.nic.in (accessed on 9 November 2009).

Sen, Ashish. 'Citizens' voices into Bangalore budget'. Available at www.indiatogether.org (accessed on 7 July 2009).

Sezhiyan, Era. 2001. 'On contentious territory'. *Frontline*, August.

Shah, Parmesh and Sanjay Agarwal. 'Participatory approaches in public expenditure management'. Available at www.sasanet.org (accessed on 27 January 2010).

Shah, Parth and Bakore Makarand. 2006. *Ward Power: Decentralised Urban Governance*. New Delhi: Centre for Civil Society.

Sharma, Bhavna. 2009. 'Voice, Accountability and Civic Engagement: A Conceptual Overview'. Discussion Paper 14, UNDP Oslo Governance Centre.

Sharma, Gokulesh. 'Crime, Punishment and Judicial Procedure in Ancient (Smrti) India'. Available at http://drgokuleshsharma.com (accessed on 8 February 2010).

Sharma, Nagendar. 2009. 'Make judges names public, say jurists.' *Hindustan Times*, 19 December.

Sharma, Nagender. 2009. 'UK. US judges declare assets. Indian judges don't want to'. *Hindustan Times*, 30 January.

Sharma, Rajvir. 2004. 'Changing notions of accountability: A good governance perspective', *The Asian Review of Public Administration*, XVI (1).

Sharma, Sadhvi. 2009. 'Fractured Narratives: Identities in a Political Vacuum'. Paper presented at 'The Nation: Narratives and Community', Workshop organized by The Centre of Excellence for National Security (CENS), Nanyang Technological University, Singapore, and The National Security Coordination Secretariat (NSCS), 2 March, Singapore.

Shourie, Arun. 2009. 'New beginnings?' *The Indian Express*, 15 June.

Shourie, H. D. 2004. 'Toothless watchdogs can only watch, not act'. *The Indian Express*, 12 November.

Singh, Mahendra Kumar. 2010. 'Govt to match netas' I-T returns with poll affidavits'. *The Times of India*, 4 January.

————. 2009. 'Govt plans independent body to evaluate aam aadmi schemes'. *The Times of India*, 16 September.

Singh, Mahendra P. and Surya Deva. 2005. 'The Constitution of India: Symbol of Unity in Diversity'. *Yearbook of Public Law*, 53, pp. 649–86.

Singh, Ritesh and Vinay Vutukuru. 'Enhancing Accountability in Public Service Delivery Through Social Audits: A Case Study of Andhra Pradesh, India'. Available at www.accountabilityindia.org (accessed on 30 June 2009).

Singh, Sanjay. 2007. 'Bench upholds expulsion of tainted MPs'. *The Economic Times*, 11 January.

Singh, Tavleen. 2004. 'How about a code for CECs—past and present'. *The Indian Express*, 9 May.

Singh, N. K. 2005. 'Bridging the gap between outlays and outcomes'. *Indian Express*, 4 September.

Singh, U. B. 1998. 'Age of Imperial Unity'. In *Administrative System in India: Vedic Age to 1947*, New Delhi: APH Publishing Corporation.

Singhal, Nishtha. 'Understanding the citizens' right to information'. Available at http://ccs.in/ccsindia/ (accessed on 15 April 2010).

Sinha, Kaustabh and Nabjita. 2008. 'Doctrine of pleasure and its proviso article 311 of Indian Constitution'. Available at www.legalserviceindia.com (accessed on 1 February 2010).

Sinha, Rajesh Kumar. 2008. 'Accountability in Rural Wage Employment Programmes in India: Case of Social Audit in NREGA'. Paper presented at the 5th International Conference on Citizenship and Governance, PRIA, 27–29 February, New Delhi.

Sirker, Karen 2006. 'General Social Accountability Concepts and Tools'. World Bank Institute. Available at www.icgfm.org (accessed on 3 May 2010).

'Social Audit Calendar'. Available at http://nrega.nic.in (accessed on 22 January 2010).

'Social audit ensured success of NREGS'. 2009. *The Indian Express*, 26 May.

'Social Audit: Gram Sabha and Panchayati Raj'. 2005. Available at http://planningcommission.nic.in (accessed on 30 June 2009).

'Statement of Election Expenditure'. Available at http://eci.nic.in/ (accessed on 1 September 2009).

'SMS and Helpline Campaign'. Available at http://nationalelectionwatch.org (accessed on 13 April 2010).

'Social Accountability in India: Moving from Mechanisms to Outcomes and Institutionalisation in Large Scale Public Programmes'. 2009. Available at www.cuts-international.org (accessed on 12 April 2010).

'Social Accountability Mechanism—A Generic Framework'. Available at http://darpg.nic.in (accessed on 12 April 2010).

'SP in tatters; Shahid Siddiqui joins BSP'. 2008. Available at http://news.rediff.com (accessed on 6 January 2010).

Sprunger, Meredith. 'An Introduction to Hinduism'. Available at http://urantia-book.org/ (accessed on 10 February 2010).

Stapenhurst Rick. 2000. 'The Media's role in curbing corruption'. The World Bank Institute.

'State not prepared to tackle bogus voting, says EC'. (2008). *The Indian Express*. April 10.

'State-society synergy for accountability: Lessons from the World Bank'. 2003. Washington, D. C.: The World Bank.

Steffek, Jens. 2008. 'Public Accountability and the Public Sphere of International Governance', RECON Online Working Paper Series. Available at www.recon-project.eu (accessed on 23 April 2010).

Stepniak, Daniel. 2008. *Audio-visual Coverage of Courts: A Comparative Analysis*. New York: Cambridge University Press.

'Strengthening NGOs through Information Technology'. Available at www.microsoft.com (accessed on 23 March 2010).

Subrahmanya, A. T. 2009. 'Lokayukta handicapped by few powers and fewer personnel'. *The Times of India*, 4 February.

Subramanian, Arvind. 2007. 'The Evolution of Institutions in India and its Relationship with Economic Growth'. Available at www.iie.com (accessed on 5 February 2010).

Subramanian, K. 2008. 'Towards free and fair elections in India'. *The Hindu*, 2 July.

'Sukrity becomes the one millionth resident whose Aadhaar Number is generated'. 2011. Available at http://uidai.gov.in (accessed on 10 March 2011).

'Summary on Kautilya's Arthashastra: Its Contemporary Relevance'. 2004. Indian Merchants Chamber. Available at www.esamskriti.com (accessed on 3 February 2010).

'Sunshine Laws: How Are States Making Lawbreakers Pay?' AEJMC Archives, Central Michigan University. Available at https://ls2.cmich.edu/ (accessed on 1 July 2009).

'Supreme Court judges agree to disclose assets'. 2009. *The Times of India*, 26 August.

Sura, Ajay. 2009. 'Cash-at-door scam: Judge gets clean chit from AG'. *The Times of India*, 27 June.

Suri, K. C. 'Parties under Pressure: Political Parties in India since Independence'. Paper for the project on the state of democracy in South Asia, Lokniti-Centre for the Study of Developing Societies. Available at www.democracy-asia.org (accessed on 9 February 2009).

Suri, Megha. 2009. 'Now, Track Driving License Status Online'. *The Times of India*, 22 February.

Surie Devasher, Mandakini. 'Performance Management and Government?' Available at http://www.accountabilityindia.in (accessed on 12 January 2011).

Surya, D. 2003. 'Fine collection targets set for traffic police'. *The Times of India*, 22 February.

'Tackling Corruption and Promoting Accountability'. Available at www.karmayog. org (accessed on 15 April 2010).

'Talking Volunteerism'. Available at www.pravah.org (accessed on 26 March 2010).

'Tarnishing the image?' 2007. Available at www.thehoot.org (accessed on 4 January 2010).

Thakur, Pradeep. 2009. 'Official travel was 75% of ministers' expenses'. *The Times of India*, 13 September.

Tiwari, Ruhi and Liz Mathew. 2009. 'RTI has hit rate of 27% finds study'. *Mint*, 22 October.

_____. 2009. 'Parliament to debate women's reservation, some pending Bills'. *Mint*, 16 November.

'The British Raj'. Available at www.netcharles.com (accessed on 4 February 2010).

'The Caste System'. 1997. Available at http://home.snu.edu (accessed on 3 February 2010).

'The E-Government Handbook for Developing Countries'. Available at www. infodev.org (accessed on 6 November 2009).

'The FY 2008 Performance Report of the Federal Government'. 2009. Available at www.whitehouse.gov (accessed on 22 June 2009).

'The Gupta Empire 320–600 A.D'. Available at www.sjci.com/ (accessed on 5 February 2010).

'The Lokpal Cycle'. Available at indiatogether.org (accessed on 20 September 2010).

'The Mauryan Empire'. Available at www.uio.no (accessed on 11 February 2010).

'The Mughal Empire'. University of California, Los Angeles: Manas Section.

'The NREGS: Power not fully comprehended'. 2009. Available at www.ima-india. com (accessed on 25 November 2009).

'The Rights to Information, Participation, and Justice: The Importance of a Voice'. 2005. Available at http://multimedia.wri.org (accessed on 6 November 2009).

Jebaraj, Priscilla. 2010. 'The spotlight is on the media now'. *The Hindu*, 24 November.

'The Vedic Age 1500–600 BC'. In *The Rough Guide to India*, 6th edn. Available at http://expediauk.travel.roughguides.com (accessed on 2 February 2010).

Thomas, Kurian. 'Social Audit'. Available at www.idgnet.org (accessed on 29 March 2010).

Thoompunkal, Agnes. 'A Case for Content: Why NGOs Need to Outsource Research and Writing'. Available at www.chillibreeze.com/ (accessed on 31 March 2010).

Tinani, Sunil. 2008. 'Sharp claws but no teeth'. Available at http://bangalore.citi-zenmatters.in (accessed on 29 April 2010).

Tiwari, Shashi. 2008. 'Democratic Assemblies in Vedic Era'. Available at www.scribd.com (accessed on 2 February 2010).

Transition Monitoring Group. 2006. 'A Handbook for NGOs on Advocacy and Lob-bying Skills to Promote Electoral Reforms'. Available at www.tmgnigeria.org (accessed on 26 March 2010).

'Transparency and Good Urban Governance'. 2004. Urban Governance Toolkit. Available at http://ww2.unhabitat.org (accessed on 16 March 2010).

'Transparency in Government Act 2008'. Available at http://publicmarkup.org (accessed on 6 June 2009).

Treisman, Daniel. 2000. 'The causes of corruption: a cross-national study'. Avail-able at http://www.policyinnovations.org/ (accessed on 7 January 2011).

'Truncated cabinet sworn in'. 2009. Available at http://news.indiamart.com/ (accessed on 6 January 2010).

Tummala. Krishna. 1996. 'The Ethos of Indian Administration'. In *Public Administration in India*. New Delhi: Allied Publishers.

'Union Home Minister P. Chidambaram speech at the inaugural function of the 40th All India Police Science Congress in Raipur'. 2010. Available at www.pib.nic.in (accessed on 8 October 2010).

'United Nations: e-Government Survey 2008'. Available at http://unpan1.un.org (accessed on 3 July 2009).

'UPA mantra: Let's fix governance'. 2009. *Business Standard*, 4 June.

Upadhaya, R. 1999. 'Communalism and Casteism in Electoral Politics'. Available at www.southasiaanalysis.org (accessed on 6 May 2010).

'Upload videos, audios to expose corruption on Central Vigilance Commission's "Vig-Eye"'. 2010. *DNA*, 9 December.

Venkatesan, V. 2004. 'Defending the whistle-blower'. *Frontline*, June.

Vadivel, V. S. 2009. 'Public Interest Litigation: A boon or a bane. Available at www.legalserviceindia.com/ (accessed on 28 April 2010).

Venu, M. K. 2007. 'Weary of fragmentation politics'. *The Economic Times*, 17 April.

Vergne, Clémence. 2009. 'Turnout in Developing Countries: The Effect of Mass Media on National Voter Participation'. Available at http://publi.cerdi.org (accessed on 29 April 2010).

Verma, J. S. 'Mechanism for Judicial Accountability'. Available at www.judicialre-forms.org (accessed on 3 February 2009).

Verma, Shivshanker. 2008. 'Are government salaries really low'. Available at www.domain-b.com (accessed on 30 January 2009).

Viju, B. 2009. '15,438 RTI appeals pending in state'. *The Times of India*, 1 June.

————. 2009. 'Use RTI to get court orders copies'. *The Times of India*, 19 Febru-ary.

_____. 2006. 'Ministers wrote to get cops transferred'. *The Times of India*, 29 September.

'Vital Stats: Pendency of Cases in Indian Courts'. 2009. Available at www.prsindia. org (accessed on 30 June 2009).

Wahi, Namita. 2008. 'Draft Discussion Paper: Regulation of Campaign Finance'. Available at www.prsindia.org/ (accessed on 6 February 2009).

Walton, Michael. 2010. 'Capitalism, the state, and the underlying drivers of human development'. Human Development Research Paper 2010/09. Available at hdr.undp.org/ (accessed on 20 January 2011).

Wasan, Dalip. 2007. 'Better People Shall Establish Better Government'. Available at www.articlesbase.com/ (accessed on 3 March 2009).

_____. 2007. 'Voters have got limited choice'. Available at www.articlesbase. com/ (accessed on 3 March 2009).

'What affects turnout? Voter turnout 1945–1999: A global survey. Available at www.idea.int/ (accessed on 29 April 2009).

'What is Good Governance?'. Available at www.unescap.org (accessed on 12 February 2010).

'What is Outcome Budget?'. 2005. Available at www.rediff.com (accessed on 6 November 2009).

'When employees act as goodwill ambassadors'. 2005. *The Financial Express*, 4 September.

'Whistle Blower Act in India'. 2008. Available at http://ngopost.org (accessed on 20 April 2009).

'Why not a retirement age for Parliamentarians?' 2009. Available at www.mer-inews.com/ (accessed on 4 February 2009).

'Workshop on the Application of Social Accountability Mechanisms in Community Driven Development and Decentralization Programs in South Asia: Experiences from Pilot Projects'. 2007. Available at www.sasanet.org (accessed on 29 March 2010).

'Workshop on RTI in Giridh'. 2008. *PRIA E-Newsletter*, 1 (6).

Wyman, Miriam. 2001. 'Thinking about Governance: A Draft Discussion Paper'. Paper for the Commonwealth Foundation Citizens and Governance Programme. Available at www.democracyeducation.net (accessed on 16 February 2010).

Zachariah, Reeba and Namrata Singh. 2009. 'Go vote, India Inc tells employees'. *The Times of India*, 12 March.

'150 newly elected MPs have criminal records'. 2009. *Hindustan Times*, 17 May.

'58 Rajya Sabha MPs seek HC judge's ouster'. 2009. *The Times of India*, 21 February.

'2G scam: Raja to blame for losing Rs 1.76L cr'. 2010. *The Economic Times*, 10 November.

Index

....

DATE DUE